Kosciuszko

Also by Anthony Sharwood

From Snow to Ash
The Brumby Wars

Kosciuszko

THE INCREDIBLE LIFE OF
THE MAN BEHIND THE MOUNTAIN

Anthony Sharwood

Note: This book makes reference to the names of Aboriginal people who have died.

Published in Australia and New Zealand in 2024
by Hachette Australia
(an imprint of Hachette Australia Pty Limited)
Gadigal Country, Level 17, 207 Kent Street, Sydney, NSW 2000
www.hachette.com.au

Hachette Australia acknowledges and pays our respects to the past, present and future Traditional Owners and Custodians of Country throughout Australia and recognises the continuation of cultural, spiritual and educational practices of Aboriginal and Torres Strait Islander peoples. Our head office is located on the lands of the Gadigal people of the Eora Nation.

Copyright © Anthony Sharwood 2024

This book is copyright. Apart from any fair dealing for the purposes of private study, research, criticism or review permitted under the *Copyright Act 1968*, no part may be stored or reproduced by any process without prior written permission. Enquiries should be made to the publisher.

 A catalogue record for this book is available from the National Library of Australia

ISBN: 978 0 7336 5097 0 (paperback)

Cover design by Luke Causby
Cover image – portrait of Tadeusz Kosciuszko by Karl Gottlieb Schweikart (1772–1855) (Wikimedia Commons)
Cover photo of the Main Range near Mt Kosciuszko by Anthony Sharwood
Typeset in Simoncini Garamond by Kirby Jones
Printed and bound in Australia by McPherson's Printing Group

 The paper this book is printed on is certified against the Forest Stewardship Council® Standards. McPherson's Printing Group holds FSC® chain of custody certification SA-COC-005379. FSC® promotes environmentally responsible, socially beneficial and economically viable management of the world's forests.

CONTENTS

Timeline   vii
A few brief notes on spelling, accents and related things   xi

Introduction: The purest son of liberty   1

SECTION ONE
America: History speaks in echoes, not memos   15
1. Pole position   17
2. A tornado in Jeffersonville   25
3. Where there's a will, there's a way out   37
4. The teeth of the issue   48
5. Cheesesteaks and high stakes   55
6. Sunshine and rainbows   59
7. Just another white guy from history   66
8. A sukmana for a sable   72
9. The bank of justice   79
10. A kind master is forgiving   86
11. The deplorable entanglement   92
12. Bad apples and good eggs   99
13. Take care of yourselves and each other   109
14. Mississippi yearning   117
15. The key to the continent   130

SECTION TWO
Poland: 'I don't want to, but I have to'   143
16 A hero still needed?   145
17 The paradise of the Jews   158
18 A delicate constitution   167
19 Too gentle for a revolutionist   179
20 A twinge of the heart   189
21 The difference between mud and dirt   202

SECTION THREE
Australia: The learning walk   209
22 Peaky blindness   211
23 'You prosper on our native soil and we are famishing!'   219
24 Of moths and myths   228
25 Tales of the garden of Kosciuszko   238
26 'And the earth itself to nobody'   251
27 'And down by Kosciusko …'   261
28 The stone from Snowy River   273
29 A Polish pickle   289
30 The last wishes of the departed   297

Sources   311
Acknowledgements   319

TIMELINE

Since this book explores key moments in Kosciuszko's life episodically rather than sequentially, we thought a timeline might come in handy.

1746: Kosciuszko is born to a family on the lowest rung of the Polish nobility in Mereczowszczyzna in the Polish–Lithuanian Commonwealth, in what today is Belarus.
1755: His formal education begins at the Piarist school in the town of Lubieszow, where the first seeds of Enlightenment thinking are sown.
1765: Kosciuszko is selected in the inaugural uptake of the Royal Military Academy's Corps of Cadets in Warsaw, where he becomes a star pupil.
1769: The young graduate arrives in Paris to continue his studies and is further influenced by Enlightenment thinking.
1772: The first partition of Poland sees a third of the country annexed by Russia, Prussia and Austria. The second and third partitions occur in 1793 and 1795.
1774: Kosciuszko returns to Poland but is unable to secure a position in the military. He tries to elope with Ludwika Sosnowska but is thwarted.
April 1775: America's War of Independence begins.
October 1775: Kosciuszko again leaves Poland for Paris, this time en route to America.

August 1776: Kosciuszko arrives in the USA after being shipwrecked. The US Declaration of Independence is signed while he is at sea.

September 1776: Having impressed Benjamin Franklin, Kosciuszko is deployed to help fortify Philadelphia.

December 1776: Washington first hears of Kosciuszko's expertise and summons him north to help defend the Hudson.

1777: Kosciuszko engineers a pivotal victory at the Battle of Saratoga, which formally brings France into the war as an American ally.

1778–80: Kosciuszko successfully fortifies the crucial elbow of the Hudson River at West Point.

May 1779: Agrippa Hull, a free Black enlisted man, becomes Kosciuszko's orderly.

1780–83: Kosciuszko serves with distinction in the Southern Theatre of the War of Independence.

July 1784: Kosciuszko sails for Europe.

1784: Unable to secure a position as an officer in the Polish military despite his celebrated feats in America, Kosciuszko becomes a farmer for four years on the family estate.

1789: Kosciuszko at last secures a position in the Polish military, becoming Major General Kosciuszko.

1792: Kosciuszko becomes a fully-fledged Polish military hero even though Poland loses the Polish–Russian War.

March 1794: Kosciuszko proclaims an uprising against Russia and Prussia.

April 1794: Kosciuszko enjoys his greatest victory on home soil at the Battle of Raclawice.

May 1794: The Proclamation of Polaniec is issued by Kosciuszko, promising new rights to Polish peasants.

TIMELINE

October 1794: Kosciuszko falls at Maciejowice, effectively heralding the end of the uprising. He is imprisoned by the Russians in St Petersburg.

1796: Catherine the Great dies and her son Tsar Paul I frees Kosciuszko.

1797: Kosciuszko arrives back in Philadelphia to a hero's welcome and drafts a will in which he leaves his unclaimed Revolutionary War pay to free and educate the enslaved, including those on Jefferson's plantation.

1798: Kosciuszko departs America for the last time, giving Jefferson a sable coat. He lives in France until 1815.

1802: The US Military Academy at West Point commences operations. It was Kosciuszko's idea.

1815: Kosciuszko fruitlessly tries to restore Poland's freedom at the Congress of Vienna.

1817: Kosciuszko dies in Solothurn, Switzerland.

1823: The Kosciuszko Mound, the artificial hillock whose shape was said to inspire Pawel Strzelecki's name choice for Australia's highest mountain, is completed in Krakow.

1825: A committee of West Point cadets selects Kosciuszko as the first person to be honoured with a monument at the US Military Academy.

1826: Thomas Jefferson dies on the 50th anniversary of the adoption of the Declaration of Independence.

1835: New South Wales Governor Sir Richard Bourke issues a proclamation which effectively implements the doctrine of Terra Nullius in Australia.

1840: Polish explorer and scientist Pawel Strzelecki climbs and names Australia's highest peak Mt Kosciuszko.

1852: Kosciuszko's will is finally settled by the US Supreme Court, with not a cent going to the enslaved as he had intended.

1890: Banjo Paterson's iconic poem 'The Man from Snowy River' is published.
1910: Kosciuszko's statue is unveiled in Lafayette Square, opposite the White House.
1917: Poland returns to the map of Europe for the first time since the third partition of Poland in 1795.
1945: The Nazis invade Poland, sparking World War II.
1967: Kosciusko State Park, which was proclaimed in 1944, becomes Kosciusko National Park (still without the z).
1972: The Thaddeus Kosciuszko National Memorial opens in Philadelphia.
1984: Australian band Midnight Oil releases its fifth studio album *Red Sails in the Sunset*, on which the song 'Kosciusko' (without the z) appears.
1990: Former electrician and trade union leader Lech Walesa is elected President of Poland, ushering his nation out of the communist era.
1992: The landmark Mabo Case is handed down by the High Court of Australia.
1997: The missing z is restored to Mt Kosciuszko and Kosciuszko National Park.
2000: The first public proposal to rename Mt Kosciuszko to an Aboriginal name.
2007: Music composed by Tadeusz Kosciuszko is played atop the summit of Mt Kosciuszko by Sydney band The Windjammers.
2020: The Kosciuszko statue opposite the White House is defaced by Black Lives Matter protestors.
2022: Your author wakes up one day and goes, 'Hang on, who was this Kosciuszko guy, anyway?' Research and travel for this book commences.

A FEW BRIEF NOTES ON SPELLING, ACCENTS AND RELATED THINGS

I do not speak Polish and I assume most of you don't either. Because most readers won't know how the accents on Polish letters affect the pronunciation of words, we have deleted them all, except in the references.

Accents do appear in this book on some words in languages like French and Spanish but that's because most people know what the accents do. For example, it's widely understood that the 'ñ' in El Niño turns the second syllable into a 'nyo' rather than a 'no' sound.

As for spelling of Aboriginal places in Section Three of this book, if you see the same place or Nation spelled two different ways, that is deliberate. For example, Iris White calls herself a Monero-Ngarigo woman whereas the most common modern spelling in relation to the region east of Kosciuszko National Park is Monaro.

You might also be interested to know that Ngarigo is technically pronounced with a soft 'ng' sound at the start of the word, like the sound at the end of the word 'sing'. The trick is to capture that sound and start the word with it, although in truth, most Ngarigo just say it with an 'n' sound to make life easier for everyone. It's also worth noting that the 'o' at the end is generally pronounced a bit more like 'u' or 'oo', and indeed some of the Ngarigo interviewed prefer it spelled 'Ngarigu', hence any apparent inconsistency.

One last comment about the term Ngarigo. Some Aboriginal people will tell you that Ngarigo is technically the name of the language, not the people. But it has come to mean both, and for the sake of avoiding a clumsy title like 'the people of the southern and eastern part of the Snowy Mountains who speak dialects of the Ngarigo language', I have just called them the 'Ngarigo' as most people do.

More broadly regarding Aboriginal people, I call them that. I do not call them First Nations people, for the simple reason that the term originated in Canada and most Ngarigo folk I spoke to find it too foreign. This is not the case with other Nations in Australia who prefer the term First Nations, but over the course of researching three books on the Australian High Country, my experience is that the Ngarigo prefer the term Aboriginal, but never the noun 'Aborigine', which is considered highly offensive.

As for me, my parents married under the unpronounceable Lithuanian name Schaiowitz before they Anglicised it to Sharwood. My maternal grandmother was from Belarus and her married surname was even harder to pronounce before she Anglicised it too. I am a person of remarkably similar ethnic heritage to Kosciuszko himself, without an atom of Anglo-Saxon blood despite my British-sounding name, and while that was not a motivating factor behind this book, it made it all the more interesting to research and write.

INTRODUCTION

THE PUREST SON OF LIBERTY

Did you know that the letter z is worth only one point in Polish Scrabble? In the native tongue of Tadeusz Kosciuszko, z is as common as the brilliant yellow canola fields which in springtime chequerboard the pole – the fertile plain from which his homeland takes its name. Kosciuszko was born on that pole in 1746, in a thatch-roofed house on the Mereczowszczyzna estate, in what today is part of Belarus. See all those beautiful z's? There are four in Mereczowszczyzna and another three in our hero's full name: Andrzej Tadeusz Bonawentura Kosciuszko. In Poland, z is as common as ziemniaki, the Polish word for potatoes. Indeed, it's the second most frequent consonant in the Polish language, after n. Suffice to say that if you correctly guessed z on *Kolo Fortuny*, the Polish version of the American game show *Wheel of Fortune*, you surely would be little closer to solving the word puzzle.

Of course a person should be remembered for their deeds, not the Scrabble tiles which make up their name, and Kosciuszko's valiant exploits were many. Long before America gave Poland *Kolo Fortuny*, Poland gave America Kosciuszko. Without his ingenuity, bravery and unwavering selflessness, America's Revolutionary War would doubtless have been prolonged, perhaps even lost, and the United States of America as we know it might never have existed. In Poland, the heroic uprising Kosciuszko led against Russia and other aggressors has become the stuff of national legend, while his snubs to the great megalomaniac Napoleon were some of history's finest screw-yous.

But who was he? Who was this man that Thomas Jefferson, America's third president and author of the Declaration of Independence, called, 'As pure a son of liberty as I have ever known, and of that liberty which is to go to all, and not to the few or rich alone'?

History is like a magazine list of the greatest music artists: it morphs over time in accordance with prevailing norms, tastes and social movements. In 2020, The Beatles' *Sgt. Pepper's Lonely Hearts Club Band* dropped from number one to number twenty-four on *Rolling Stone* magazine's 500 greatest albums, replaced at the summit by Marvin Gaye's *What's Going On*. In the new list, twenty-four of the top fifty albums were by Black artists – double the twelve in the inaugural 2003 list – as popular music's taste curators adjusted their white-tinged perspective in line with the broader cultural climate. History's great leaders have been far from immune to this sort of upheaval. The collective esteem for Thomas Jefferson and George Washington once seemed as indestructible as their granite likenesses on Mt Rushmore in South Dakota's Black Hills. But even stone crumbles, and the two Founding Fathers have faced intense scrutiny for their ownership of enslaved people. Meanwhile, Kosciuszko's life has endured no such reappraisal. He remains morally unimpeachable. Nobody has 'cancelled' him and it's likely they never will.

Kosciuszko grew up in the eastern part of what was then the Polish–Lithuanian Commonwealth, the youngest of four children in a family which occupied a place toward the base of the pyramid of the Polish nobility, or szlachta. A bright student, he was plucked from relative obscurity at eighteen to attend the Royal Military Academy's Corps of Cadets in Warsaw. He furthered his studies in France before briefly returning to Poland, then crossed the Atlantic to fight in America's Revolutionary War, where his military engineering skills proved invaluable to the ragtag Continental Army, which was desperate for experts schooled in the technical arts of war. Kosciuszko would go on to serve longer in the war than any other foreign officer, eventually attaining the rank of brigadier general. He is best known for his fortifications of Philadelphia, the pivotal victory he engineered at the Battle of Saratoga – which brought the French into the war on America's side – and for his impenetrable defences at West Point on the Hudson River north of New York City.

Later, Kosciuszko became a national hero in Poland for leading the 1794 Kosciuszko Uprising against Russia and Prussia, winning hearts and minds in his own country and across Europe for inspiring his countrymen and women to fight for freedom, with the promise of equal or enhanced rights and social and economic status. Ultimately, the uprising was unsuccessful and after spending two years imprisoned in Russia, Kosciuszko returned to America, where he penned a will, edited and signed by Jefferson, in which he pledged his unclaimed Revolutionary War salary to purchase the freedom and education of enslaved people, including those owned by Jefferson at his plantation, Monticello. After this brief second stint in America, Kosciuszko again returned to Europe, spending the last two decades of his life fruitlessly trying to reinstate his homeland in dealings with various European dictators and dignitaries, including Napoleon. He never married, dying in exile in the Swiss town of Solothurn at age seventy-one in October 1817. Each morning for the last three years of his life, he would ride around town handing out coins to poor people from the back of a black pony called Dobry, which means 'good' in Polish.

The image of the old freedom fighter doling out small change from a black pony called Good tells you plenty. Here was a man who served humanity until the end, willingly and with good cheer. Here, in short, was a good guy. That's the sort of wishy-washy phrase your high school history teacher would strike out of your essay with a big red swipe, but Kosciuszko's genial nature is a key aspect of his story.

It goes without saying that Kosciuszko led an important, accomplished and celebrated life but he also pops up in all sorts of unexpected places. In French author Jules Verne's 1870 sci-fi classic *Twenty Thousand Leagues Under the Sea*, the mysterious Captain Nemo has a portrait of Kosciuszko on his cabin wall. When America's Congress decided to 'stage an illumination' to celebrate Independence Day in 1783, Kosciuszko was the friendly pyrotechnician at hand. Yes, Kosciuszko staged the fireworks for the first ever 4th of July celebrations. Every American schoolchild knows and hisses at the name Benedict Arnold, the American-born Revolutionary War general who became a despised figure by selling out to the British. But who knew that the bargaining chip used by America's most notorious traitor was Kosciuszko's meticulous drawings of the fortifications at West Point? West Point itself is of course now home to the United States Military Academy. The man who first proposed the academy's existence, based on his experiences as a cadet in Warsaw, was none other than Kosciuszko. Down the Hudson toward New York City, one of the first American schools for formerly enslaved people and their children opened in Newark, New Jersey, in 1825. It was called the Kosciuszko School and was funded by the sale of land in Ohio which Kosciuszko had been granted for his war service.

The more you look into Kosciuszko, the more he looms as a figure in the manner of Forrest Gump, the titular character of the 1995 Oscar winner for Best Picture. The fictitious Gump lived a great if mostly anonymous American life, his talents many, his dual superpowers universal likeability and unwavering hope. Kosciuszko and Forrest Gump even share an amusing military injury: Gump was shot in the buttocks in Vietnam while Kosciuszko was rear-ended with a bayonet in the southern theatre of the Revolutionary War of 1775 to 1783. Kosciuszko cut things close a couple of times in the South. In what many historians argue was the final skirmish of the eight-year war at James Island, South Carolina, four British musket balls pierced Kosciuszko's coat but not his body. Could there be a more poignant symbol of defiance than the great freedom fighter remaining unscathed after being struck near the heart by musket balls, as the infant America gulped its first mighty breath of liberty?

Away from the military arena, Kosciuszko was a Renaissance man, widely read and fluent in four languages. He was a capable composer and painter, and was even the subject of art and literature himself. *Thaddeus of Warsaw* by the English writer Jane Porter was one of the earliest historical novels and was inspired by Kosciuszko's life. The 1803 book, published during Kosciuszko's lifetime, was such a smash hit that at least eighty-four editions were printed. According to Briton Monica M Gardner, who published the first English language biography of Kosciuszko in 1920, Kosciuszko read *Thaddeus of Warsaw* and liked it. He even complimented Jane Porter on it, joking that he was glad his exploits were set 'in a romance, because no-one will believe them'.

There was indeed something irresistibly romantic about Kosciuszko's life, and it's therefore no surprise that Romantic poets wanted in on the action. Three revered English masters of verse – Coleridge, Keats and Leigh Hunt – each wrote sonnets entitled 'To Kosciuszko'. He also featured in longer poems, such as Lord Byron's 'Age of Bronze', where the poet left out the z but perfectly captured the zeitgeist:

'That sound that crashes in the tyrant's ear –
Kosciusko!'

Kosciuszko's name and legacy were evoked in 'Pan Tadeusz' (Master Thaddeus), the 1834 epic poem by Poland's national poet, Adam Mickiewicz. To this day, it is a mainstay of the Polish school syllabus. In 1799, Scottish poet Thomas Campbell wrote a lengthy poem in heroic couplets called 'The Pleasure of Hope', capturing the widely held esteem for Kosciuszko as a symbolic figure in the struggle against tyranny by referencing the moment when he was near-fatally wounded in the Kosciuszko Uprising (even if Campbell, too, made the old error of omitting the z):

Hope, for a season, bade the world farewell,
And Freedom shriek'd — as KOSCIUSKO fell!

And freedom shrieked as Kosciuszko fell. The inversion of subject and object in that line is like the old joke about Hollywood tough guy Chuck Norris taking a shower. Not the one about how Chuck Norris doesn't take showers, just blood baths. And not the other one about how Chuck Norris doesn't turn on his shower, he just stares at it till it cries. Freedom shrieking as Kosciuszko fell is like the joke that Chuck Norris doesn't get wet in the shower; the water gets Chuck Norris'd! In Campbell's verse universe, it's not Kosciuszko who shrieks as he falls on the battlefield in pursuit of freedom; freedom itself shrieks in despair at the demise of its standard-bearer.

'I pledge not to use these powers to oppress any person, but to defend the integrity of the borders of Poland, regain the independence of the nation, and to strengthen universal liberties,' Kosciuszko proclaimed in Krakow's Main Square on 24 March 1794, announcing the uprising that would bear his name. This was not the first or last time that Kosciuszko would invoke America's noblest ideals in his native Poland. Indeed, most people have no idea that in 1791 Poland introduced Europe's first modern constitution, based largely on America's. And Kosciuszko meant every word of that March 1794 Krakow pronouncement and subsequent proclamations promising greater freedoms for Polish citizens. Here was a leader who was never going to make a screeching U-turn and become tyrannical as the blood of power rushed to his head. When Kosciuszko said he wouldn't abuse his powers, he meant it. When he spoke of equality, he lived it. Indeed, Kosciuszko spent large parts of the uprising fighting alongside peasants, most of whom were equipped with nothing more than agricultural scythes. He even took to wearing a wool peasant robe in battle rather than his military regalia. Kosciuszko's legend was forged on inclusivity long before it became a buzzword, and on solidarity long before trade unionist and later Polish President Lech Walesa ushered his country out of the darkness of communism with a movement taking that name. Thomas Jefferson might have penned the immortal words 'all men are created equal' but as a lifelong owner of more than 600 enslaved people, TJ ultimately only talked the talk. But TK walked the walk, eventually freeing the serf families on his modest Polish estate and dedicating his life to securing the dignity, wellbeing, freedom and opportunity of every man, woman and child, no matter their ethnicity, religion, nationality or social standing. While he didn't win every battle, and indeed ultimately failed to preserve his country's very existence, never did he compromise on his ideals.

'I have tired of the endless discussions of Jefferson and believe that time would be better spent on the true son of liberty, Tadeusz Kosciuszko, who never turned away from his dreams of human equality and the end of slavery,' historian Graham Russell Gao Hodges wrote in 2014 in the American journal *The Polish Review*.

'He was a kind of human rights activist, well ahead of his times. Personalities of this kind are desperately needed today,' Polish diplomat Wojciech Flera wrote in the same publication in 2007.

'He was a social reformer who was an abolitionist before it was cool. The dude lived a metal life and I have no idea why there hasn't been a movie made about him,' wrote a US military blogger who goes by the pseudonym of Angry Staff Officer in 2019.

It feels like Kosciuszko's hour has arrived. Andrzej Tadeusz Bonawentura Kosciuszko is the hero the world needs now, a hero we can all believe in regardless of our political leanings. In a polarised world, this Pole is the kind of unifying figure we seem incapable of producing anymore. So why don't contemporary history books thunder his name?

Within Poland, twentieth-century heroes like Pope John Paul II and Lech Walesa loom much larger than Kosciuszko in minds both young and old. Outside of Poland, detailed knowledge of Kosciuszko's life is largely confined to expatriate Polish communities and a smattering of historians. Kosciuszko is celebrated with something like 360 plaques, pedestals, slabs, statues, sculptures, markers, mounds, busts and obelisks scattered in at least a dozen countries, but who apart from diehards makes pilgrimages to these places? Australia's highest mountain, an Alaskan island, a bridge connecting Brooklyn and Queens in New York City, and Oprah Winfrey's Mississippi hometown are among the landmarks to carry Kosciuszko's name, yet who in those places knows the first thing about him? This book by this author is proof that you can spend a lifetime traipsing on ski and foot around Australia's Kosciuszko National Park, write two books about the area's ecology and history and the culture wars being fought over the only alpine landscape in the hottest, driest continent on Earth, yet still wake up one morning and ask for the very first time: 'Wait a minute, who actually was this Kosciuszko fella and what did he stand for?'

Maybe our blind spot is because of that hard-to-pronounce surname which, for the record, is something like Kos-chyoozh-koh (to their credit, most Poles don't mind how you say it, just as Kosciuszko himself never took offence at mangled attempts by his American comrades). Maybe the man remains too Eastern European for western tastes, despite the fact he was not just a Polish patriot but an American citizen and an honorary French citizen. Maybe history, like sport, is too obsessed with conquerors and stories that end in glory rather than good guys who had as many successes as failures and who ended up riding a pony around town like the mythical Yankee Doodle. And maybe our brains only have room for so many historical figures beyond leviathans like Washington and Jefferson, or their equivalents in our own countries, even in an age when their legacies are being reevaluated. But as mentioned, our take on history can change.

Hamilton creator Lin-Manuel Miranda elevated Alexander Hamilton from a lesser-celebrated Founding Father to superstar American Dreamer who resonated with modern youth. 'This is a story about America then, told by America now, and we want to eliminate any distance between a contemporary audience and this story,' Miranda told *The Atlantic* in 2015. Kosciuszko deserves the same treatment. The cultural and temporal distance between us and Kosciuszko should be eliminated. His life and legacy should be made inspiring, thrilling, relevant, indispensable to a modern audience no matter where we live.

Relax. We are not about to break into rap. The only faint hat-tip here to Miranda's spectacularly successful *Hamilton* is that we're employing a popular modern storytelling genre. In this case, not the musical but the road trip. That's right, we're hittin' the road. Pack your corn dogs, your kielbasa, your Toblerone and your Vegemite, because we're embarking upon a journey across three continents and four countries to places where Kosciuszko fought, lived, or which bear his name.

What can we hope to discover on the road, when Kosciuszko's life story has already been painstakingly pieced together down the years by Polish, Swiss, British and American authors, including many of Polish descent? Why travel to places like the town of Kosciusko, Mississippi or Mt Kosciuszko in Kosciuszko National Park when the man himself never visited the region that became the state of Mississippi or the faraway land of Australia, whose highest peak was named in his honour by the Polish explorer Pawel Strzelecki?

One important reason is because everything's more interesting with geography, especially historical biography, and while that sounds like it could be the opening line of *Kosciuszko! The Musical*, it's true. A long-gone historical figure comes to life when you add people and places to the scholarly world of history books, journals and old letters. You can't understand the strategic brilliance of Kosciuszko's works at West Point until you've hiked up to Redoubt Four, high above the Hudson. You can't truly feel Kosciuszko's passion for a free Poland until you walk the bustling cobbled streets of Krakow's Old Town on a perfect spring afternoon, following Planty Park down toward Wawel Cathedral, deep inside of which lies his marble tomb. Kosciuszko's unpretentiousness becomes believable, relatable, when you visit his modest quarters in Philadelphia and Solothurn, Switzerland.

But the main reason to hit the road is because this is a journey into Kosciuszko's legacy as much as his life. Road trips are magical things. The dual promises of road trips are taco sauce on your lap and enlightenment of one form or another as the road reveals truths about the world around us and ourselves. Those big ideas that Kosciuszko fought for – liberty, opportunity, dignity for all – how are they faring today? Can we refresh and reimagine our world view through the lens of Kosciuszko's life? Can Kosciuszko inspire us to be better? Can his life's work remind us of what's really worth striving for?

From afar, it's so easy to despair at the current state of America. But up close, has America evolved in a manner that would please Kosciuszko? Alex Storozynski, the Polish American Pulitzer Prize-winning journalist and author of the excellent 2009 biography *The Peasant Prince: Thaddeus Kosciuszko and the Age of Revolution*, wrote a 2017 piece in the *New York Daily News* in which he argued that 'Kosciuszko would be crushed that the country he fought for has devolved into a system where politicians care more about ideology, and their own parties, than the Republic.' Few would disagree that American politics has gone to hell, but what about America beyond Capitol Hill? Has the country become a horribly contorted version of what the Founding Fathers envisioned and what Kosciuszko fought for? Is there reason to hope? The road will reveal all.

Poland also has a traumatic history, from being wiped off the map of Europe for 123 years after the unsuccessful Kosciuszko Uprising in 1794, to the horrors of World War II and its post-war repression under communism. Located either in central Europe or eastern Europe depending on which mapping or administrative body you place your faith in, Poland is currently enjoying its longest unbroken stretch of freedom and prosperity in centuries. What would Kosciuszko make of that? How would he view the convoluted political landscape of a nation which in late 2023 swung back toward the left after eight years under a populist right-wing government which chipped away at basic freedoms? How relevant is Kosciuszko today in this key nation straddling eastern and western European values, culture and geography?

In Australia, there's a simmering debate over the potential name change of Mt Kosciuszko to an Indigenous name favoured by the local Ngarigo people, who lived there for tens of thousands of years before Europeans arrived, and who were far from the only Aboriginal Nation to visit or name the mountain. What would Kosciuszko make of this? Would taking a leaf out of his playbook of respect for the rights of Indigenous people make a difference to the way the issue plays out?

As we hit the trail of Thomas Jefferson's purest son of liberty, it's worth noting that Jefferson was neither the first nor last American president to heap praise on Kosciuszko. William Howard Taft, Dwight D Eisenhower, Theodore Roosevelt, both George Bushes and Lyndon B Johnson are among the presidents to have extolled Kosciuszko's virtues in various contexts. Even Donald Trump had a go at pronouncing his name in a speech and he didn't mangle it as badly as some. In 1818, future ninth president William Henry Harrison – then a US representative from Ohio and a former general and hero of the War of 1812 – delivered Kosciuszko's eulogy, passionately arguing that the hero of two continents deserved to be recognised alongside no less a giant of history than America's first president, George Washington.

Washington himself said as much. By the end of the Revolutionary War in 1783, his regard for Kosciuszko was so high that at his official farewell to Revolutionary War officers in the Long Room of Manhattan's Fraunces Tavern, he presented Kosciuszko with two pistols and a sword engraved in Latin with words that translated as 'America and Washington are joined with our friend T. Kosciuszko'. He even pulled a ring off his own finger and gave it to Kosciuszko, inducting Kosciuszko into the Society of the Cincinnati, an organisation of former Revolutionary War officers, named after Cincinnatus, the Roman statesman who, like Kosciuszko himself, was at varying times in his life both a military hero and a farmer.

Washington first heard of Kosciuszko late in 1776, a few months after the Pole's arrival in Philadelphia. In those chaotic early years of revolution, the Commander-in-Chief of the Continental Army was doubtless too busy trying to fashion willing but untrained bands of militia into a fighting force capable of taking on England's well-drilled redcoats to waste time trying to spell a name like Kosciuszko correctly. 'I have been well informed, that the Engineer in the Northern Army (Cosieski, I think his name is) is a Gentleman of science and merit,' he wrote to Congress a year or so after Kosciuszko's strategic brilliance engineered victory in the pivotal Battle of Saratoga in autumn 1777.

You can imagine Washington in his military field office, his attention scattered like shotgun pellets: 'Cosieski? Kawolski? Kransky? Oh, they'll know who I mean!'

It's said that Washington misspelled the Pole's name eleven different ways in various correspondences in those early years of war. He wasn't alone: Kosciuszko's comrades-in-arms were like men trying to eat alphabet soup with a fork when they tried to spell or pronounce his name. But by 1778, after touring Kosciuszko's impregnable fortifications at West Point, Washington had well and truly joined the fan club. With admiration came respect, and with respect came attention to detail. In his correspondences immediately after his visit to West Point, Washington started spelling Kosciuszko's name correctly for the first time. Tellingly, he included the z.

Just like in Polish Scrabble, that z made a point.

Section One

America: History speaks in echoes, not memos

CHAPTER 1

POLE POSITION

When you've eaten every overpriced burrito and chugged every can of root beer and aimlessly perused every shelf of the bookstore in Terminal 7 at Los Angeles International Airport waiting hours for a delayed connecting flight, one thing becomes very clear: Americans love self-help books. Turns out they consume them in larger numbers than any other country, both in total and per capita. What to make of this hunger to fashion the 'best version of yourself', as the cringeworthy saying goes? On the one hand, you could cast it as a modern expression of American Individualism, that as you stride across life's pastures seeking the Life, Liberty and the pursuit of Happiness promised in the Declaration of Independence, it's fundamentally up to you to make those fields fertile. On the other hand, you might see it as a response to the increasing dysfunctionality of major public and private American institutions from gluttonous Wall Street to money-grubbing megachurches to the hopelessly entangled health system, the self-serving legal system, the prohibitively expensive education system, government officials beholden to donors and lobby groups perpetuating the very swamp they claim they want to drain, you name it. Amid such broad-scale structural entropy, who's left to help individuals but themselves? Either way, when Americans sit on the loungeroom floor of life with the IKEA sofa of their dreams in a million unassembled pieces, self-help books can look a lot like the Allen key to success.

If Tadeusz Kosciuszko were alive today, you can bet your last zloty he'd be contributing to public life in a more constructive way than writing self-help books. That's not to say he wouldn't make a great fist of it. Exhibit A: the letter he wrote to the eighteen-year-old son of his friend Peter Zeltner, in whose Swiss household Kosciuszko spent his twilight years:

> Rise at four in the summer and six in the winter. Your first thoughts must be directed towards the Supreme Being; worship Him for a few minutes. Set yourself to work with reflection and intelligence, either at your prescribed duty carried out in the most scrupulous manner, or perfect yourself in some science in which you should have true mastery. Avoid lying under any circumstances in your life, but always be frank and loyal and always tell the truth. Never be idle but be sober and frugal, even hard on yourself while indulgent to others. Do not be vain nor an egotist. Before speaking or answering on something, reflect and consider well in order not to lose your point and say something stupid. Never fail to give due recognition under any circumstances to the person who is in charge of your wellbeing. Anticipate his desires and his wishes. Pay close attention with proper humility. Look for an opportunity to be useful. As you are a foreigner in the country, redouble your concern and efforts to gain trust and preference over the natives legitimately by your merit and superior knowledge. If a secret is entrusted in you, keep it

religiously; in all your actions you must be upright, sincere and open; no dissimulation in your speech. Do not argue but seek the truth calmly and with modesty, be polite and considerate to everyone, agreeable and obliging in society, humane and helpful to the unfortunate according to your means. Read instructive books to embellish your mind and improve your spirit. Do not degrade yourself by making bad acquaintances, but rather those with high principles and reputation, thus your conduct should be such that the whole world approves it and that wherever you may be it will be considered irreproachable.

How good is that? Those are 297 words both sensible and inspirational that deserve to be stuck on a big yellow post-it note on everyone's fridge. Better still, you could take that letter, break it into themed chapters, pad the chapters out with a blend of sensible advice and psychobabble, do the cookbook thing and intersperse the text with images of quintessential Polish scenes – Krakow's Disneyesque Wawel Castle at sunset, a plate of potato pierogi scattered with chopped onions, the Polish white-tailed eagle soaring over the Baltic plains of Pomerania, Warsaw's imposing mock-Art Deco Palace of Culture and Science, the towering Tatra Mountains as viewed from Zakopane, the huge industrial crane-like Monument to the Fallen Shipyard Workers in Gdansk – then give the thing a snappy title with a nod to Kosciuszko's nationality like *Pole Position: Your Head Start in the Race of Life*, and old Koz would surely be sitting atop the *New York Times* bestseller list until Christmas 2080. And if you're thinking, 'Okay, so he talked a good game in a letter to an eighteen-year-old but did Kosciuszko live up to half of his own advice?', you'd best go visit the man himself at eighteen.

The year was 1765. Kosciuszko had just secured his first big break in life, granted a scholarship in the inaugural intake of the newly established Corps of Cadets at the Royal Military Academy in Warsaw thanks to local priests and noblemen who had connections to Prince Czartoryski, head of the academy and cousin to Poland's new king, Stanislaw Augustus Poniatowski. Kosciuszko had a humble background compared to most of his academic peers and worked hard to get ahead. Like Miranda's Alexander Hamilton, he was young and hungry and he was not throwin' away his shot. Polish historian Tadeusz Korzon's 1906 Kosciuszko biography records that the young man would tie a thin cord to his wrist each evening and trail it into the hallway so the nightwatchman could tug it to wake him at 3 am. Given that in his letter Kosciuszko encouraged Zeltner's son to rise at 4 am in summer and 6 am in winter, he didn't just live up to his own words of advice, but exceeded them.

Those pre-dawn starts paid off. Kosciuszko became the Military Academy's star pupil, studying subjects including engineering, mapmaking, trigonometry and drawing. He even learned about fort construction, which would eventually become — you have to say it — his forte. Combat skills were also part of the curriculum and by all accounts Kosciuszko fought hard but within the bounds of good sportsmanship and was popular among his colleagues. He had friends in high places too. As the academy's patron, King Stanislaw himself took a shine to its keenest scholar, meeting regularly with young Tadeusz. On graduation, the king awarded Kosciuszko one of just four royal scholarships to further his studies in France.

The 23-year-old Kosciuszko arrived in Paris in 1769 with another Polish officer, Captain Joseph Orlowski. The duo enrolled in the Royal Academy of Painting and Sculpture. Kosciuszko wanted to further his military studies, but as a foreign officer he was unable to attend military schools, so he privately studied architecture and structural engineering under leading civil engineer Jean-Rodolphe Perronet. Included in his studies were the fortifications of Sebastien le Prestre de Vauban, whose famous works still adorn many provincial cities, strategic hilltops and mountain passes in and around France.

In addition to his studies, Kosciuszko devoured Enlightenment literature. He was heavily influenced by the French economist François Quesnay, one of the leading lights of a theory called physiocracy, which argued that nations derive their wealth from the land and the agriculture practised upon it. The theory would eventually diminish in prominence as the Industrial Revolution spread across Europe and labour and capital superseded land in the hierarchy of the means of production, but physiocracy spoke to Kosciuszko's soul. In it, he found the intellectual rationale behind what he always saw as the cruel injustice of serfs working the land for little more than a few crumbs of the wealth this key asset generated.

From an early age, Kosciuszko was uncomfortable with the feudal system operating in much of Europe. His father, Ludwik Tadeusz Kosciuszko, died when he was twelve but he never forgot how the old man had treated the thirty-one peasant families fairly and with dignity on their estate at Mereczowszczyzna. As a child, Kosciuszko played with the serf children. Polish American author Antoni Gronowicz wrote in his 1947 biography, *Gallant General: Tadeusz Kosciuszko*, that Kosciuszko was nicknamed 'chlopek roztropek', which roughly translates as 'the lively little peasant' according to American scholar Lindsey Grudnicki.

'Kosciuszko experienced equality firsthand as he ran through the fields and house accompanied by children who, though destined to suffer under an oppressive system, were no different from himself in their capacity to grow and play,' wrote Grudnicki in 2013 in her thesis 'True to a single object: the character of Tadeusz Kosciuszko'. 'This intermixing was common on many estates, yet the notions of equality triggered by interaction with the peasant children remained with Tadeusz Kosciuszko into adulthood and shaped his views of what "citizenship" should mean in Poland.'

Meanwhile, as Kosciuszko studied in France, Poland had entered a period of turmoil. In 1772, around a third of Poland's land area and half its population was subsumed by Russia, Prussia and Austria in what became known as the First Partition of the Polish–Lithuanian Commonwealth. Returning from France to his hollowed-out homeland in 1774, Kosciuszko was dismayed by both the state of his country and his family estate, the latter in poor order due to his brother's financial mismanagement. Short of cash and unable to serve as an officer in the Polish army as such positions had to be purchased, Kosciuszko took a tutoring job. His students were the daughters of the Polish nobleman Lord Sosnowski. Remarkably, the sisters had recently translated a book by the physiocrat François Quesnay from French into Polish. Could a louder clap of thunder possibly have boomed from above?

Legendary playboy Casanova had spent two years screwing his way through Warsaw society a few years earlier, and would later refer to 'the great Kosciuszko' in a rare section of his memoirs that covered events outside the bedroom, yet the Italian's lustful desires were a mere candle to the bonfire of true love between Kosciuszko and Lord Sosnowski's elder daughter, Ludwika. The two seemed made for each other.

Things would doubtless have turned out differently in Kosciuszko's life, and world history, if Ludwika's stern father had approved of the relationship. But he did not. Kosciuszko occupied too low a rung on the Polish nobility ladder despite the royal connections he'd made at the academy, and anyway, Ludwika was already betrothed to Prince Jozef Aleksander Lubomirski, a prominent member of Poland's upper nobility. 'Pigeons are not meant for sparrows and the daughters of magnates are not meant for the sons of the common gentry,' Lord Sosnowski famously said of the two lovebirds, a cruel slur to Kosciuszko but also a disrespectful slight upon either pigeons or sparrows, as it's hardly clear which species is the lower in the avian pecking order.

Kosciuszko was in his late twenties and hopelessly in love. As he would throughout his life, he took his fate into his own hands, dashing to Warsaw to seek the intervention of his old benefactor, King Stanislaw. No luck. Stanislaw was in effect a puppet monarch, having been placed on the Polish throne by Catherine the Great, whose bed and favour he'd enjoyed as a younger man while serving as a Polish diplomat in St Petersburg. The king had to tread warily with powerful nobles like Lord Sosnowski, many of whom were sympathetic toward Russia. With no help from on high, Kosciuszko faced a choice: pragmatism or defiance. Was Pope John Paul II a Catholic? Do endangered Carpathian brown bears poop in the woods of Poland's Bieszczady Mountains? Kosciuszko of course chose defiance and he and Ludwika tried to elope, until the nobleman's henchmen chased the couple down and delivered Kosciuszko a severe beating. Broke, broken and heartbroken, he made his way back to Paris.

It was now 1775 and the French capital was abuzz with news of the nascent American Revolution. The early Revolutionary War skirmishes in the Massachusetts towns of Lexington and Concord would in time come to be known collectively as 'the shot heard round the world' after a line in Ralph Waldo Emerson's 1837 'Concord Hymn'.

In Paris, where there was no love for the imperial British, the proverbial shot was heard almost as soon as it was fired. To a Polish idealist trained in military arts, the idea of a freedom-loving nation fighting to unharness itself from Britain's colonial yoke was irresistible. Apart from all that, this was an age of mercenary militarism. If war didn't find its way to the country of trained officers, they'd often go and find one. The fact that America's revolution was justified in Kosciuszko's eyes only strengthened his resolve. The shot heard round the world was another shot that Kosciuszko was not throwing away.

CHAPTER 2

A TORNADO IN JEFFERSONVILLE

Flying from Australia to the east coast of the United States, you lose a day of your life but gain most of it back with the time difference. That is, unless east coast storms delay your connecting flight and you depart Los Angeles for Newark four hours late, divert to Washington because those stubborn storms still haven't cleared, sit on the plane in the middle of the tarmac eating the world's saltiest peanuts for three hours at the aptly named Washington Dulles Airport, then finally depart for Newark, arriving who knows when but it starts with a small number.

A later inspection of the National Weather Service log for 22 April 2023 will reveal that the weather that wreaked havoc with air travel in the northeast was so severe that a tornado touched down outside the tiny village of Jeffersonville in upstate New York. A tornado in Jeffersonville. If that's not an omen, it'll do till we get a better one.

Chris, a commercial airline pilot, has also been delayed for hours by the storms, which means he's en route from New

York's JFK Airport to his home in leafy Hillsborough, New Jersey, and it's no inconvenience to pick up his Australian cousin by marriage at Newark. He arrives in a large, white, sleek Rivian electric pickup truck. The brand's slogan 'Keep the world adventurous forever' is surely a nod to America's fear that the inevitable phase-out of the internal combustion engine will somehow translate to a loss of freedom, excitement and good times. If the Rivian is any guide, good times are here to stay. Chris can't resist showing off how the noiseless monster accelerates from zero to warp speed in a finger snap. Nor does he mind sharing that he voted for Donald Trump in the 2016 presidential election, then didn't in 2020. While a sample size of one can never prove or disprove a broader demographic trend, Chris nonetheless helps you to understand how the 2020 United States presidential election was won, not stolen, by Joe Biden. Not that proof is needed after literally dozens of judges – Republicans among them – ruled in literally dozens of courts that there was not the faintest shred of evidence of coordinated foul play. Indeed, there's compelling evidence that Trump himself tried to affect the election result with his phone call urging Georgia's Secretary of State to find 11,000 votes, an act which eventually led to one of his indictments and the famous 'Blue Steel' mugshot, which really should have taken on the name 'Blue Steal'.

The point is that Chris is the sort of successful, hardworking American from a migrant family who is naturally inclined to vote for a pro-business candidate. He works hard when he's working and plays hard when he's playing, his garage full of skis, mountain bikes and other outdoor toys as sleek and shiny as the Rivian. But four years of Trump chaos was too much for him, and there were clearly millions of swing voters like him who swung cautiously, or even enthusiastically, toward

Trump in 2016, then away from him in 2020. How they will swing next is anyone's guess.

Daylight is a slap in the face. Cousin Karen, Chris's wife, is poring over college applications at the kitchen table with their eldest child, Kayla. For now, the applications can wait. Karen is leaving her kids Jared and Kayla at home and coming to Philadelphia to learn about Kosciuszko before taking her Australian cousin out for cheesesteak. Philadelphia's Thaddeus Kosciuszko National Memorial is the only museum in America dedicated to Kosciuszko, and we want to get there early before hunger gets the better of us.

Highway 76 is like the episode in *Better Call Saul* where Saul, or Jimmy as he's still called at that point in the series, takes out a billboard beside the freeway. The freeway is lined with enormous pictures of lawyers with airbrushed cheeks like seedless hamburger buns, each promising to maximise your payout from all manner of shocking mishaps, perhaps like that terrible repetitive strain injury you suffered while filling out forty-seven college applications. Personal injury lawyers generally take twenty-five per cent if there is a settlement or a third if the case goes to trial and they win. The legal system eats even its most deserving clients, and always has. There's no better example than the matter of Kosciuszko's will, which he wrote in conjunction with Thomas Jefferson in what is now the Thaddeus Kosciuszko National Memorial.

We make it to the memorial right on the midday opening time. It's situated within an attractive but unassuming three-storey brown brick building on the corner of 3rd and Pine in Philadelphia's historic Society Hill neighbourhood. We're greeted by a chirpy fella called Sean Stout, who explains that his employer, the United States National Park Service, administers the memorial. At just eighty square metres, the

Thaddeus Kosciuszko National Memorial is the smallest of the 425 'units' in the system that includes such icons as Yellowstone and Yosemite national parks. The memorial is also the least visited, generally attracting fewer than 100 people per day when it's open on weekend afternoons in the warmer months. But to Stout, the Thaddeus Kosciuszko Memorial is as important as any other unit, if not more so. Bearded and energetic with a background in archaeology and military history, Stout enthusiastically engages the trickle of visitors this fine spring Sunday, most of whom are drop-ins with zero knowledge of this unpronounceable historical figure. Stout says the memorial sees its fair share of Poles. It also attracts the occasional person who is ticking off every National Park Service unit. On hearing an Australian accent, he instantly makes the connection between the mountain and my interest. The source of his own interest?

'Obviously I'm drawn to Kosciuszko because of his military exploits specifically here during the American Revolution,' he says. 'But also he's a fascinating individual who fought for causes that he believed in. There have been military heroes across all countries and cultures over the years, but it seems to me few had the character of Kosciuszko.'

Kosciuszko first came to Philadelphia late in the summer of 1776. Due to the British blockade of key ports on America's Atlantic coast, European freedom fighters had to detour via the Caribbean and sneak in the back door on smaller boats. Kosciuszko's ship was wrecked near the coast of the east Caribbean island of Martinique, which was in British hands. Little is recorded about how he survived or how many others perished, but it's known that Kosciuszko eventually took a fishing boat to Philadelphia, which was then America's most populous city. The Declaration of Independence had been signed at the Pennsylvania State House while he was at sea and its most famous phrase – 'all men are created equal' – would prove to be the guiding principle of Kosciuszko's life. Indeed it was right here in this building that Kosciuszko would challenge Jefferson in his will to prove that he meant it.

But that would happen years later. When Kosciuszko walked off the docks in 1776, he was a stranger. He knew nobody and nobody knew him. Well-connected French officers expected or even demanded to be welcomed into the Continental Army with instant promotions but Kosciuszko had no such expectations. Some say he had not so much as a letter of recommendation, while others have suggested that Kosciuszko brought with him a recommendation from Prince Czartoryski, the head of his old school in Warsaw and the friend of Continental Army General Charles Lee, who had spent time in Czartoryski's household in Poland a decade earlier. Whatever the case, Kosciuszko managed to gain an audience with Founding Father Benjamin Franklin, who was a member of the Second Continental Congress, the body coordinating the early war efforts. Depending on which source you take as gospel, the meeting took place either in Franklin's print shop or Independence Hall. The two conversed in French, as Kosciuszko was not yet proficient in English, and the Pole asked to sit the engineer's exam. 'What sort of sophisticated operation do you think we're running here?' was the general gist of Franklin's response, so Kosciuszko instead sat, and nailed, a geometry test, which proves that all those x's and y's are valuable in any language even if the letter z is worth only one point in Polish Scrabble.

Franklin was also the head of the Pennsylvania Committee of Safety and wasted little time tasking the enthusiastic young engineer with bolstering the blockades and fortresses that were already underway on the New Jersey side of the Delaware River. This Kosciuszko accomplished with aplomb. He drafted plans for forts, built underwater defences called chevaux-de-frise — clusters of iron-tipped spiked logs sunk in the river, designed to rip open the hulls of British ships — and generally proved himself competent in all endeavours.

By late October 1776, he was Colonel Kosciuszko, on a United States Army salary of sixty dollars per month. By December, his expertise had come to the attention of General Washington, who at first assumed Kosciuszko was a Frenchman, perhaps because so many foreign officers were French, and possibly because Kosciuszko preferred to speak French over English, in which he was not yet proficient. Washington desperately needed engineers of any nationality and deployed Kosciuszko north of New York City to help defend the Hudson River Valley from General John Burgoyne's British redcoats surging southward from Canada. The British hoped to divide the thirteen rebellious colonies in two by controlling the crucial corridor of the Hudson, which Washington famously called 'the key to the Continent'. Thanks in large part to Kosciuszko, that key would remain firmly in Washington's hands and the door locked to the British.

We'll get to the Hudson soon enough. Indeed, we're off to the twentieth annual conference of the American Association of the Friends of Kosciuszko at West Point for an insider's tour of West Point and surrounds. But for now, let's skip forward twenty-one years to Kosciuszko's second visit to Philadelphia, as the Thaddeus Kosciuszko National Memorial commemorates that chapter of Kosciuszko's life. Remember that Kosciuszko first arrived in Philly in 1776, fought in the Revolutionary War until 1783, returned to Europe in 1784, fought in vain for Poland's independence, was imprisoned in Russia from 1794 to 1796, then returned briefly to America, residing in this building from November 1797 to May 1798.

Kosciuszko's landing in Philadelphia in late 1797 was a stark contrast to his anonymous arrival twenty-one years earlier. After two months of rough sailing from Bristol aboard a small freighter called the *Adriana*, cannons boomed a thirteen-gun salute as his ship sailed up the Delaware, while a large dockside crowd cried, 'Long live Kosciuszko!' The *Philadelphia Gazette* captured the occasion on 17 August 1797, as Kosciuszko was afforded the late-eighteenth-century equivalent of a lift into town in a sleek white Rivian electric pickup truck:

> On his landing, he was received with three cheers, and, as a further mark of great respect for this popular character, the citizens who were present insisted on drawing him to his lodgings.
>
> The General appears to be in good spirits but has suffered very materially from his wounds and inhuman imprisonment. We trust, however, he will long live to enjoy on these peaceful shores that liberty and happiness which he assisted in fighting for, but which he fought in vain to obtain for his native country.

You might imagine that Kosciuszko's Revolutionary War heroics had dimmed in the public imagination in the fourteen years since the end of the war, but his legend had in fact grown. His bravery in the Polish uprising in the name of universal liberty, his severe wounding on the battlefield and his subsequent captivity in Russia had all been widely reported in American newspapers.

'I beg you to be assured that, no one has a higher respect, and veneration for your character than I have; or one who more sincerely wished, during your arduous struggle in the cause of liberty and your country, that it might be crowned with success,' George Washington wrote to Kosciuszko on his arrival.

The incumbent president John Adams also contacted the Pole, writing: 'Give me leave Sir, to congratulate you on your arrival in America, where, I hope, you will find all the consolation, tranquility and satisfaction you desire after the glorious efforts you have made on a greater theatre.'

Not everybody welcomed or looked kindly upon Kosciuszko. Some among Adams' Federalist Party, founded by Alexander Hamilton, were wary of the Pole's revolutionary ways and his French sympathies at a time when they favoured building relations with the more stable English. But to the average person, Kosciuszko was a hero who had played a key role in America's birth, then taken its noblest aspirations to Europe. His story was known and it was celebrated. And now he was back, primarily to lobby Congress to cough up his unclaimed Revolutionary War pay, but also to reflect, rekindle friendships, recuperate and reset.

Kosciuszko's old room on the second floor is cosy, homely, even a little cluttered. It is furnished as it was back in the day, strewn with his personal effects. It's almost as though old Koz has just ducked out for a stroll, assuming he was able to do so. Kosciuszko was severely wounded in the uprising in Poland, and his wounds were slow to heal during his Russian detention. Arriving in America, his movement remained severely limited but there's evidence he was more nimble than he let on. One general in the Kosciuszko Uprising wrote in his memoirs that when Kosciuszko was in America the second time, he exercised vigorously at night while alone in his quarters, keeping his improving mobility a secret from even his close confidants. This is not to suggest that Kosciuszko faked the severity of his injuries, or indeed that he was duplicitous or sneaky, but he knew when to keep his cards close to his chest. Kosciuszko had just been freed by Tsar Paul I and if the Tsar, or anyone who might report to him, believed that Kosciuszko was still bedridden and in no condition to return to Europe to meddle in Polish affairs, all the better.

Kosciuszko's simple wooden double bed takes up about half the space in his old room. Beside it stands a small tripod table holding two silver plates, an apple, a teapot and a candlestick. Under the window is a chaise longue upholstered in a tasteful rose-coloured fabric. A lovely touch is the cheery mint-green floral wallpaper which the National Park Service recreated from old discarded fragments. Three things deserve closer scrutiny: the coffee pots, the strange object on the chessboard and the scattered papers from the Pennsylvania Abolitionist Society.

There is no coffee pot in the actual bedroom but there's one on display on a table just outside it and another just down the hall, a clear statement that here lived a coffee connoisseur. And it's true. Kosciuszko, a figure ahead of his time in so ways, was definitely a man of today when it came to caffeine addiction. In *The Peasant Prince: Thaddeus Kosciuszko and the Age of Revolution*, Alex Storozynski unearthed a letter from the latter years of the war written by Kosciuszko to a certain Doctor William Read after a shipment of supplies arrived without coffee. Bear in mind that Kosciuszko never asked for much. He didn't pester his superiors about promotions, he never whined about the scanty provisions and he often willingly shared rations and threadbare blankets with men of lower rank. But we all have our weaknesses and there's something incredibly endearing and relatable about the uncomplaining Pole writing to Doctor Read speaking of his 'great mortification' at the absence of coffee. 'I cannot live without coffee,' he wrote. 'I beg you to send me six pounds of Coffee with Sugar in proportion.' Never mind all the other hardships of warfare, not least the daily threat of being killed or maimed: send Coffee with a capital C! And for mercy's sake, don't forget the Sugar with a capital S!

The chessboard is set up ready to play, with elaborately carved red and white pieces squared off against each other on a classic black and white surface. But before you could start the game in the classic manner by moving the king's pawn forward two spaces, you'd need to shift the mysterious object in the middle of the board, a ceremonial peace pipe tomahawk, as in both a tobacco-smoking implement and a weapon. And when you think about your typical nicotine addict, it's hardly the least useful two-in-one contraption, because what smoker doesn't turn murderous when they're out of tobacco? Smoke. Run out. Rampage homicidally. Rinse and repeat.

The story behind the peace pipe tomahawk is as intriguing as the object itself. It was a gift from Chief Little Turtle of the Miami people, whose name in his Algonquian dialect was Mihsihkinaahkwa, which makes you think that the letters k and h wouldn't be worth much in Algonquian Scrabble. Chief Little Turtle was a great military leader and, despite having led Native American forces who fought for the British in the Revolutionary War, the great warrior and humanist came to pay homage to his foe of two decades earlier. Kosciuszko wasn't a smoker but was so taken with the unusual gift that he presented his guest with a cloak, a pair of reading glasses and his favourite pair of pistols. 'These pistols I have carried and used on many a hard-fought battlefield in defence of the oppressed, the weak, the wronged of my own race. I now present them to you with the injunction that with them you shoot dead the first man who comes to subjugate you or to despoil your country,' Kosciuszko told the wildly appreciative chief.

Classic Kosciuszko. How often in history did a white guy tell an Indigenous guy to kill anyone who tries to enslave him or take his land?

Little Turtle became quite the fan after his encounter with Kosciuszko. He couldn't stop talking about his mate 'Kotscho', and there's a great account of the chief's response to the unexpected trio of gifts in the American diary of Julian Niemcewicz, Kosciuszko's loyal Polish comrade who was imprisoned with him in Russia and accompanied him to America:

> He came to see General Kosciuszko and presented him with a tomahawk. Kosciuszko gave him his felt cloak. The chieftain saw some eye-glasses and seemed to be eager to acquire them. Nothing could equal his joy when Kosciuszko presented them to him. He could not understand how glasses can enlarge objects and seemed to experience an endless pleasure in seeing them so changed. 'You have given me new eyes!' he exclaimed.

Kosciuszko, too, was seeing America more clearly than ever before on his second visit, and especially its hypocrisies.

He had first begun to think deeply about slavery in his twenties in Paris, where he moved in the same circles as French Enlightenment figures like Abbé Raynal, who wrote on the injustice of slavery and colonial cruelty in general, and the Marquis of Condorcet, who wrote a celebrated pamphlet denouncing slavery. The abolitionist spark lit by the French became a raging hot flame as Kosciuszko journeyed through plantations during the Revolutionary War in the late 1770s and early 1780s. Two decades later, with around three-quarters of a million people enslaved in America, slavery was on his mind again. This is why replicas of papers of the Pennsylvania Abolitionist Society are today strewn on the chaise longue in Kosciuszko's room. Founded in 1775, the society is the oldest abolitionist organisation in the United States and still exists to this day, now tackling issues like the over-representation of African Americans in prison.

The presence of those papers on the chaise longue is telling us something. Sean Stout says they would likely have inspired Kosciuszko's American will, in which he left every cent of his American estate — which essentially meant his Revolutionary War pay and the interest accrued — to free and educate enslaved people. If Thomas Jefferson had executed the will, as he had promised to do, it would unquestionably be one of America's most famous documents. But Jefferson welched on the deal, and what's truly remarkable is that hardly anyone knows this story.

CHAPTER 3

WHERE THERE'S A WILL, THERE'S A WAY OUT

Kosciuszko was a polyglot, which sounds like a person who eats too much Polish sausage, though it of course means he spoke multiple languages. Four with fluency – Polish, French, German and English – plus a few words in other tongues. So giggle at the typos in the first draft of his will if you must, but ask yourself how your English would be if you'd learned it among soldiers and hadn't used it for the best part of fourteen years.

Here's the text of the will as Kosciuszko originally drafted it in 1797.

> I beg Mr. Jefferson that in case I should die without will or testament he should bye out of my money So many Negroes and free them, that the restante Sums should be Sufficient to give them aducation and provide for thier maintenance. that is to say. each should know before; the duty of a Cytysen

in the free Government. that he must defend his Country. against foroign as well internal Enemies who would wish to change the Constitution for the worst. to inslave them by degree afterwards. to have good and human heart Sensible for the Sufferings of others. each must be maried and have 100. Ackres of Land. wyth instruments. Cattle for tillage and know how to manage and Gouvern it as well to know behave to neybourghs. always wyth Kindnes. and ready to help them to them selves frugal. to ther Children give good aducation i mean as to the heart, and the duty to ther Country, in gratitude to me to make thems'elves hapy as possible.
T Kosciuszko

Now here's the final version of the will which Jefferson – once a highly regarded attorney who had been admitted to the Virginia bar thirty years earlier in 1767 – used his legal expertise to touch up:

I, Thaddeus Kosciuszko, being just in my departure from America do hereby declare and direct that should I make no other testamentary disposition of my property in the United States, I hereby authorize my friend Thomas Jefferson to employ the whole thereof in purchasing Negroes from among his own or any others and giving them Liberty in my name, in giving them an education in trades or otherwise and in having them instructed for their new condition in the duties of morality which may make them good neighbors good fathers or mothers, husbands, or wives and in their duties as citizens teaching them to be defenders of their Liberty and Country and of the good order of society and in whatsoever may make them happy and useful, and I make the said Thomas Jefferson my executor of this.

While Jefferson did the legal i-dotting and t-crossing, Kosciuszko made a subtle but significant change. The first version of the will had mentioned freeing and educating enslaved people. The final version specifically mentioned the option of freeing and educating some of the enslaved people owned by Jefferson. This was Kosciuszko tapping his buddy on the shoulder, using a legal document to convey words which were perhaps too awkward to express in conversation. Jefferson surely intended to honour his friend's wishes. Why else did he agree to be executor?

Kosciuszko died in October 1817, aged seventy-one, after falling from a horse which may or may not have been his trusty pony Dobry. He tumbled into the chilly waters of a river and when he caught a fever, the fever caught him twice as hard.

Months earlier, Jefferson had written to Kosciuszko, inviting him to spend his final days at Jefferson's Monticello plantation, urging his old friend to 'close a life of liberty in a land of liberty'. Kosciuszko had politely declined, preferring to use his last flickers of life in Solothurn, giving pennies to the poor and advising anyone who sought his counsel on matters relating to Poland. Then, a month before his death, Kosciuszko wrote the last of the forty-one known letters between him and Jefferson. Of his American funds, he wrote 'after my death, you know the fixed destination'. It was his final reminder that this was what really mattered to him.

Jefferson learned of Kosciuszko's death via American newspaper reports in December 1817, two months after the event. He was working at that time to establish the University of Virginia, the last great project of his public life, and while he knew it would be energy-sapping probating even the most straightforward American will of a European who had died in Europe, he declined to engage a lawyer and started going through the motions himself. His first act was writing to William Crawford, the Secretary of the Treasury, and William Wirt, Attorney-General of the United States and Jefferson's personal legal adviser. Jefferson had numerous reasons for contacting them. For example, he sought clarity on the appropriate court in which to prove the will, yet the wording of his letters leads some to believe that Jefferson was being a little cagey.

'Jefferson concealed the precise language of Kosciuszko's will,' historian Graham Russell Gao Hodges argued in his 2008 book *Friends of Liberty: Thomas Jefferson, Thaddeus Kosciuszko and Agrippa Hull*, which was co-authored with the late historian Gary B Nash. The book is brilliant. It pulls off the nifty trick of reshaping the way we view history by giving roughly equal space to Jefferson, Kosciuszko and Hull, a free Black man from Massachusetts who was Kosciuszko's Revolutionary War assistant before living a comparatively anonymous life. Hodges contends that Jefferson was 'deliberately vague' in his letter to Wirt, stating only that he had been asked to dispose of Kosciuszko's funds 'in a particular course of charity'. He argues that Jefferson was 'similarly opaque' in his letter to Crawford, in which he again neglected to mention Kosciuszko's specific intent to free and educate the enslaved.

On 12 May 1819, 76-year-old Thomas Jefferson walked into the Albemarle County Circuit Court in Charlottesville, Virginia, just down the hill from Monticello. The court was in session but everyone dropped what they were doing when they saw who'd just shown up. Jefferson told the court he'd been named executor of Kosciuszko's will but that he couldn't fulfil his obligation, ostensibly due to old age. 'Your will is important to us,' he effectively told his late great mate Kosciuszko, 'please hold.'

Graham Hodges is a lanky New Yorker who rocks a mean baseball cap. In conversation with him, you can feel the search engine of his mind darting between millions of American history data points. One minute, you're talking about how Jefferson's reputation has diminished in leftist circles without plummeting off a populist cliff in the manner of, say, America's seventh president, Andrew Jackson, whom Hodges calls 'an enslaver with a deep hatred of Native Americans'. Then you're on to the 1824 presidential election, which Jackson lost to John Quincy Adams amid claims of electoral shenanigans, which of course teleports you directly to the 2020 presidential election and Trump, for whom Hodges has few kind words. When asked whether his views on Trump expressed here or elsewhere might get him in hot water, Hodges defiantly snarls, 'Trump is a traitor, that good enough for you?'

Hodges sees the worst of America in Trump and, while it might seem extreme to draw parallels between a bookworm like Jefferson and an unabashed populist like Trump, Hodges did exactly that in 2019, invoking the cronyism of the Trump administration in Jefferson's reticence to follow through with Kosciuszko's will in an article for the website historynewsnetwork.org:

> In a time when we are accustomed to seeing the current president reject scientific analysis on fearsome problems, stack regulatory commissions with those devoted to non-regulation, and stake out policy positions on the basis of insider friends and their deep-pocket interests, this earlier abandonment of an honor-bound pact with Kosciuszko has a peculiar odor.

Hodges argues that Jefferson chose to look after his Virginia cohort for fears of upsetting what he calls the 'Old Dominion aristocracy', whose lavish lifestyle, based on the profits of slavery, might have been threatened had Jefferson set the example of freeing the enslaved. The other obvious reason for Jefferson's reticence to execute Kosciuszko's will was the state of his personal finances. The man on America's two-dollar bill spent much of his life without two dollars to his name and was close to bankrupt after Kosciuszko's death.

Kosciuszko's funds – which had ballooned out to more than $17,000 from the original $12,280.54 due to interest – would have compensated Jefferson for freeing some of his enslaved workers. But who would harvest the crops? Who would manufacture nails in the plantation's nail factory? Who would cook the lavish dinners? Who would staff the dumb waiter in the basement to send up a fresh bottle of Château Lafite when Jefferson and his guests had drained the first one?

Without question, operations at Monticello would have been compromised if Jefferson had executed Kosciuszko's will. But he also had some perfectly valid reasons for relinquishing his duty, because there's a whole other side to this story.

In the introduction to his 2009 magnum opus *The Peasant Prince: Thaddeus Kosciuszko and the Age of Revolution*, Alex Storozynski notes that his editor advised him to ensure his book was not a hagiography – a word which originally meant an uncritical biography of a prominent person in a religious order, but which now generally means an uncritical biography of anyone – yet in the very next line, Storozynski confesses that it was 'tough to find blemishes'. He's right. It is tough. Combing through old texts and journal articles, Kosciuszko's character comes across as beyond reproach. But that doesn't mean he was perfect in all respects. If a performance review into his life's work were conducted in the afterlife, a white-winged middle-manager might point out that old Koz could be a little scatty on the administrative side of things, as evidenced by the fact that he made four wills. That's right, *four*. The result, obviously, was chaos.

'It was a veritable probate nightmare,' wrote District of Columbia lawyer Louis Ottenberg in the January 1958 issue of the *American Bar Association Journal* in an article entitled, 'A Testamentary Tragedy: Jefferson and the Wills of General Kosciuszko':

> And all this trouble arose because General Kosciuszko wrote and executed four unrelated testamentary dispositions with different beneficiaries for three small estates in three different countries. Even a great military engineer was a very poor will draftsman.

Ottenberg's entire article contains tones of deep admiration for Kosciuszko and genuine regret that Jefferson was unable to execute the will. But the lawyer in him just can't get past the legal complications of the four wills which, as he points out, Kosciuszko neglected to tell anyone about, Jefferson included.

The first Kosciuszko will was the one he made with Jefferson in Philadelphia in 1798.

In 1806, he made a second will leaving $3704 to the son of his Revolutionary War comrade General John Armstrong. Kosciuszko had rekindled his friendship with Armstrong in Philadelphia in 1797, and again in 1804 after Armstrong was appointed ambassador to France by President Jefferson. Armstrong must have thought extremely highly of Kosciuszko, because his son was not christened Thomas or George or Sebastian or Billy Bob, but Kosciuszko Armstrong.

Kosciuszko wrote his third will in French in 1816 in Paris, leaving his Polish properties to members of his family. The will contained no reference to his American estate. In it, there was a standard revocation clause which read: 'Je révoque tous les testaments et codiciles que j'ai pu faire avant le présent auquel seul je m'arrête comme contenant mes dernières volontés.' Translated, this rendered all his previous wills null and void. Why, the following year, he then reminded Jefferson of his obligation to the 1798 will is a mystery. Polish American historian James Pula suggests that Kosciuszko perhaps failed to realise that the French attorney had included the pro forma revocation clause.

The fourth will was dated 10 October 1817, about a week before Kosciuszko's death. This one left his money and assets to his Swiss host family, the Zeltners, and contained no revocation clause or reference to any assets in America. This was the will in which he granted freedom to the serfs on his family estate (sadly, Poland was under the thumb of Russia's Tsar Alexander, who denied this wish).

Unsurprisingly, the three subsequent wills wreaked legal havoc on Kosciuszko's American will, which was contested in US courts for thirty-five years. Imagine the actor William Shatner as a buff young Captain Kirk in *Star Trek*, then Shatner as portly veteran lawyer Denny Crane in *Boston Legal*: that's how long it took to get this thing settled. Numerous claimants emerged over time, including the children of Kosciuszko's elder sister, Anna, who argued they were legally entitled as Kosciuszko had no direct descendants. In 1852, the Supreme Court finally delivered its judgement, ruling that the 1816 will invalidated the two before it, which meant that Anna's descendants ended up receiving what was left of Kosciuszko's American funds. Sadly, by then, that equated to not much.

As late in the piece as 1847, the estate was worth a whopping $43,504 thanks to the ongoing magic of compound interest. Alas, the funds were almost certainly pilfered. In 1832, a certain Colonel George Bomford was appointed executor of the will. By the time he died in 1848, just $5,680 of the $43,504 could be found. The administrator who came after Bomford reported to the court that Bomford had 'wasted or converted to his own use' $37,924.40. That's comfortably in the vicinity of a million dollars in today's money, swindled or frittered away in the finest traditions of the American legal system.

'The ideals of this Polish American hero, his hopes for liberty and education of the oppressed and his choice of Mr Jefferson – all these were superb. They were the sublime expression of his American experience,' concluded Ottenberg. 'But the implementation of those ideals was at fault. There were just too many wills.'

That's more or less how Annette Gordon-Reed, Professor of History at Harvard, sees it. Gordon-Reed won the Pulitzer Prize for History for her 2008 book *The Hemingses of Monticello: An American Family*. Sally Hemings was an enslaved woman who was Jefferson's sexual partner after his wife, Martha, died, and who gave birth to six of his children yet was never freed, even after Jefferson's death. This should make it clear that Annette Gordon-Reed is no pom pom–shaking cheerleader for Jefferson but she remains pragmatic on the matter of the Kosciuszko will, as evidenced by her contribution to *The Atlantic* in December 2012.

Gordon-Reed's article was a response to the journalist and author Ta-Nehisi Coates, who wrote an *Atlantic* piece entitled 'Thomas Jefferson and the Divinity of the Founding Fathers', in which he argued that he didn't think much of the line that

Jefferson would have subjected himself and his family to some amount of financial hardship by emancipating his enslaved workers in accordance with Kosciuszko's wishes. 'I find that argument about as morally compelling as claiming that a billionaire banker must continue dealing fraudulent balloon-payment mortgages, lest he sink into poverty,' Coates wrote. 'Doing the right thing hurts. That's the point.' Coates then doubled down in a similar story the next day, implicating Gordon-Reed as a defender of Jefferson.

In an article headlined 'Thomas Jefferson, Tadeusz Kosciuszko, and Slavery: Annette Gordon-Reed Responds', the Harvard law professor's tone was admirably good-natured and breezy as she rifled off three quick points in Jefferson's defence after noting that she, too, was initially inclined to be critical of Jefferson when she first learned of Kosciuszko's will.

Her first point was that being the executor of a will is a role that 'mixes power with responsibility and risk' and that will administrators must post a bond, which Jefferson was hardly in a position to do, given his precarious finances.

Second, she pointed out that the 'heart-tugging language' often used in relation to Jefferson's duty to his friend unfairly stacked the deck:

> Your friend asks you to perform a task that seems simple enough at first. Then he/she proceeds to do things, without telling you, that substantially increase the difficulty of carrying out the task. Indeed the friend's actions may involve you in long-running litigation.

In a throwback to the old US road safety slogan that went 'Friends don't let friends drink and drive', she concluded: 'Friends don't implicate friends in litigation.'

Third, Gordon-Reed argued that the stages of life matter. She wrote that founding the University of Virginia and executing Kosciuszko's will might have been too much for someone who was in his twilight years, which is why he sought a younger person to replace him.

Gordon-Reed ended her piece with a broader point about people's reticence to face the fact that white supremacy was part of America's founding ideology: 'Beating up on TJ, as if he were some singular case, is part of the denial.'

CHAPTER 4

THE TEETH OF THE ISSUE

The bestselling recent biography of Thomas Jefferson is 2012's *Thomas Jefferson: The Art of Power* by the distinguished American journalist Jon Meacham. You could break a window with the 802-page volume, yet in his brick of a book, Meacham does not dwell upon the matter of Kosciuszko's will.

Meacham swirls into the ballroom of your attention like a romance novelist, painting a vivid portrait of the Master of Monticello as a sort of George Clooney of yesteryear, ageing but more screwable than ever, with a crow's foot or two and a country squire's natural wear and tear:

> His sandy hair, reddish in his youth, was graying. His freckled skin, always susceptible to the sun, was wrinkling a bit. His eyes were penetrating but elusive, alternately described as blue, hazel or brown. He had great teeth.

Oh, those penetrating but elusive eyes. The guy belonged on a Mills & Boon cover. And those great teeth. Thomas Jefferson kept at least 600 people enslaved in his lifetime and didn't hesitate to pay a debt by selling off a human being who would never see their family again, but by god, he had immaculate oral hygiene. In dreams, the loss of teeth symbolises vulnerability, insecurity, even shame. Old TJ experienced none of that because he had chompers like Zeus in a Colgate ad.

'America has always been torn between the ideal and the real, between noble goals and inevitable compromises,' Meacham muses in the introduction to his book. But was Jefferson's shunning of his duty as executor really an inevitable compromise on the noble goal of Kosciuszko's will? Not according to legal historian Paul Finkelman, author of the 2014 book *Slavery and the Founders: Race and Liberty in the Age of Jefferson*. In 2017, Finkelman delivered an animated, highly entertaining talk in his pleasing, somewhat gravelly voice, at an Historical Society of the New York Law Courts event at Fraunces Tavern, a Lower Manhattan eatery and watering hole which as stated earlier was where Washington inducted Kosciuszko into the Society of the Cincinnati in 1783.

> The first thing to understand ... is that if there was any single man in the United States who you should not entrust money to, not only for investing but for the purpose of fighting slavery, that single man was Master Thomas of Monticello.

Bam!

> This is a man who bought and sold human beings the way some of us go to the grocery store, and it is important to understand this when we understand the will, because when our emancipationist Polish general is in Philadelphia, being good friends with Jefferson ... they were undoubtedly

talking about the problem of slavery and I am sure that Jefferson is nodding and saying, 'Oh yes, of course slavery is something we need to deal with, yes it's terrible about these poor slaves' and at the same time he is writing letters to his overseer, telling him to sell human beings because of his constant importation of fine wine and antiques and art from France.

Oof!

Now, I appreciate Jefferson's taste in wine ... But one might think that the taste of the wine would be a little off when you realise that it was paid for in misery, because selling a slave always meant that families would be divided ... people you've known your whole life, you would never see again.

Thwok!

We get Thomas Jefferson in the textbook as the man who wrote, 'we're all created equal', and 'we're endowed with the rights of life, liberty and the pursuit of happiness.' We don't get the Jefferson who writes to his overseer and says, 'I'm tired of the behaviour' – and then he names a slave – 'I want you to go to his cabin at three in the morning and sell him' ... and sadly, this is the man that is entrusted with carrying out this will.

Zing!

And so when Jefferson hears that his friend has died, he doesn't take the money ... he goes to court and says,

'Relieve me of this burden because I am too old to accept this burden.' The only problem is that he's not too old to be actively involved in politics, he is not too old to be lobbying for the creation of the University of Virginia, he is not too old to be fighting with people politically all over the country. He is too old to lift so much as his pinky finger to help slaves and to end slavery.

Kapow!

When I catch Finkelman at home on a quiet weekday evening, he is no less feisty. He simply can't get past the fact that this was *Thomas Jefferson*. Courtrooms cleared for him. No-one in the whole of America held more sway.

'If Jefferson wants to be the executor, he walks into the Chancery Court and he says, "Here's the will, Kosciuszko's made me his executor, I'm going to do it and I'm not even going to take the executor's fee because I don't want to make money off the death of my friend. I will do it because I'm an honourable man. Does the court have any objections?" And the judge says, "Mr Jefferson, we're so honoured that you're in our court. Of course we have no objections." And nobody raises the question of the bond. Why? Because it's Thomas Jefferson!'

As for the legal complications of the other wills, Finkelman reckons Jefferson could have sorted out that kind of mess with his eyes shut. 'He has a very long career as a lawyer. He's a very good lawyer. Read the Declaration of Independence – I mean, this is a crackerjack legal mind! And what do you think a lawyer in Virginia in 1817 did? Contract disputes, land transactions, slave transactions and wills. Writing wills and being executors were things lawyers regularly did.'

Nor does Finkelman put much stock in Jefferson's claims that he was too old.

'All you've got to do is look at his correspondence to know how vigorous he is. He's completely vigorous. He's writing ten letters a day. And then he was designing UVA but that was later. That was after the will.'

Finkelman often brings up 'the Coles letter' – an 1814 letter from Edward Coles, a much younger neighbour who had just inherited enslaved people from his father, who was also the private secretary to President James Madison. Coles had decided to free his enslaved, in part because he was influenced by Jefferson and the Declaration of Independence. In the letter, Coles asks Jefferson to endorse his plan. He spends about ten lines saying 'I'm not worthy' before daring to urge the former president to:

> employ your pen to eradicate this most degrading feature of British Coloniel policy, which is still permitted to exist, notwithstanding its repugnance as well to the principles of our revolution as to our free Institutions.

Jefferson's response to the Coles letter? To use the succinct, all-purpose Australian phrase which means the arrow on your cerebral dial briefly veers to yes before flicking firmly back to no, Jefferson went, 'yeah, nah'.

'Coles says to Jefferson, "You're free of politics, you're free to do this now. You've led us this far, take the next step",' Finkelman explains. 'And Jefferson writes back this five-page letter. And in the first two pages, he talks about the problem we're facing and you think that Jefferson is about to become an abolitionist. Then he turns around and says, "Screw them. We don't care about them. They're pests on society."'

This is true. Finkelman obviously has the gift for painting a colourful version of history, but 'pests on society' were

Jefferson's actual words, and there was worse in his letter to Coles, including the part where he wrote:

> Their amalgamation with the other colour produces a degradation to which no lover of his country, no lover of excellence in the human character can innocently consent.

How Jefferson reconciled those words with his decades-long sexual relationship with the enslaved Sally Hemings is anyone's guess.

Coles himself was not perfect. In the *Atlantic* in 2012, Annette Gordon-Reed referenced an 1831 letter that Coles wrote to Jefferson's grandson, in which he called African Americans an 'ignorant, immoral & degraded race'. Those were strange days indeed, when even an avowed abolitionist was on the record calling African Americans inferior. But at least Coles walked the abolitionist walk. Eventually, he took his enslaved people to Illinois, emancipated the lot of them, bought them land and ended up governor of that slavery-free state. When Jefferson was Governor of Virginia, from 1779 to 1781, no state in the union held more people enslaved.

'Jefferson could have said, "Okay, I'm going to free twenty-five slaves and I'll even let the slaves live on Monticello free while they get settled because Kosciuszko gave me all this money. It solves my financial problem. It's a tip of a hat to my friend Kosciuszko. And for the only time in my life, I will have done the right thing with regard to slavery." He could have done that.'

Those are Paul Finkelman's words toward the end of a long, lively conversation, and when you've been around writing and journalism long enough, you get a sense of when someone has provided a great quote to end a chapter or story. But the urge to ask one more question is too strong. When you've got an eminent legal historian at your disposal, how can you not present him with the binary courtroom choice of guilty or not guilty on the matter of Jefferson's conduct on Kosciuszko's will?

'Guilty!' Finkelman exclaims with not a nanosecond of hesitation. 'In fact, he's completely guilty, which is even worse than guilty!'

CHAPTER 5

CHEESESTEAKS AND HIGH STAKES

After a healthy serve of Kosciuszko at the Thaddeus Kosciuszko National Memorial, it's time for cheesesteaks and root beer. Root beer is hard to find in Australia, while cheesesteaks are popping up here and there but you always want to try a famous dish in its place of origin.

A neighbourhood or two south of the Memorial, Philadelphia changes from pretty to gritty. This is South Philly, home to iconic cheesesteak rivals Pat's and Geno's. The two restaurants occupy opposing triangular blocks at an intersection where the diagonal East Passyunk Avenue slashes though the city's orderly grid pattern, carving little arrowheads of real estate. It feels like they're facing each other in an ongoing cheesesteak stand-off. But which establishment to try? Pat's calls itself the King of Steaks® and purports to be the inventor of the cheesesteak. Geno's goes 'Meh, who cares who dreamed it up? We've perfected it' and claims to make 'the best cheesesteak in Philadelphia'. So then, Pat's or Geno's? Geno's or Pat's? In the end, the parking gods make the decision and we take an outdoor seat at Pat's.

The cheesesteak is great. The flavour is a little one-note, but this is cheese and steak on a bread roll we're talking about, not Michelin-starred cuisine. The root beer complements it perfectly, with just the right amount of crushed ice to keep the drink cold without diluting it.

Opposite Pat's is a park with a couple of pick-up games in progress on the basketball courts. The local players aren't much. Their shooting sucks and they catch and pass like their hands are covered in cheesesteak grease. Definitely no Philadelphia 76ers in this lot, the NBA team named for the year the Declaration of Independence was signed. In the late 2010s and early 2020s, the Sixers had a strong roster but never won a title, always falling a rung or two short of glory. In 2021, their star point guard Ben Simmons, originally from Australia and twice an NBA All-Star, mystifyingly lost his mojo. Late in game seven of the best-of-seven conference semifinals against the Atlanta Hawks, he got himself into a great position under the rim and just had to dunk to tie the scores. It was absolute bread-and-butter stuff, no cheese or steak required. But to everyone's shock, Simmons dished off to teammate and fellow Aussie Matisse Thybulle, who was fouled and made just one of the two ensuing free throws. The Sixers lost the momentum, the game and the series. Their coach, Doc Rivers, and the team's best player, Joel Embiid, both turned on Simmons. For failing to drive to the hoop himself, the city of Philadelphia turned on Simmons. Every American sports fan, and plenty worldwide, turned on Simmons. Nobody with even half an eye for the NBA has forgotten that moment.

Why is this relevant?

Because Simmons threw away his shot. Literally and figuratively, he threw away his shot. Not because he failed to pull off a regulation move which would have constituted a garden-variety sporting fail, but because he didn't even try, which was a cultural fail, and nothing less than an existential fail in the popular folklore of American life. Did not Miranda's Hamilton tell us that the essence of an American life – of the American dream – is to take your shot? Did not Eminem sell the same message with his line in 'Lose Yourself', the signature tune from the movie *8 Mile*, where he rapped about only getting one shot and about opportunity only arriving once and all that? Did not Thomas Jefferson set the tone for this entire American ethos with his words in the Declaration of Independence that you have 'unalienable rights' to 'Life, Liberty and the pursuit of Happiness'? An often overlooked but key word there is 'pursuit'. It means happiness is not guaranteed. You are not entitled to happiness, but by almighty god, you are entitled to a crack at it. You get your shot. On 20 June 2021, at the Wells Fargo Center right here in Philadelphia, Ben Simmons didn't take his shot. For this, he remains a villain.

Thomas Jefferson never took his shot at ending slavery either. Kosciuszko gave him his shot on a platter, also right here in Philly. And whatever Jefferson's considerable excuses, the bottom line is that he didn't take it, thus denying who knows how many people their pursuit of happiness. That's the tragedy here, and if the story were better known, perhaps more Americans would consign Jefferson to the same basket as Simmons.

'Had Jefferson felt stronger about the object, he would have ventured the experiment, despite statutory obstacles and the shortness of years,' wrote University of Virginia history professor and all-round Jefferson fan Merrill Peterson in his 1970 biography *Thomas Jefferson and the New Nation*.

'What an all-conquering influence must have attended his illustrious example …' wrote William Lloyd Garrison, the noted abolitionist, writer and publisher of anti-slavery newspaper *The Liberator*.

'One may wonder if the course of history would be different if Jefferson had freed his slaves in keeping with the will of Kosciuszko? Would we as a nation be farther ahead in social progress today?' Anita Solak, Archives Technician at the National Archives in Washington, DC, pondered more than two centuries later in the Blog of the National Archives Textual Records Division.

Now there's a provocative thought. What, apart from the destiny of the enslaved people themselves, might Jefferson have changed? Journalist Israel Losey White followed that thought track in a 1908 *Newark Evening News* article, 'It is possible that if [the will's] suggestion had been followed, there might have been no Civil War in the United States …'

Graham Hodges flirted with the idea when researching *Friends of Liberty*. By liberating the enslaved, might Jefferson have set off a chain reaction among wealthy Southern planters that hastened emancipation and even averted the Civil War? Hodges quickly put the theory to bed after speaking to Adam Rothman, author of *Slave Country: American Expansion and the Origins of the Deep South*: 'Would the planters in the South have done the same thing as Jefferson?' Hodges asks. 'Rothman said no.'

So Thomas Jefferson freeing and educating his enslaved in accordance with the 1798 Kosciuszko will might not have achieved much in the big picture of the America of his day. But history speaks to us in echoes, not memos. If Jefferson had actively sought and found a way to honour his dear departed friend's wishes, who knows how long the echoes may have lasted, and who they may have reached?

CHAPTER 6

SUNSHINE AND RAINBOWS

At some point in an American life, or in any life, the pursuit of happiness might become the less ambitious but no less worthy arc of moving on from unhappiness, or even just getting by. The recent story of Cousin Karen's sister, Debbie, is a little like that. Debbie lives in Princeton, New Jersey, which is only about fifteen minutes from Chris and Karen's place in Hillsborough. We're stopping off to visit her after we're done in Philly but first, we need to walk off those cheesesteaks. The area just north of cheesesteak corner is a largely Mexican neighbourhood. One restaurant is closing for the day and has left a stack of free homemade lentil soup in plastic containers on an outside table. We grab one to take to Debbie's then hit the road, stopping in downtown Princeton for a quick look-see.

In January 1777, General Washington led the Continental Army to victory over the British in the Battle of Princeton, just outside town. Ironically, Princeton today feels quite British, or at least it feels like an American version of Oxford. There is even a smattering of Tudor-style houses among the immaculately restored two-storey timber residences. Downtown Princeton is unabashedly upmarket, bordering almost on Disneyfied. But it's undeniably pretty, even if you have to be a Kennedy to afford a single scoop of gelato.

Debbie's condo is in a less posh part of town. It's half a room too small but it's homey and it's home. Debbie had dreams. You'd better believe Debbie lived those dreams. She was a rising star of Philadelphia TV news and then wham! Bam! Life socked her with a one-two punch. First, her daughter Lydia died of Neuroblastoma just before her third birthday. Then Debbie had a severe stroke. 'I had the floating up and away experience and all,' she says. Life can be unfair and life can be tough. Having just visited Philadelphia, it seems appropriate to illustrate this with the words of Sylvester Stallone's fictional Philadelphia fighter, Rocky Balboa, who in the 2007 film *Rocky Balboa* – the sixth instalment of the Rocky series – tells his son:

> The world ain't all sunshine and rainbows. It is a very mean and nasty place ... You, me or nobody is going to hit as hard as life. But it ain't about how hard you hit, it is about how hard you can get hit and keep moving forward ... That's how winning is done!

If getting hit and moving forward is the measure of success, then Debbie is a world champion. It's all about family now. There's her partner, Brad, a New Jersey good guy who likes Bruce Springsteen and baseball. There's her son, Adam, a livewire teenager with a heart of gold and enough bright-eyed energy to power the whole state. There's her mum, Lilian, in Florida, a great lady whose friendship with my mother helped bring together the two strands of our family, which had originated in Eastern Europe. And then there's Karen, the rock of the family and newest member of the Tadeusz Kosciuszko fan club. The two sisters are as close as identical twins, although they are definitely not that — Karen a caramel blonde, Debbie a flaming redhead. The five of us share pizza and the free Mexican lentil soup. The pizza is fine but the soup is the best thing any of us have eaten for ages. Like love and family and a home run caught in the stands, some things money can't buy.

Early the next morning, amateur chauffeur extraordinaire Karen chirpily drives her bleary-eyed Aussie cousin through light pre–rush hour traffic to the Amtrak Station in the small city of New Brunswick, New Jersey. Kosciuszko stopped off here in 1797 when escaping a serious outbreak of yellow fever that spread through Philadelphia. A yellow fever epidemic four years earlier had killed 5000 people in the city that then held 50,000, so Kosciuszko and his Polish comrade Julian Niemcewicz skipped town shortly after the *Adriana* docked, journeying to New York City to visit Kosciuszko's old Revolutionary War friend and commander, Major General Horatio Gates, at his estate in Rose Hill, Manhattan. Gates was commander of the Northern Department of the Continental Army in 1777 during the triumphant victory in the Battle of Saratoga, for which he generously, and accurately, credited Kosciuszko's brilliant engineering feats. Gates' military career and reputation would be ruined in 1780 with a devastating defeat in the Battle of Camden in South Carolina but Kosciuszko wasn't the type to abandon an old friend whose stature had diminished. Besides, in 1790 Gates had freed the enslaved people on his Virginia plantation, so the two doubtless had much to discuss.

Kosciuszko was super excited to see his old mate. We know this because *The Peasant Prince* author Alex Storozynski unearthed in the Gates Papers of the New York Historical

Society a great quote in a letter from Kosciuszko to Gates which read: 'I have only one friend and one servant with me, and with such army I will attack your house unless you will set your dogs at me, and by force throw me out from your house.' It's a rare snapshot of Kosciuszko in light-hearted banter mode. You can feel his enthusiasm and just about taste the nacho cheese corn chips or whatever snacks you took in the carriage on a road trip in 1797.

It's 100 miles, give or take, from Philadelphia to New York, and New Brunswick is a little over halfway, which made the New Brunswick home of Brigadier General Anthony Walton White, another of Kosciuszko's war buddies, the perfect stopover point. Both White and his wife, Margaret, were great admirers of Kosciuszko. Their grandson, Anthony Walton White Evans, conveyed that esteem in his 1883 memoir of the Pole's life. From page one, its tone was glowingly reverential:

> Among the men of modern times there was, perhaps, in Europe none whose fame was more brilliant, whose patriotism was more pure, and whose character for fierce bravery, gentle acts and virtuous conduct through life, was more unsullied than that of Thaddeus Kosciuszko.

The memoir chronicled Kosciuszko's visit to New Brunswick, as recounted by Evans' grandparents. Evans wrote that his grandmother considered Kosciuszko second only to Washington. 'Kosciuszko appeared to have some magnetic property about him, for he endeared himself to all he met, and the attachment remained throughout life,' he gushed.

It's true that almost everyone who met Kosciuszko adored him. And that begs the question: why did he never marry? Being broke for much of his life didn't help. That's what killed his hopes of marriage with Ludwika, and it kyboshed his mid-life proposal to another Polish woman, Tekla Zurowska, when he was again thwarted by a nobleman father seeking a suitor with deeper pockets. Were there really no other suitable women in Kosciuszko's life? He was certainly handsome enough, slightly taller than average, with his curly hair and pleasant features which were enhanced, not ruined, by that slightly upturned nose. Apart from bad luck and bad timing, was there another reason for his lifelong bachelorhood?

Prussian officer Friedrich von Steuben – who was among the Continental Army's most celebrated foreigners – is now widely considered to have been openly gay but there's only the faintest such suggestion with Kosciuszko, and you've got to go a fair way off-piste to find it. In the 2003 book *The Great Tradition and its Legacy: The Evolution of Dramatic and Musical Theater in Austria and Central Europe*, Halina Filipowicz, professor of Polish literature at the University of Wisconsin–Madison, argued that it's impossible to tell from the sketchy historical accounts whether Kosciuszko's attempted elopement with Ludwika Sosnowska was gossip or fact, arguing that the story has been amplified to maintain the image of a hero with a 'respectable' sexuality:

> Even his most devoted biographers note that he was seen as an 'effeminate' figure, soft and emotional. The Sosnowska story at once removes the imputation of Kosciuszko's gender bending and reasserts his heterosexuality. He is safely returned to his all-male world where he substitutes the love of country for would-be pleasures of the flesh.

But what if love of country really was a surrogate for the love of a woman? What if, even in his own lifetime, women tended to view Kosciuszko as more of a symbol than as living flesh and blood – as hero material, not husband material?

In a 2018 article in the journal *Polish American Studies*, the academic Jill Walker Gonzalez argued that the Anthony Walton White Evans memoir about Kosciuszko 'offered late nineteenth-century American readers a sentimental portrait of the man who epitomized Poland as America's beau ideal'. The phrase 'beau ideal' is interesting. It basically means America's best version of itself. Having led an uprising which tried to instil universal liberty in Poland at a time when no other European nation – not even France – was attempting anything quite as progressive, Kosciuszko remained the embodiment of American ideals long after his death. But perhaps, in his lifetime, he was just too committed to those ideals for people to commit to him. Like a fighter in the ring, a freedom fighter's life is not all sunshine and rainbows, especially not the rainbows part in Kosciuszko's case, on the basis of all available evidence. Not that the man himself would have thought there's anything wrong with that.

No-one ever said the neighbourhood in the vicinity of New Brunswick Amtrak Station was all sunshine and rainbows, or if they did, they had a good dealer. The watery coffee at the station's Dunkin' Donuts does nothing to improve the ambience. Why can't America make coffee? That noted caffeine addict Tadeusz Kosciuszko would doubtless be dismayed at this significant modern deficiency in the nation he helped found. Then again, perhaps the uncomplaining Pole would be thrilled to find even the most insipid brew readily available on any street corner.

The train to Washington is swift and full of laptop-tapping types this Monday morning. Window seat guy is a classic post-Covid hybrid commuter/work-from-homer – a couple of days in the DC office, the rest of the week in Brooklyn.

There's Princeton, Trenton, Philadelphia, Wilmington, Baltimore. There are lines recalled from *The Wire*, which was set in Baltimore – 'A man got to have a code' – a credo which Washington, DC lawmakers would do well to remember. And then there's Washington, a city that feels surprisingly familiar to this traveller, and not just because of landmarks familiar from TV and movies.

CHAPTER 7

JUST ANOTHER WHITE GUY FROM HISTORY

In 1901, Australia shrugged off its colonial past, at least constitutionally, and became a fully federated nation. In 1913, its capital city, Canberra, was founded in a valley where sheep still grazed – the location chosen essentially to end the bickering between the two largest cities, Sydney and Melbourne. Washington, DC was also founded as a compromise, and that's not the only similarity between the two capitals. As someone who grew up in Canberra, it soon becomes clear upon exiting Washington's Union Station and walking the streets of America's capital that Canberra, or at least its planned central area, resembles a mini-Washington. Both are places of statues, monuments, lawns, gardens, water and low-slung buildings with reflective glass, more boxy than skyscraping. Both have their residential neighbourhoods and suburbs strewn well out of sight of the governmental part of town, lest the elected representatives be reminded of who they're actually representing. And in both cities, the point of these manicured spaces and unspectacular office blocks seems to be to tell a calm, controlled story of the nation, and of the government's role in shaping that narrative.

Thomas Jefferson referred to the US government as 'the world's best hope' in the inaugural address of his first presidency in 1801, a phrase echoed by Lincoln in his 1862 speech to Congress and many times since. But the white-domed neoclassical Capitol building, housing the legislative arm of the world's best hope, became a place of despair and violence on 6 January 2021, as 'stolen election' ideologues and assorted riffraff stormed the Capitol, hardly dissuaded by Donald Trump and, according to at least one judge, egged on by him. The result was five deaths, injuries to more than 100 police officers and many others, and damage in the millions. It's surreal to be a foreigner ascending the gentle slope of Capitol Hill on a sublime spring morning, warm enough for ice cream, cool enough for soup, and contemplating the chaos that unfolded here. But America has never been a dormant volcano, and Washington is one of its most active vents.

Prior to the attack on the Capitol, the most recent large-scale outburst of unrest in Washington had been in May 2020 after the murder of Minneapolis man George Floyd, who was choked to death when police officer Derek Chauvin refused to remove his knee from his neck despite Floyd's increasingly desperate cries of 'I can't breathe' and 'I'm about to die'. While onlookers urged Chauvin to ease off, Floyd somehow found the grace to entreat his soon-to-be murderer: 'Please, the knee in my neck, I can't breathe.' The white cop was physically and emotionally unmoved at the plight of the prone Black man. Before long, Floyd lay limp and lifeless. In response to the killing, people took to the streets in protest, first in Minneapolis, then around the country, then around the world as part of the Black Lives Matter movement, which had begun in 2013.

In Washington, as elsewhere, protestors defaced statues of old white guys. They didn't miss the Kosciuszko statue, located in the northeast corner of Lafayette Square, opposite the White House. After walking more than four kilometres down the National Mall from the Capitol to the Lincoln Memorial, then veering right up past the White House, I munch a food truck taco on a bench opposite the statue.

Not much is happening at the Kosciuszko statue. No-one kneels in reverence having completed a pilgrimage. No-one even stops out of passing interest. Not that old Koz seems to mind. He stands atop his pedestal, alert and ready for action, the sun warming his shoulders. He sports the uniform of a brigadier general of the Continental Army, an outfit he would have worn on ceremonial occasions after the war, but not during it as he wasn't promoted until the war had ended. But the purpose of such monuments is symbolism, not verisimilitude. And the symbolism here is rich, from the map in his right hand of his famous fortifications at Saratoga to the base of the pedestal where on one side an eagle guards a flag, a shield and a sword against a backdrop of a map of America, while on the other side an eagle battles a snake against a backdrop of a map of Poland. Eagles are, of course, freedom symbols in both America and Poland.

The statue was unveiled in 1910 by US president William Howard Taft, on the same day as he inaugurated a statue on nearby Pennsylvania Avenue of Casimir Pulaski, the Pole known as 'The Father of American Cavalry' who fell on a Revolutionary War battlefield in Georgia. Esteemed Polish historian and Kosciuszko biographer Tadeusz Korzon was in attendance at both events, while Theodore Roosevelt, the president before Taft, sent a telegram from Germany stating that Kosciuszko and Pulaski would 'forever be associated on the honor roll of American history'.

JUST ANOTHER WHITE GUY FROM HISTORY

To the protestors in May 2020, Kosciuszko was just another white guy from history. And they made a good mess of the statue, scrawling *BLM* and *Burn this bitch* in black spray paint and *Fuck 12* in red spray paint that left drip marks like blood (the phrase means 'Fuck the police' because police enforce the law and law starts with 'l' and 'l' is the twelfth letter of the alphabet).

Many high-profile Poles were aghast, including Polish radio journalist Pawel Zuchowksi, who shared a video of spray-painters clambering all over the statue. The then Polish ambassador to America, Piotr Wilczek, posted on social media that he was 'disgusted and appalled'. That elicited a feisty response from Polish American Kosciuszko biographer Alex Storozynski, who said, 'Kosciuszko would have been more disgusted that hundreds of Black people are killed by police each year than the fact that frustrated kids wrote *Black Lives Matter* on his statue.' A similar response came via the Kosciuszko Foundation, a non-partisan American group which has built cultural bridges between the USA and Poland since 1925. It released a statement which gave the statue's defacers a pass, while also explaining why they chose the wrong white dude on a plinth:

> While deeply saddened by the desecration of the Kosciuszko statue in Washington D.C., we understand the pain of the African American community about police killing unarmed Black people. Graffiti can be washed off. The loss of a loved one is eternal.
>
> But Kosciuszko was the wrong target for this frustration. Kosciuszko dedicated his salary as a General from the American Revolution for the emancipation and education of enslaved Africans. He asked that his money

be used to buy land, livestock and farming tools for liberated slaves so that they could make their own living as free citizens of the United States. He knew that Black Lives Matter ...

Kosciuszko was a man ahead of his time. That's why the Kosciuszko Foundation will contribute to the cleansing of the Statue in Lafayette Park, and we urge all Americans to learn more about Kosciuszko's vision of tolerance. Kosciuszko led by setting an example that we should all try to follow.

Meanwhile, two Polish philosophers were so convinced that Kosciuszko would understand the reasons behind the Washington, DC statue's besmirchment that they believed it should never be cleansed. Lukasz Moll and Michal Pospiszyl sent a petition to the Polish government, arguing that the graffiti should be left in place to highlight the plight of African American victims of American police brutality. 'We are certain that had Kosciuszko been resurrected, he would himself write "Black Lives Matter" in big bold letters across his statue,' they wrote on Poland's left-leaning *Krytyka Polityczna* website.

It's an interesting thought, which after all is what philosophers are supposed to have: would a resurrected Kosciuszko make a statement by defacing his own statue? And here's a provocative thought from an Australian writer pondering all things Koz: would the great republican Kosciuszko be denigrated by modern-day Republicans as 'woke'? America's Merriam-Webster dictionary defines woke as being 'aware of and actively attentive to important facts and issues especially of racial and social injustice'. Is that not precisely what Kosciuszko stood for?

As if deliberately to pop the thought bubble, a loudspeaker barks from over near the White House. 'Leave the park now!' The reason for the sudden eviction is unclear, but what can you do? Onward to the Jefferson Memorial on the banks of the Potomac, a solid half-hour's walk and an excellent opportunity to de-taco.

CHAPTER 8

A SUKMANA FOR A SABLE

The Jefferson Memorial is an airy, unenclosed space with fifty-four columns, a domed roof like the Capitol's, albeit much smaller, and the words of the Declaration of Independence etched into the white-marble wall panels. It feels like this place was designed to reassure Americans that it's their right as free citizens of a free country to be as solemn or as light-spirited as they see fit, to linger reverentially or breeze on through as they pay homage to the six-metre-tall bronze Founding Father who commands the room from the centre, arms by his side, pursed lips hiding those great teeth. Thomas Jefferson looks resplendent in his full-length coat, which would no doubt please Kosciuszko, as the coat was once his.

Kosciuszko hastily gave the black sable coat to Jefferson at the end of his second stint in America in 1798. Before that, it had belonged to Tsar Paul I. The story of how Kosciuszko got the coat dates back to what was effectively the end of the Kosciuszko Uprising at the Battle of Maciejowice on 10 October 1794, not far south of Warsaw. In that battle,

Kosciuszko fell from his horse and Cossacks thrust pikes into him three times as he lay on the ground. Because he was dressed in the woven sheep's wool peasant robe called a sukmana, the Cossacks didn't realise they were spearing the supreme commander of the Polish forces until it was almost too late. In despair, Kosciuszko put his pistol in his mouth. Depending on whose account you read, it either failed to fire because it was out of bullets and he then lost consciousness face down in the mud, or Kosciuszko lost consciousness before he was able to pull the trigger. The key fact is that the pistol never fired and he survived.

Kosciuszko's fall at Maciejowice is the moment captured in Thomas Campbell's line: 'And Freedom shriek'd — as KOSCIUSKO fell!'

Not that Poland's enemies put it in quite those terms. Remember that Poland was fighting the Russians, Prussians and Austrians. The home territory of the Prussians included large parts of today's Germany, and they were the ones who spread the rumour that Kosciuszko had cried, 'Finis Poloniae!' – Latin for 'Poland is finished!' – as he fell from his horse, no doubt hoping that if it were widely believed that the uprising's leader had given up on a free Poland, all Polish citizens would surrender arms. But the cry was a fabrication; we know this because Kosciuszko himself addressed the lie in a letter to the Comte de Segur, a Frenchman and fellow American Revolutionary War veteran and Society of the Cincinnati member:

> When the Polish nation called me to defend the integrity, the independence, the dignity, the glory and the liberty of the country, she knew well that I was not the last Pole, and that with my death on the battlefield or elsewhere Poland could not, must not end ...

Then, as now, truth was the first casualty of war.

Kosciuszko's identity was eventually discovered as he lay prone in the dirt and he was attended by a Russian surgeon. Captured with him were many close comrades, including his valet Jean Lapierre – a Black man who was probably from Saint-Domingue, the former French colony in what today is Haiti – and Julian Niemcewicz, Kosciuszko's aide-de-camp. Niemcewicz was of noble birth and had played a significant role in the Kosciuszko Uprising and events leading up to it. A poet, playwright, politician and patriot, he penned many of the speeches that Kosciuszko delivered and the proclamations to which he put his name. Niemcewicz had a gift, writing with passion and realism well ahead of his time. His account of the maimed and severely wounded Kosciuszko at Maciejowice, published in his 1844 book *Notes of My Captivity in Russia: In the Years 1794, 1795 and 1796*, is vivid and emotive:

> His head and body covered with blood, contrasted in a dreadful manner with the livid paleness of his face ... He could scarcely breathe. This was very painful to me; the silence, or rather sullen stupor, was, at last, interrupted by the sobs and cries of a grief as violent as sincere. I embraced the General, who had not yet recovered his senses, and from this moment until we were thrown into solitary prisons, I remained with him.

Kosciuszko, Niemcewicz, Lapierre and many others were marched off to Russia, with Kosciuszko and the less badly wounded Niemcewicz afforded the relative luxury of travelling in carriages through the late autumn snows as the Russians ransacked villages along the way. The captives were eventually imprisoned in the Peter and Paul Fortress on an island in St Petersburg's Neva River, opposite the Hermitage Museum, which was then thirty years old. Inconsolable at the loss of his country's freedom and at his wits' end after constant interrogation, Kosciuszko again tried to take his own life, this time by hunger strike. Catherine the Great put an end to that, transferring him to the palatial home of a wealthy banker, then to another family's mansion. She never granted Kosciuszko an audience but she wanted her prize alive. Niemcewicz continued to languish in prison, but both men did it tough. Anywhere in Russia was captivity for the Polish patriots.

Then after two years, their luck turned. In November 1796, Catherine the Great died, aged sixty-seven. Her son, Tsar Paul I, was no fan of his mother, probably because she had overthrown his father to take the throne, then likely sanctioned his killing in prison. But the Tsar held deep admiration for Kosciuszko, whom he pardoned and freed within two weeks of his mother's death.

It might seem unusual that Russia's monarch would hold in such high regard the leader of an uprising against his own nation, but Kosciuszko had that sort of effect on people. In a 2014 article in US journal *The Polish Review*, Polish academic Michal Burczak compared Kosciuszko and Washington as symbolic national heroes and unearthed a quote from one of Kosciuszko's Polish comrades-in-arms, General Jozef Zajaczek, who wrote:

> Kosciuszko had the gift of gaining the respect of those who had a high sense of honor without antagonizing the feelings of those who had previously been acting against the interests of Poland.

Making your enemies not just respect but admire you was indeed some gift. You can feel the depth of Tsar Paul I's admiration in a fascinating fly-on-the-wall dialogue captured in Polish historian Korzon's 1906 biography of Kosciuszko, as translated by Storozynski. Riddled with effusive honorifics which, in Kosciuszko's case, probably had all the sincerity of your average LinkedIn profile, the passage captures the moment when the Tsar freed Kosciuszko:

> Tsar Paul I: I have come my general to restore your freedom. I always pitied your fate, but under the rule of my mother, I could not help you. Now I can as the first act of my rule restore to you Sir, freedom. You are now free.
>
> Kosciuszko: Your Royal Highness, I never grieved for my own fate, but I will never stop grieving the fate of my Fatherland, Sir.
>
> Tsar Paul I: Forget about your Fatherland, Sir. Her turn has come as with some many other states, of which their memory remains in history, in which you will always be beautifully remembered.
>
> Kosciuszko: I would rather be forgotten and have my Fatherland remain free.

Again, classic Kosciuszko. What use was his personal freedom with Poland in chains? Alas, this was the reality. The uprising was brutally subdued after its leader's fall, with an estimated 20,000 Polish civilians massacred by the Russians and their merciless allies, most of them in Warsaw. In 1795, the Polish–Lithuanian Commonwealth was officially carved up in what's known as the

Third Partition of Poland. That meant that Kosciuszko, freed in 1796, literally had no homeland to which to return.

'I no longer see my Fatherland in the country in which I was born, but instead, the country in which I will die, America,' Kosciuszko told the Tsar, according to Polish historian Jan Lubicz-Pachonski's 1986 book *Kosciuszko After the Insurrection: 1794–1817.*

This was Kosciuszko's little white lie. Poland was never far from his heart or mind, and while he had to return to America to settle the matter of his unclaimed Revolutionary War pay, it was above all a place to lie low, keep healing and consider his next move, far from the Tsar's vast European web of spies.

It was early winter when Kosciuszko departed Russia for America, via Scandinavia and England, which is why Tsar Paul I furnished him with the sable coat that he ended up giving to Jefferson. Russian sables are small, dark, arboreal omnivores in the same animal subfamily as wolverines, and their pelts are considered more luxurious than mink. And the Tsar's largesse did not end there. Kosciuszko was penniless – a problem he would solve when he got to America – but he needed money to tide him over and the Russian ruler duly obliged, giving him the sizeable sum of 60,000 roubles: 12,000 in cash, the rest awaiting him in a London bank. The Tsar even ordered a special carriage to be configured so that the incapacitated hero could travel lying down. Lastly, the Tsar agreed to free more than 12,000 Polish prisoners in Russia, many of whom had been transported to Siberia, after Kosciuszko pushed for their release. But there was a major catch: Kosciuszko and Niemcewicz both had to swear an oath of loyalty to Russia. What choice did they have? Pledging allegiance to the belligerent bully that had overrun his homeland was probably the hardest and easiest decision Kosciuszko ever made.

Before his departure, the royal couple held a function at the Winter Palace at which Kosciuszko was wheeled around in Empress Catherine's old wheelchair. The Tsar's wife, Maria, had requested the peasant sukmana that Kosciuszko had worn throughout the uprising, which he duly gave her. Even if a sheep's wool sukmana for a silky sable was a great deal on paper, this must have pained him as the garment surely held enormous sentimental value.

And then the Poles said do svidaniya, do widzenia and goodbye.

Though shrunken in physical stature by his wounds, Kosciuszko's personal status had grown immeasurably since he had led Poland's insurrection. In Stockholm, London and at countless stops in between, people from all strata of society swarmed to see the great champion of liberty. Lapierre was also a great hit, as many Scandinavians had never seen a Black man, and the loyal, multitalented valet was given his leave by Kosciuszko in Sweden. Accounts vary of what happened to him from there, although the most common version is that he returned to Poland, where he worked as a bookkeeper for the important Radziwill family, who so respected him that he was given a small share of one family member's estate. What we know for sure is that Jean Lapierre's life mattered, not least to Kosciuszko.

CHAPTER 9

THE BANK OF JUSTICE

Just up the way from the Jefferson Memorial is the United States Holocaust Memorial Museum, where a sign on the door urges *NEVER STOP ASKING WHY*. Another sign out the front says *UNDENIABLE TRUTH*. These, quite literally, are signs of the times, when the industrial-scale murder of millions can be denied by a video somebody just posted on social media.

Onward to the base of the Washington Monument, the 555-foot-tall obelisk which was the world's highest building when it opened to the public in 1888, a reign which lasted barely a year before the Eiffel Tower soared more than 400 feet higher. Down to the Lincoln Memorial Reflecting Pool, where it's well worth reflecting on the huge throng, estimated at a quarter of a million, which gathered here at the March on Washington in August 1963 for Dr Martin Luther King, Jr's 'I Have a Dream' speech. Just thirty-four years old at the time, King was the final speaker and while everyone knows the famous anaphora – the repeated phrase which serves as the speech's unofficial title – there's no shortage of other memorable phrases in the iconic oration. Here's a brief early section:

When the architects of our republic wrote the magnificent words of the Constitution and the Declaration of Independence, they were signing a promissory note to which every American was to fall heir. This note was a promise that all men — yes, Black men as well as white men — would be guaranteed the unalienable rights of life, liberty and the pursuit of happiness.

It is obvious today that America has defaulted on this promissory note insofar as her citizens of color are concerned. Instead of honoring this sacred obligation, America has given the Negro people a bad check, a check which has come back marked insufficient funds. But we refuse to believe that the bank of justice is bankrupt ...

The president who first proposed the Civil Rights Bill to Congress was none other than John F Kennedy, via a nationally televised address, two months before King's speech. Shortly after Kennedy's assassination, President Lyndon B Johnson addressed a joint session of Congress, urging lawmakers to honour Kennedy's memory by passing the bill. In July 1964, the Civil Rights Act became law despite 130 members of Congress voting against it. The Act outlawed discrimination based on race, colour, religion, sex and country of origin and it prohibited segregation in schools, businesses and other public places. Next came the Voting Rights Act of 1965, which bolstered the rights which had been enshrined to African American people in 1870 in the Fifteenth Amendment. For example, the new Act outlawed literacy tests as a prerequisite to voting.

The outbreaks of white violence which had raged since the 1950s intensified. In 1968, Martin Luther King, Jr was assassinated in a Memphis motel room. The Southern Baptist preacher and Nobel Peace Prize laureate died a young man, just three months beyond his thirty-ninth birthday. Like the architect of emancipation Abraham Lincoln, who was assassinated at the theatre in 1865, King was yet another pivotal civil rights figure whose story ended with a bullet, that ubiquitous metal exclamation mark at the end of so many reformist American lives.

When you're researching a figure like Kosciuszko, who fought for the rights of all people, including African Americans, and when you view the timeline of American history, with its big steps forward, like the Emancipation Proclamation in 1863 and the Civil Rights Act in 1964 and the backlashes that followed, and when you consider the still-troubled state of American racial equality in the present day, a question inevitably forms in your mind: why?

In fact, there are a lot of whys. Why did more than a century elapse between Emancipation and the Civil Rights Act? Why did it take so long for true equality to be written into law? Why – despite giants of American life like Oprah Winfrey and Barack Obama and Toni Morrison and Neil deGrasse Tyson and too many iconic athletes and entertainers to name – do the majority of African American folk still not enjoy the equal status for which Kosciuszko and others fought, and which is now enshrined in law?

The National Museum of African American History and Culture aims to answer such questions. It's just across the road from the Washington Monument and with this being a working Monday, tickets should be available without booking, which will fill the next four hours nicely until the train to Charlottesville, the base for Jefferson's Monticello.

Have you ever been into one of those houses where the walls are covered with well-meaning but inane wall art with phrases like 'LIVE, LAUGH, LOVE'? The National Museum of African American History and Culture is a bit like that, only the stuff on the walls is a skewer to the soul: There's the closing line from the 1926 Langston Hughes poem 'I, Too' and if you need the poem's title decoded, you need plenty more explained besides that.

There's also a stanza from Hughes' 1943 poem 'Beaumont to Detroit' where he deliberately puts bad guys like Hitler and the Ku Klux Klan in lower case as a subtle 'Screw you'. Later in the poem he does the reverse, capitalising the word 'Negroes' in what was probably a nod to civil rights activist WEB Du Bois, who in 1918 pushed for the upper-case N in Negroes to become ubiquitous, saying, 'Eight million Americans are entitled to a capital letter.'

'Beaumont to Detroit' cuts deep. Hughes ends the poem with a line about having to fight both Hitler and Jim Crow. The whole line is in capital letters as though he's a REALLY ANGRY PERSON ON THE INTERNET, and his point that Black folk have had tormentors enough in their own backyard would be famously repeated by Muhammad Ali's famous quip around the time of his conscientious objection to the Vietnam War: 'No Viet Cong ever called me n****r.'

If Hughes screams defiance, the lines on the wall from Maya Angelou's 1978 poem 'Still I Rise' breathe resilience. And that sums up the tone of the museum's exhibits: a story of resilience and pride in the monumental contributions of Black folk to American life despite chapter after chapter of American history where white folk tried to keep them down. The museum shocks, moves, educates and entertains in equal measure. Facts come thick and fast, especially with regard to slavery and the slave trade. Enslaved people had a life expectancy of just seven years once they started working the sugar plantations. The cotton gin – that great American invention which turbo-charged the Southern economy – also turbo-charged the demand for enslaved labourers. As many as 700 human beings were crammed like matchsticks aboard slave transport ships, with one in six dying along the way. Louisiana State Penitentiary is the nation's most populous prison with over 5000 inmates, more than three-quarters of them African American. It takes its nickname, 'Angola', from the plantation which once occupied the site, itself named for the West African country from which so many were forcibly taken. Angola is a working prison farm today, and many say conditions now aren't too different from back in the day.

There are lighter, more uplifting sections of the museum that celebrate the culture and achievements of African Americans but the overall emotional weight of this place is heavy.

Never buy anything in a museum gift store unless you hate money or desperately need a coffee mug at any price, which is unlikely in this part of the world, given the calibre of said beverage. That said, one particular coffee mug catches the eye. It has a picture of Frederick Douglass, a prominent abolitionist who escaped the bonds of slavery and penned three books about his enslaved life, and it bears the phrase: *It is easier to build strong children than repair broken men.* Douglass was a key figure around the time of Reconstruction, when America tried to unravel slavery and everything that went with it. In his speech to the 1876 Republican Convention, Douglass asked, 'The question now is, do you mean to make good to us the promises in your Constitution?' It was a good question and a book in the museum store explains how America answered it, its title *Make Good the Promises: Reclaiming Reconstruction and its Legacies*.

Long story short, Reconstruction was a mess. Even a quick flick through the book leads you to understand why Doctor

King's bank of justice is still barely solvent. All those constitutional amendments that ushered in things like the abolition of slavery, birthright citizenship, voting rights for Black men and equality before the law regardless of race were great on paper, not so much in reality. Laws, after all, are only as effective as the people who enforce them. While hundreds of Black folk were elected to public office in the South and the the KKK was suppressed by the Enforcement Act of 1871, the Reconstruction period in the 1860s and 1870s was a time of violence, vengefulness and wilful disobedience by many white people.

'Principles which we all thought to have been firmly and permanently settled by the late war, have been boldly assaulted and overthrown by the defeated party,' Frederick Douglass said shortly before his death in 1895. It's worth noting that Douglass knew about Kosciuszko and cited his work many times in speeches during his life.

'The idea of Black people enjoying American freedom so offended white nationalists that they overthrew Reconstruction by waging war on them and it,' history professor Kidada E Williams wrote in the essay 'Legacies of Violence' in *Make Good the Promises*. She illustrates this statement with the story of Warren Jones, a former enslaved man in Georgia who negotiated a contract with a white man to work his cotton fields in exchange for half the yield. He was never paid, and then a white gang came for Jones and his family. They escaped with their lives but how many didn't?

'Advancing the promise of full freedom was thwarted by hardship, terror, violence, and white backlash,' Candra Flanagan, Paul Gardullo and Kathleen M Kendrick wrote in the intro to *Make Good the Promises*.

Terror, violence and white backlash reared their ugly heads at the Unite the Right rally in Charlottesville, Virginia, in

2017. Thomas Jefferson's Monticello is fifteen minutes out of town and that's the next stop. The train to Charlottesville leaves in ninety minutes.

There's something depressing and end-of-days about even the most upbeat food court, and the food court at Washington Union Station is not one of the cheerful ones. It feels like no-one wants to be eating here, no-one wants to be working here and the barn-raised chickens at Chik-fil-A definitely didn't ask to end up as chicken burgers here without getting a chance to see the sky falling. But the hypocrisy of the hungry carnivore and former backyard chicken owner knows no bounds, and so in the grim basement-level dining hall, a limp, tasteless chicken sandwich is joylessly consumed. How Chik-fil-A has spread to almost 3000 stores in forty-eight states is anyone's guess. The company's founder, the late S Truett Cathy, was a Southern Baptist who insisted that his store close on Sundays, a rule that persisted after his passing in 2014. There's an argument they should shut up shop the other six days too. Old Cathy wrote five books. The third of them, published in 2004, based on his work as a foster parent and grandparent, was called *It's Better to Build Boys than Mend Men* – a title that, at a glance, owes much to Fredrick Douglass and his coffee mug quote.

America owes much more to Black folk than it often admits. Too often, that debt has gone unpaid. When Kosciuszko worked with Black people, he always displayed gratitude and respect, and there's one terrific story that proves it.

CHAPTER 10

A KIND MASTER IS FORGIVING

When Kosciuszko and Jean Lapierre parted ways in Sweden, it was not the first time he had served alongside a Black man for a prolonged period. His first assistant of African origin was a free Black man from Massachusetts called Agrippa Hull. 'Grippy', as he was known to all, claimed to be the son of an African prince. He enlisted in the Continental Army at the age of eighteen and was originally assigned to Major General John Paterson before he and Kosciuszko struck a rapport and Grippy was transferred to Kosciuszko in 1779. They would stay together for more than four years of freezing winters, scorching summers and all the travails and horrors of war.

The story that best demonstrates Kosciuszko's warm regard for Hull surfaces in virtually every telling of Kosciuszko's life. In fact, the story's so good, it deserves to be told twice.

One day, in the period when Kosciuszko was supervising the construction of what turned out to be his impregnable West Point fortifications, he departed on an overnight scouting trip along the Hudson. For one reason or another, he returned unexpectedly the same evening to discover Hull throwing a party for Black enlisted men in his quarters. It must have been quite the scene. Everyone except the teetotaller Hull was drinking, and there was raucous laughter as Hull dressed in Kosciuszko's Polish military regalia, in what you've really got to call 'Kosplay'. Little did the men realise that Kosciuszko watched it all unfolding from outside, pondering his next move.

What happened next would make a mockery of the old aphorism, attributed to German philosopher Georg Hegel, that goes 'No man is a hero to his valet.' Indeed Hull spent the rest of his eighty-nine years recounting the tale.

Let's start with the version by Thomas Egleston, the great-grandson of Major General Paterson, who colourfully captured the episode in his 1894 biography of his great-grandfather, even if, like so many others, he made the rookie error of omitting the z in Kosciuszko:

> The General had brought with him from Poland a costly uniform, said to have been brilliant with adornments, with a chapeau or crown-shaped cap and a showy cluster of nodding ostrich plumes. On one occasion Kosciusko went from West Point down the river some miles, expecting to cross over and be gone two or three days. In the meantime Grippy improvised a dinner-party and invited to it all the Black servants in camp. He dressed himself in General Kosciusko's Polish uniform. As a substitute for boots or black stockings, he blacked his legs in order to make them shine like boots. Kosciusko, for some reason finding he could not cross the river, returned unexpectedly the same day to camp. Before reaching his quarters he was apprised of what was going on, while the dinner was in progress.

He left his horse and reached the front of his quarters at the bend of the river, without being discovered.

The weather was warm, the windows all open, with a screen placed before the open door to exclude the entertainment from the view of passers-by. The party were drinking wine freely and were very hilarious. The General managed to get behind the screen unobserved, just as the party, all standing, were ceremoniously drinking Grippy's health and calling him by the name of his master. Kosciusko suddenly sprang in among them, causing such commotion that had Satan himself appeared in their midst it could not have resulted in a greater stampede. Some of the party escaped by the door, but more of them jumped through the windows, falling to the ground heels over head. Grippy fell prostrate at the General's feet, crying, 'Whip me, kill me, Massa; do anything with me, Mr. General.'

General Kosciusko, taking hold of his hand with great formality, said, 'Rise, Prince, it is beneath the dignity of an African prince to prostrate himself at the feet of any one.' He made him put on his cap of plumes (Grippy meanwhile pleading to be whipped or killed) and marched with him across the grounds to General Paterson's quarters at the base of the hill. The uniform attracted much attention, and to those they met the General introduced Grippy as an African prince, and some thought he was one in fact. They erected a temporary throne at General Paterson's quarters and placed Grippy upon it. After going through many mock ceremonies of presentation to royalty that afforded the throng a world of sport, they closed by smoking with him the calumet of peace. This was equal to crucifixion to Grippy, and was rare sport to the large military party that had assembled.

He never forgot it, and was careful after that never to assume any false position. When he was an old man he delighted in telling this story himself.

The second version comes from a story called 'West Point' written by Catharine Maria Sedgwick, a popular novelist and short story writer who hailed from Hull's hometown of Stockbridge in the Berkshire Mountains of western Massachusetts. Hull worked as a servant for her father after the war before he found his feet as a landholder and respected community leader. Hull must have shared the tale while working in the Sedgwick household, and Catharine Sedgwick did a great job of conveying the theatrical nature of Grippy's storytelling, which included rhyming couplets like an early form of rap:

> If you wish it, young ladies, you shall have a tale; for when it's about the General, love and memory never fail.
> The General was going away to be gone two days. 'When the cat's away, the mice will play!' as the proverb says. The servants wanted a frolic. They persuaded me to dress up in the General's Polish clothes. So I put on his laced coat, his Polish cap, sash, sword and all. His boots I could not wear; so they black-balled my legs and feet. Then I strutted about, took a book, and stretched myself on the sofa, ordered the servants here and there, and bade one of them bring me a glass of water. He did not return soon; and I, to play my part well, rang and rang again; the glass of water came, brought by General Kosciusko himself! I was neither red nor pale; but my knees began to fail.
> 'I deserve to be punished, sir,' said I.

'No, no, Grippy,' said he, 'come with me. I'll take you round to the officers' tents, and introduce you as an African Prince. Don't speak, but mind my signs and obey them.'

'I shall die, sir,' said I.

'Oh, no Grippy, you will not die; follow me.'

The General had his beautiful smile on; but I was past smiling. I looked solemn enough. The General took me from one tent to another, called me by a long name, made me shake hands and sit down by the first of the army. Mercy on us! The blood run through my heart like a mill-race. One officer gave me wine, and another brandy and another offered me a pipe. General Kosciusko motioned to me to take them all. (Poor Agrippa! This was the hardest trial of the gauntlet he had to run; for smoking and drinking were ever odious to him.)

My heart was sick, and dizzy grew my head, and I looked to the General, wishing I were dead; and he took pity on me; for he was not a man to enjoy riding on a lame horse. So he laughed out; clapped me on my back, and told me to go about my business.

From that day to this, I have never tried to play any part but my own. I have made many mistakes in that; but a kind Master is forgiving.

Remember that this was the late 1770s. Kosciuszko would have been well within his rights to punish Hull severely. Whipping or another form of corporal punishment would have been appropriate at the time, perhaps even de rigueur. But Kosciuszko chose to deal with the matter in good humour. In Egleston's telling, Kosciuszko gently humiliated the modest Massachusetts man by playing up Hull's royal blood. In Sedgwick's version, Kosciuszko employed booze and tobacco in the manner of a dog owner rubbing a puppy's nose in its own poop, which was a form of punishment but in the most playful way possible. Either way, Kosciuszko's response spoke to his humanity, to his good nature and to the fact that, as Grippy said, a kind master is indeed forgiving.

CHAPTER 11

THE DEPLORABLE ENTANGLEMENT

But there are masters and there are masters. Grippy might have called Kosciuszko 'Master' but the Pole was more like a friend to his assistant. To the enslaved at Monticello, Thomas Jefferson was considerably less forgiving.

As a young man, Thomas Jefferson met a woman on a plantation called The Forest, just east of Virginia's state capital, Richmond. That woman, Martha Wayles, became his wife.

Jupiter Evans, another young man born at Monticello around the same time, also met his wife at The Forest. The two boys quite possibly played together as children. And that's where their stories diverge, like Robert Frost's two roads in a yellow wood.

Evans was an enslaved man at Monticello. He was an expert stonemason who hand-carved the four Doric columns on the portico of Monticello's beautifully restored Classical Revival mountaintop mansion that looks like a Parthenon that never crumbled. Later, Evans was in charge of the stables. He was a capable, versatile, hardworking man and we don't know much more about him except for one thing: we know how he died.

Archaeologists have dug up close to a million artefacts down the years at Monticello, among them the foil capsules that covered the corks on Jefferson's Château Lafite and Tuscan Montepulciano and southern French white Limoux. One item unearthed at Mulberry Row – the area lower down the hill which was the industrial nerve centre of the plantation and home to its enslaved families and communities – was a cowrie shell. A prized object used as currency in some African communities, the cowrie tells us that Monticello's enslaved folk held on to traditions from the countries from which they had been violently abducted. Jupiter Evans was no exception. One day, probably when he was still relatively young, Evans became sick. A standard practice of western medicine in the 1700s was bloodletting, when doctors cut open a vein in the deluded belief that the illness might bleed out before the patient did. Perhaps Evans knew this and wisely wanted no part of it. Whatever the case, he sought not a white doctor but an African healer, trekking more than twenty miles to see one. He was given an antidote and told it would either kill him or cure him within a matter of hours. Evans slipped into a coma and died. No-one will ever know if it was the sickness or the cure that killed him.

Naturally, Jefferson was devastated.

Kidding. When Jefferson heard of Evans' death, he wrote a letter saying, 'I am sorry for him, but he leaves a void in my domestic administration which I cannot fill.'

Jefferson was meticulous with lists and inventories. The man who governed a state and then an entire country was known as the Master of Monticello for good reason, as he still found time and energy to be the Micromanager of Monticello. He once discovered to his great satisfaction that he was making a four per cent profit each year on the birth of enslaved children. The great Renaissance man had a dispassionate, calculating side. With the death of Jupiter Evans, he had lost not a human being but a commodity. While Kosciuszko spent his childhood playing with serf children and his adulthood trying to free them, Jefferson spent his childhood playing with enslaved children and his adulthood calculating the value of their labour.

The story of Evans is recounted by Ashley Hollinshead, an historian and Monticello tour guide with a delightful Southern drawl. She starts the From Slavery to Freedom tour by explaining that the only context is viewing Monticello through the lens of Thomas Jefferson the enslaver. 'Is this what y'all signed up for?' she asks on the off-chance a visitor to Disney World took a wrong turn at Orlando and found themselves 800 miles north.

Clint Smith, author of the mega-bestselling *How the Word is Passed: A Reckoning with the History of Slavery Across America*, made the truly shocking point that tour guides at Monticello used to be African American people dressed up in 'livery' – a word he admits he didn't previously know. If you're not sure either, perhaps you recall the scene in Quentin Tarantino's *Django Unchained* when Jamie Foxx's free Black man Django goes into character as a valet and picks out a ridiculous frilly blue-and-white outfit, which prompts a perplexed enslaved woman to ask, 'You mean you wanna dress like that?'

The point is, Monticello has come a long way. Back in 1993, legal historian Paul Finkelman – who you'll recall for his scathing comments on the matter of Kosciuszko's will – was asked to write a paper on Jefferson and slavery for a conference at the University of Virginia for Jefferson's 250th birthday. He originally planned to write a paper that essentially said Jefferson didn't like slavery but was a man of his times and had to put up with it, never quite able to do the right thing and end it. But the more Finkelman read, the more he found Jefferson to be what he calls a 'monstrous hypocrite'. Finkelman ended up delivering quite the provocative paper. In November 2023, he started a two-month residency doing research on site. Monticello is owning its history now, good and bad.

> Jefferson and many other patriots believed slavery should be abolished in the new American nation. Emancipation would fulfill the ideal that 'all men are created equal'. Yet over the course of his life Jefferson himself owned 600 people. He was unable to extricate himself from what he called the 'deplorable entanglement' of slavery.

That's a snippet from the 'Paradox of Liberty' section of the Monticello website which almost says it all. *Almost*. What it fails to capture is the way that Jefferson calcified; how he became detached, cold-hearted. Early in his career as a statesman, Jefferson occasionally talked the abolitionist talk and even briefly walked the legislative walk. 'You know that nobody wishes more ardently to see an abolition not only of the trade but of the condition of slavery: and certainly nobody will be more willing to encounter every sacrifice for that object,' he wrote to French journalist, revolutionary and abolitionist Jacques Pierre Brissot in 1788. But in the end, there were no sacrifices. It's not that Jefferson was 'unable to extricate himself from what he called the "deplorable entanglement" of slavery' as the Monticello website says. It's that, after some brief legislative flirtations early in his political career, he completely stopped trying.

'With five simple words in the Declaration of Independence – "all men are created equal" – Thomas Jefferson undid Aristotle's ancient formula, which had governed human affairs until 1776: "From the hour of their birth, some men are marked out for subjection, others for rule."' That's journalist and historian Henry Wiencek in an article entitled 'The Dark Side of Thomas Jefferson' in the October 2012 issue of *The Smithsonian Magazine*. Put like that, it's amazing to think how much of a line in the sand of human progress those five words really were, or promised to be. But Jefferson arguably spent his last five decades making a mockery of them.

When he drafted the Declaration of Independence, he was thirty-three. He died aged eighty-three on the fiftieth anniversary of the first 4th of July, still a slaveholder. Even Sally Hemings, his long-time sexual partner and mother of six of his children, remained enslaved after he died.

'What time do you get off work?' asked a smitten Jefferson, played by Robert De Niro, in a 2002 *Saturday Night Live* skit set at Monticello.

'Um, never,' replied Hemings, played by Maya Rudolph.

There are worse ways to spend a fine late April Tuesday morning than walking the grounds of Monticello. You catch glimpses of the distant Blue Ridge of the Appalachians from the well-tended gardens of the flat mountaintop, which was levelled by incalculable hours of human labour. Dropping down the hill toward the visitor centre, you pass through groves of native and exotic trees. As a somewhat overwhelmed international visitor trying to make sense of where American history and mythology overlap, you're left with emotions, impressions, factoids and fragments that lodge in the mind like pebbles in your shoe.

There's the large map of Africa on the wall in the main residence foyer which lacks basic detail like cities and mountain ranges, but which has areas of blue shading around the mouths of the continent's great rivers. This, of course, was a map of where people could be abducted and forced into slavery – and why Jefferson thought this was a terrific thing to display is anyone's guess. There's the exterior brick of the main house with a child's delicate fingerprints, the legacy of an enslaved kid whose job was to turn over freshly made wet bricks that were laid out in the sun so they would dry evenly before being fired in the kiln. Monticello is the only US presidential home on the United Nations World Heritage Site list, and its main house literally bears the marks of unpaid child labour.

Meanwhile in a drawing room at the front of the residence hangs a small portrait of Jefferson's great friend Kosciuszko, who was invited to rest eternally at Monticello but politely declined. Indeed, he never visited.

Jefferson loved books and his house is full of them. Indeed his famous collection contributed to his precarious financial state. Though he wrote America's founding document, he only ever wrote one book himself. *Notes on the State of Virginia* was originally published anonymously in Paris in 1785 when Jefferson was serving as a diplomat and was an eclectic mix of facts and musings, covering everything from Virginia's natural resources and economy to Jefferson's general thoughts on everything from the state of Virginia society to the nature of racial differences. In it, he wrote: 'I advanced it, therefore, as a suspicion only, that the blacks, whether originally a distinct race, or made distinct by time or circumstances, are inferior to the whites in the endowments of both body and mind.'

If you're looking for the ideological essence of everything that underpins Jefferson's lifelong holding of enslaved people, it's right there in *Notes on the State of Virginia*. Thomas Jefferson absolutely believed to his core that Black folk were a lesser race. Call him a white supremacist. Call him a man of his times. Just don't call Thomas Jefferson 'as pure a son of liberty as I have ever known, and of that liberty which is to go to all, and not to the few or rich alone' because that of course is the compliment that Jefferson himself paid to Kosciuszko, and it was no boomerang.

CHAPTER 12

BAD APPLES AND GOOD EGGS

It's about a seven-hour drive from Charlottesville to Ohio, which is what two members of today's tour group face after they drop this here ride-bumming Aussie in Charlottesville, about fifteen minutes down the hill. The Democrat couple drove all the way from their very Republican state to Monticello, and it's fair to say they've had their view of old TJ's legacy challenged, or perhaps confirmed.

So here's what comes next. Food, hopefully edible, then transport, because Mississippi, my next destination, ain't going to drag its own flat ass to Virginia. Breakfast at the Big Overpriced Chain Hotel near Charlottesville Station was terrible. American breakfasts at their best are wonderful. Crispy, almost snappable American bacon is so much better than the slimy, half-cooked British version. Pancakes in most countries are served in ones and twos but American stacks are like ten-storey parking lots, and while that might seem gluttonous, these stacks speak to American generosity, even honesty. You are after all eating food with the word 'cake' in it, so stack 'em high, shovel 'em in and worry about tomorrow, tomorrow. Regrettably, the pancakes at the Big Overpriced Chain Hotel near Charlottesville Station were lifeless flying saucers of barely browned dough. Don't even ask about the rubbery eggs, or the apples so floury you could have baked a muffin out of them. And did the local cows pee black this morning? No, that was the 'coffee'. Kosciuszko would surely have cursed in Polish as he tipped this stuff into the dirt.

As for cutlery, forget it. America has a plastic problem, and the Big Overpriced Chain Hotel near Charlottesville Station has it bad. The chilli sauce for the rubbery eggs came not in bottles but sachets. The cereal came in small plastic sachets. Even the plastic cutlery came in individual plastic sachets. America generates the most plastic waste in the world, both overall and per capita, and it's a failure of everything the country stands for.

Charlottesville is a good-looking town or small city or whatever you want to call it. Typical of most American university towns, this is Democrat country. In the 2020 presidential election, Joe Biden received 42,466 votes to Donald Trump's 20,804 in Albemarle County, and it wouldn't be the world's wildest presumption that the owners of the Blue Moon Diner on West Main Street lean blue in political terms. The diner's decor is a mix of art deco, Southern iconography and hipster chic, with everything from Elvis to rainbow flags to a sticker on the ceiling saying *Nazi Punks Fuck Off*, the title of an old Dead Kennedys song. On the second weekend of August 2017, the Nazi punks marched right the fuck into town.

The rally was organised by local Charlottesville white supremacist Jason Kessler, a charming Southern gentleman who called Heather Heyer – the woman mown down by a murderous motorist toward the end of the event – a 'fat, disgusting communist'. Attendees included Richard Bertrand

Spencer, the dapper head of white supremacist think tank the National Policy Institute, who is credited with inventing the term 'alt-right' in the late 2000s. There was Augustus Sol Invictus, a 'goat-slaughtering, warmongering, repeat Senate candidate from Florida', as nonprofit legal advocacy group the Southern Poverty Law Center called him. There were Southern secessionists like Michael Hill, a former history professor who in 1994 co-founded the League of the South, a group which has publicly espoused white supremacist and anti-Semitic rhetoric. There was long-time Ku Klux Klan leader and Holocaust denier David Duke. And there were many, many more of his hate-filled ilk. Together the crowd chanted, 'Sieg Heil!', the white supremacist slogan, 'You shall not replace us!' and the anti-Semitic slogan 'The Jews shall not replace us!' There were also counter-protestors representing at least a dozen groups opposed to racism and other forms of prejudice.

Inevitably, clashes ensued. At least thirty were injured and, as mentioned, Heather Heyer was killed. Born in Charlottesville, she died on its streets aged thirty-two. Immediately after the event, President Trump famously said there were 'very fine people on both sides'. On the four-year anniversary of the rally in 2021, President Biden said, 'The most lethal terrorist threat to our homeland in recent years has been domestic terrorism rooted in white supremacy.'

Domestic terrorism rooted in white supremacy was behind the Charleston, South Carolina, church massacre of 2015, when nine people who were doing Bible study at Charleston's Emanuel African Methodist Episcopal Church were shot to death by white supremacist and neo-Nazi Dylann Roof, whom prominent Unite the Right rally attendee Matthew Heimbach called a 'victim'.

Charleston was a key moment that led to the Charlottesville Unite the Right rally, as it caused a surge in the removal of Confederate memorials and monuments across the South, just five of which had been removed in the century and a half between the end of the Civil War in 1865 and 2015. The thousand or so protestors who descended on Charlottesville were ostensibly in town to oppose the proposed removal of the town's Robert E Lee statue. Lee was the great Southern Civil War hero, an astute tactician who led the Army of Northern Virginia. He won several battles but his eventual surrender in 1865 signalled the end of the war. Little could he have imagined that the Civil War would still be raging as a sort of domestic cold war 150 years later, lethally flaring up over the removal of his bronze likeness.

You can't understand the mindset of those opposed to removing Confederate statues without understanding the mythology of the Lost Cause. The Lost Cause basically holds that the Confederacy had noble aims in the Civil War. In Lost Cause narratives, the Civil War is framed as a fight over states' rights, the lie often padded out with propaganda depicting the enslaved as faithful, devoted, even willing servants. Such disinformation has appeared often in American history and still pops up today. In July 2023, the Florida State Board of Education enacted new standards whereby kids would learn that slavery benefited some enslaved folk by teaching them useful skills like blacksmithing. You don't often see shrug emojis in books about historical figures, but this wouldn't be the worst place to put one.

'There's a difference between history and nostalgia,' wrote Clint Smith at the beginning of his Monticello chapter in his bestselling book *How the Word Is Passed: A Reckoning with the History of Slavery Across America*. That's exactly what the Lost Cause narrative is all about: a misty-eyed view of history, where the lost right to enslave is framed as a confiscation of freedom. But it was anything but that.

'Alexander H Stephens, the Confederate vice president, forcefully set out the reasons for secession in his famous "Cornerstone Speech",' historian Paul Finkelman explains. 'Here, Stephens tied slavery to race, making clear that the cornerstone of the Confederacy was not merely chattel slavery, but the total subordination of Black people for the benefit of white people. In this sense the Confederacy was the political grandparent of Nazi Germany and apartheid-era South Africa – regimes founded on the assumption of the racial and ethnic superiority of the ruling class and the utter inferiority and subordination of other races and groups.'

So what should be done with monuments to Confederate leaders? Should they all be taken down because the history they represent is blatant white supremacy disguised as a noble struggle for Southern freedom?

In the July 2017 issue of *Civil War Times* magazine published just before the Charlottesville violence, various experts offered opinions in a story titled, 'Empty pedestals: what should be done with civic monuments to the Confederacy and its leaders?' James J Broomall, Director of the George Tyler Moore Center for the Study of the Civil War at West Virginia's Shepherd University, argued that Confederate monuments could be left in place and used as tools for education, deliberation and even protest, especially if augmented by interpretive signage and other elements to provide greater historical context: 'Confederate monuments remind audiences of a painful past but can also give voice to contemporary social concerns and needs if they are allowed to speak.'

Michael J McAfee, Curator of History at the West Point Museum, did not share that view:

The political and military leaders of the Confederacy ... were traitors. They turned their backs on their nation, their oaths and the sacrifices of their ancestors in the War for Independence ... They attempted to destroy their nation to defend chattel slavery and from a sense that as white men they were innately superior to all other races. They fought for white racial supremacy.

That is why monuments glorifying them and their cause should be removed. Leave monuments marking their participation on the battlefields of the war, but tear down those that only commemorate the intolerance, violence and hate that inspired their attempt to destroy the American nation.

Those are strong words. If, like McAfee, you view key figures of the Confederacy through the lens of white supremacy and treason, then it's hard to argue such people should be commemorated in civic spaces. And bear in mind that those damning words come from a man, sadly recently passed, who worked at the US Military Academy at West Point for forty-eight years where, for the record, one monument towers above all others. Situated in a commanding position overlooking the kink in the Hudson River, the statue is of the great Polish military engineer Tadeusz Kosciuszko, who of course first proposed the existence of the academy at the site of his impenetrable Hudson River fortifications, an idea Jefferson latched onto, establishing West Point in 1802 during his first presidency.

A monument to Kosciuszko was first installed at West Point in 1825, with an eight-and-a-half-foot statue added in 1913. In 1825, a committee of five cadets was selected, tasked with choosing the first person to be honoured with a monument at the academy. They didn't pick Washington, Lafayette or Hamilton. Without hesitation, they chose to honour Kosciuszko. And in a delicious irony, one of the cadets on that committee was none other than Robert E Lee. You can't help wondering whether he ever heard about the Kosciuszko will and what he made of it, or what he would make of Lee Road on the West Point campus recently having its name changed to Grant Road.

Lee's statue is gone from the park in Charlottesville now too, and his name with it. In 2017, Lee Park and nearby Jackson Park were renamed Emancipation Park and Justice Park respectively. Those names lasted only a year, with the parks blandly renamed Market Street Park and Court Square Park by Charlottesville City Council in 2018. Meanwhile, the part of Fourth Street where Heather Heyer was killed is now called Heather Heyer Way. In Market Street Park, there's no sign showing where the Lee Statue was, just a telltale patch of dirt with a few scattered weeds where America came to ideological and physical blows.

Charlottesville's Downtown Mall, just a couple of blocks from the square, is surely one of the loveliest pedestrian malls in the USA. Time and money permitting, you could loll about all day, shopping for knick-knacks and eating too-salty Thai food or whatever takes your fancy. But time in particular is an issue. It's time to pick up the rental car, then drive it twelve hours or so to Mississippi, with an overnight stop somewhere in Tennessee or Alabama. A couple of days in the town of Kosciusko (no 'z') should be plenty. Then it's northward for six hours along the famously scenic historic route called the Natchez Trace to Nashville, Tennessee, where the rental car will be left. Then a quick flight to New York, just in time for the twentieth annual conference of the American Association of the Friends of Kosciuszko at West Point. It's a tight schedule but possible.

Rental car guy wears khaki pants and a polo shirt with no name tag but is surely called Chad. He has glasses, sensible hair and not the faintest sense of humour or willingness to be flexible. The deal is this: the car was booked from Australia with a debit card. It turns out they only accept credit cards, which doesn't explain how the booking was secured but whatever. Anyway, Chad is not budging. Pressing the issue is like arguing with a vending machine whose spiral dispensing mechanism left your chips one twist short of dropping.

On to the next agency. This must be done in person because a call to their local number diverts to head office which diverts to a menu which diverts to insanity. On being presented a debit card, the guy at the next agency wears an expression like someone just rented the best car in the place to run the ice road to Inuvik in Canada's Northwest Territories. Debit cards are dirt over here. The main rule of American financial life is that you can use the bank's money, not your own, which of course explains how Wall Street bankers get obscenely rich.

The next agency is a forty-minute walk but why not? You get the feel of a place when you walk it. This part of Charlottesville feels a lot different from the Downtown Mall and the University of Virginia end of town. This is literally the wrong side of the tracks. At the address where the rental car is supposed to be, all that's visible is a wrecking yard where the local mafia boss is probably turning compromised vehicles into car wafers. It's not immediately obvious where to go but at the bottom of a long driveway, there is indeed a rental car agency in a large shed-like structure. The dude staffing the office has a mullet and a tie with a half-assed knot that looks like it was tied on prom night about seven years back. His name is definitely not Chad. Jimbo, perhaps? Anyway, Jimbo listens to the sad story, and god bless America! He starts the booking process despite his company also having a no debit card policy. Then the system goes 'beep' and you just know that the beep is trouble. Jimbo says there will be a twenty-four-hour wait while they do a credit check. Forget it. Nice try, though. It's good to meet a service industry employee who is at least willing to try to solve a customer's problem. There are fewer such people in America than you'd think.

Time for Plan B, which doesn't exist right now, but that's nothing that a chocolate thickshake back at the Downtown Mall can't fix. Okay then. Seems there's a train each evening at 8 pm that runs through to New Orleans, stopping en route at a city called Meridian, Mississippi, which is about an hour from Kosciusko. The trick will be to get someone from town to come pick me up for a moderate fee, which should be doable.

The next problem is how to get to Nashville three days later to catch that plane to New York in time for the Kosciuszko conference. Perhaps Donna, the Kosciusko tourism director who is hosting me in town at her Airbnb, will have an idea. Time to call Donna.

'I'm expecting you in tomorrow.'

'That's right, yeah.'

'And you need a lift into town from Meridian?'

'Happy to pay one of your friends whatever it costs.'

'And then you need to get to Nashville?'

'That's right, yeah.'

'What day are you going to Nashville?'

'Got to be there by Sunday evening because my flight to New York is early Monday morning.'

'You need to be in Nashville on Sunday night.'

'That's right.'

'I'll drive you.'

'What?'

'I'm already going to Nashville on Sunday.'

'No way!!!!'

In hiking, there is a thing called trail magic, and it's as real as the rocks and streams. You're in a wilderness area and you snap the little widget at the end of your phone charging cord, then the first person you've seen in three days gives you their spare cord. You're thirsty as hell in an area that has no water, and five faded cans of perfectly good Coke appear in the bushes next to you. When you commit to the trail, trail magic commits to you, and that's clearly as true for this Kosciuszko trail as on any of the world's great treks. Time to celebrate at the Blue Moon Diner, maybe with a Southern favourite like crumbed catfish sandwich or perhaps mac and cheese, a dish Thomas Jefferson is said to have brought back from France via his enslaved personal chef, James Hemings, an older brother of Sally Hemings. They say that James Hemings was the first American chef to train in France. Somebody really should make a cookbook/Netflix series on his life and recipes.

In the end, it's impossible to resist ordering the all-day eggs, and you'd better believe when you order those free-range organic cackleberries over-easy, they cook 'em just right, the yolks firm on the outside and bursting with hot runny goodness.

CHAPTER 13

TAKE CARE OF YOURSELVES AND EACH OTHER

The American Revolutionary War ran from April 1775 to September 1783. The early years are mostly remembered for conflict in the North but battles and skirmishes raged in the South throughout virtually the entire war. Patriot militias took up arms against the British in the South from late 1775, then in the final years of the war the South became the main theatre.

From 1778, the British began to implement what they called their 'Southern Strategy', focusing on controlling the key ports of Charleston, South Carolina and Savannah, Georgia, the latter of which they captured in December 1778. The South had more Loyalists than the North – colonists who remained loyal to the British Crown. Powerful plantation owners were more likely to be Loyalists. While they saw themselves first and foremost as Americans rather than British subjects, they were reluctant to overthrow the British Crown under whose governance they had grown wealthy, believing independence would come in its own good time. The British believed they could harness Loyalist support to subdue the rebellion in the Southern colonies. If they did that, they could again turn north and quash the rebellion across all thirteen colonies.

Kosciuszko and Agrippa Hull journeyed south in October 1780, doubtless grateful to avoid the oncoming harsh northern winter. Kosciuszko was keen to apply his talents on the battlefield and Washington personally approved his request to leave West Point. The Pole had been looking forward to linking up with his friend Major General Horatio Gates in the South, but after Gates' disastrous loss at the Battle of Camden in August, he was relieved of command. Major General Nathanael Greene replaced Gates as commander of the Southern Department in December 1780. He had seen Kosciuszko's work at West Point and needed no convincing to retain him as chief engineer.

Enslaved people were treated worse in the South than in the northern states, and travelling through the plantations must have been distressing for Kosciuszko and Hull, especially the latter, who was far from obliged to extend his service in the South but chose to accompany Kosciuszko. There were other free Black men serving in the army and there were also enslaved men on both sides. Some enslaved men had been loaned to the Continental Army by their masters. Sometimes the service of enslaved men came with the carrot of freedom at war's end, sometimes not. Sometimes that promise was upheld, sometimes not. As many as 20,000 runaway enslaved people served with the British, figuring fighting was better than slavery. Some were given their freedom after the war while others were taken to the Caribbean and enslaved again.

Enslaved men in the Continental Army usually weren't armed, instead serving as labourers, wagoners, craftsmen, spies, scouts, couriers, orderlies, cooks, medical assistants, drummers, flag-bearers and more. Many lacked such basic items as blankets and shoes. Kosciuszko often shared his clothing and blankets but there was only so much to go around. When the anti-slavery proponent, officer and good friend of Alexander Hamilton, John Laurens, was killed in a British ambush at the Battle of the Combahee River in South Carolina in the final months of the war, Kosciuszko sought to distribute some of Laurens' clothes to the African Americans serving under him. 'They are naked. They want shirts and jackets and britches, and their skin can bear as well as ours good things,' he wrote in a letter to Greene.

In the South, Kosciuszko again proved himself useful in all sorts of ways. The Continental Army had few horses or wagons and Gates understood that South Carolina's rivers would provide the best way to move troops, so Kosciuszko oversaw the construction of a fleet of flat-bottomed boats. Their clever design meant that the boats were light enough to be carried across land, while in the water they could navigate shallow streams. They also provided stability when heavily laden with supplies and equipment. 'Kosciuszko appeared to be everywhere ... planning lines of march, gathering and dispatching crucial boats, and seeking little known shortcuts,' the Polish American historian James Pula wrote in his book *Thaddeus Kosciuszko: The Purest Son of Liberty*.

But even the naturally gifted Polish engineer had his failures. As the Continental Army successfully eliminated British outposts in South Carolina, Greene readied the troops to attack the British stronghold in a town called Ninety Six, whose unusual name's origins are disputed to this day. The British had constructed a five-pronged fortification called the Star Fort. There were other defences in and around Ninety

Six but if the Colonials took the Star Fort, they knew the rest would likely fall.

Over the course of a 28-day siege, Kosciuszko oversaw the construction of a series of parallel zigzag trenches. Work was slow as the red clay soil was more like stone. Kosciuszko also tunnelled toward the Star Fort, with the plan to put explosives underneath the fort. On detonation, Greene's soldiers would storm the fort from the trenches. But the work was undone by British scouts, who discovered the tunnel. The British attacked, which was when Kosciuszko was bayoneted in the backside. Some historians consider that Kosciuszko's complex plans cost victory at Ninety Six. Major General Greene supported his man, praising Kosciuszko for his 'assiduity, perseverance and indefatigable exertions in planning and prosecuting the approaches which were judiciously designed' and which would have 'gained success if time had admitted of their being completed.'

Every high achiever has their low points. Just ask Jerry Springer, and if that seems like the strangest segue you've read this week, you should know that the train from Charlottesville is passing through the Carolinas – hence tales of Kosciuszko in South Carolina – and news just came through that former talk show host Jerry Springer has died. Actually, 'talk show host' is not quite the right term for Springer. What exactly was he?

Springer's show launched in 1991 and originally tackled topics like homelessness and guns. But there's only so much discussion of serious issues the public can stomach and by the end of 1994, ratings were flagging. Thus began the transition to freak show. By *The Jerry Springer Show*'s heyday in the mid-to-late 1990s, a typical episode would have two or more guests on stage. Maybe a guy would reveal to his female partner that he's gay. Maybe a woman would tell her partner that he was not actually the father of their child but it was actually some guy she hooked up with in a dimly lit Burger King parking lot and she wasn't in the least bit sorry. Maybe one of the guests would unzip their skull and reveal that they were actually a green alien lizard creature. Anything could happen, and usually did. And after the big reveal, things would always end in a scuffle, with guests allowed to wrestle without ever quite landing serious blows as they were separated by the very good-natured security guards. Meanwhile, women in the audience would flash their breasts at the cameras while the whole room chanted, 'Jerry! Jerry! Jerry!'

What did it all mean? Was it the clearest sign yet of America's demise? A quarter of a century on, there's something almost quaint about it. In those days, the guests were the weirdos. Watch or listen to some of America's more extreme podcasts or cable shows nowadays and it's the hosts who are batshit crazy. But there's something else that made *The Jerry Springer Show* not entirely terrible and, in its own way, quite lovely. At the end of the show, Springer would deliver a monologue in which he tried to weave some sort of moral thread from the deranged goings-on. What did we see today? What can we learn from it? How can we be better? He then signed off with 'Take care of yourselves and each other,' a well-meaning decency that seems to have been lost in just about all forms of broadcasting, narrowcasting, podcasting, any kind of casting you can name – and god forbid you should ever see good manners on social media.

Sleep doesn't come easy. The train left Charlottesville at 9 pm and is due in to Meridian at 4 pm. Then it's just over an hour to Kosciusko, birthplace of Oprah Winfrey, the most famous talk show host of them all, whose studio audience always kept their shirts on.

Charlotte, North Carolina, is much bigger than expected. The Bank of America Corporate Center towers over the city, lit up like a big red rocket ship. The train toilets are already in a questionable condition. The guy next to me is going to see his girlfriend in Alabama and has never met an Australian or heard an Australian accent. We watch highlights of the latest round of NRL games on my phone. He's obviously never heard of Australia's National Rugby League but he likes it, so we watch highlights from the previous round too. Occasionally the train stops in the middle of nowhere to let a huge freight train thunder on by. The big freight companies own the tracks and Amtrak is just borrowing them, so freight trains have right of way. Such is American capitalism. The business of running America always, but always, comes first.

A neck-cricking sleep eventually comes. Atlanta is a word on a sign and the rest of Georgia doesn't exist. Then it's morning and the forests of Alabama are the most beautiful thing in the world. The internet says that Alabama is America's fifth-leafiest state in terms of the percentage of its land covered with forests. Maine, New Hampshire, West Virginia, Vermont and Alabama are the top five in that order. Who knew?

My journey technically entered the mythical South as soon the Potomac River was behind me and Washington, DC melded into Arlington, Virginia, but it didn't feel like a magic threshold had been crossed. Even Charlottesville felt a lot like places much further north. But the South feels like the South now. It's in the accents of the train conductors. It's in the houses and barns that could use a coat of paint. It's the Libertarian beside me spouting what's on his mind at eight in the morning after the other guy got off around dawn. It's the Republican who takes the Libertarian's seat a few hours later and who doesn't understand why Ukraine should get a cent of US money which, when you think about it, kind of makes the entire Cold War a waste of time, money and angst since the Russians are apparently now entitled to invade whoever they like.

Fortunately, you can walk away from a dud conversation on a train.

There's not much worth dining upon in the dining car but the car is alive. A family has started a game. The rules are simple. Guess the word without saying the word, get as many as possible before the egg timer runs out.

'It's what I earn.'

'Money!'

'You got a pit in your backyard and it comes up out of the pit.'

'Fire'

'No, it's what the fire's made of.'

'Flames!'

'Um, um, um ... it's what I love gettin' at a store.'

'Sale!'

'There ya go.'

'Hahahahahahahahahahaha.'

Somebody knows what his wife likes. And this whole family knows how to make a train journey not just entertaining but inclusive. They're a Black family and they've gathered several white people around them to play, myself included. These folk are colourblind. That might seem a small thing but in the South, every small or large act of inclusivity counts for something.

After the final skirmishes of the Revolutionary War in November 1782 on James Island, South Carolina, when Kosciuszko's coat was pierced by four British musket balls, the Pole negotiated a prisoner swap. In return for a captured British officer, he asked for the return of William Smith, a soldier described as 'Mulatto' – a word meaning mixed race which has been considered inappropriate since about the time it appeared in Nirvana's 'Smells Like Teen Spirit'.

The point of the story is that a mixed-race life equalled a human life in Kosciuszko's eyes. And while it turned out Smith had died of wounds while held by the British, Kosciuszko, as ever, had tried to take care of his fellow man no matter the colour of their skin.

You'd have to think Jerry Springer could fashion a great closing monologue out of that episode of Kosciuszko's life.

CHAPTER 14

MISSISSIPPI YEARNING

Rows of corn and babies are born.
Chicken is fried and grandpa died.

So begins a poem entitled 'Tylertown' by Mississippi schoolboy Bentley Brumfield, who at the time was in the ninth grade. The poem featured in the 2022 *My Town Mississippi Poetry Project* – an anthology by students in America's so-called Magnolia State on the subject of their hometowns. In Brumfield's case, that town was Tylertown, a community of 1600 residents about 90 minutes south of the state capital, Jackson. *Rows of corn and babies are born. Chicken is fried and grandpa died*. Can you imagine a more perfect opening couplet written by anyone, let alone a ninth-grader?

It's an encapsulation of the life cycle in America's agrarian south. It's a salute to everydayness. The fried chicken and corn make it seem like it might be a celebration of Blackness too. But does the poem also imply a certain bleakness? Is it saying that's all there is? You're born, you work the cornfields, you eat some fried chicken, you die. British post-punk band The Godfathers had a brief blip of success with their 1988 song

'Birth, School, Work, Death' from the album of the same name. Are we in similar territory here, in the state with the lowest life expectancy in America?

One thing can be stated with great certainty. The poem induces the irresistible desire to eat fried chicken, and soon. Fortunately, we have a booking this evening at Jason's Southern Table in Kosciusko, Mississippi. Like any self-respecting Southern chef, Jason has fried chicken on the menu and they say he is not renowned for his small portions.

Donna's friend Dave is waiting patiently at Meridian Station. At the gas station, he lets me buy snacks but rejects my offer to purchase gas. We soon clear the city limits of Mississippi's eighth-largest city. If Mississippi were a rectangular dartboard, Kosciusko would be the bullseye. From Meridian in the state's East Central Hills region near the Alabama border, we drive in a steady northwesterly direction toward the only town of any significant size in the world named after Andrzej Tadeusz Bonawentura Kosciuszko, even if his surname is misspelled. There's a tiny so-called 'unincorporated community' called Kosciusko south-east of San Antonio, Texas, which was founded by Poles, but it's barely a speck on the map. Kosciusko, Mississippi, population 7400, is a thriving little town. The area was briefly known as Redbud Springs and as the small settlement grew, Paris was suggested as a name as it was believed people might be attracted to a town sharing a name with the glamorous French capital. In the early 1800s, Mississippi state surveyor William Dodd settled on Kosciusko. His grandfather John Dodd had fought alongside Kosciuszko in the Revolutionary War, and like many of Kosciuszko's colleagues, he must have passed down stories about the great Polish engineer and all-round good guy.

The four-lane road curves through undulating farmland. You wouldn't quite call any of these gentle humps a hill but these are definitely not the marshy coastal plains of the state's south, or the fertile flatlands of the Mississippi Delta on the state's western fringe, where the river forms the border. The conversation swings between work, country, family and anything but guns and politics until, inevitably, we talk about guns and politics. There is nothing an American can say to convince any Australian that America's gun ownership laws are a good idea. John Howard, perhaps the most conservative prime minister in Australian history, effectively outlawed automatic and semi-automatic weapons in Australia after thirty-five people were killed in an horrific 1996 massacre at Port Arthur in Tasmania. Not a single mass shooting has occurred in Australia since then. But there's not much that'll change the mind of a staunchly pro-gun American, so it's best to move on and enjoy the companionship and the light.

Twilight in Mississippi seems like the sky's natural state of being. Late afternoon is mellow, early evening wistful and dusk would bring a watery tear to a bronze statue's eye. The sky is clear with only high wispy clouds and is not criss-crossed with vapour trails. Traffic thins as the road narrows from four lanes to two and it feels like no-one is coming, going or even passing through. Let the rest of the world rush around; Mississippi does things on Mississippi time and when Mississippi is good and ready, a sign tells us we've arrived in *Kosciusko, Home of the Whippets*, as in the mascot for the local high school sports teams. As a whippet owner and fan of all things Kosciuszko, it's immediately apparent to me that souvenir shopping will occupy part of the next two days. Whatever else happens, happens.

Donna makes it clear that plenty will happen because plenty is happening. This is a great weekend to be in town. It's the Natchez Trace Festival, Kosciusko's annual shindig named after the famous road that passes through town en route from southern Mississippi to Tennessee. The festival starts tomorrow, which is Friday. Then on Saturday evening, there's a concert featuring Charlie Musselwhite, the Grammy-winning bluesman who's the town's most famous product after Oprah. As the town tourism director, Donna's helping to organise that. First things first: we're off to Jason's Southern Table and you'd better believe the joint is rockin' ahead of festival weekend. The beer is cold and the fried chicken strips are piled so high that Jason surely sought a building permit. The strips are tender inside and crispy outside but the highlight is the side of green beans fried in bacon grease. The beans are soft but not soggy, a tiny bit sweet but mostly salty. Every green bean deserves this treatment. In fact, it should be mandatory.

Donna's spacious home is located on the fringe of town in a leafy neighbourhood where many gardens are so large, you'd almost call them acreages. Her Airbnb accommodation is in a wing of her house, partially separated for privacy. The comfy double bed has a cacophony of cushions and there's a beautiful en suite bathroom with an aqua-blue bike under the basin, its basket niftily set up as a hand towel holder. Ample local reading material is laid out, including the *My Town* student poetry anthology. *Rows of corn and babies are born. Chicken is fried and grandpa died.* There are one or two good poems in the collection but that one is an absolute standout.

Donna is up early brewing coffee, its aromatic, slightly sweet scent filling the house. She also plays light Christian rock music. It's lovely that she welcomes her guests to the new day in this manner and shares a cup with them, even if the languid songs of praise and the brew tinged with some sort of almond or vanilla essence are not to this visitor's tastes. But any hospitality is a beautiful thing when you're on the road. The leftover fried chicken strips from Jason's were in Donna's fridge but she tips them into the bin, and that's that. Chicken is fried and my lunch plans died. No biggie. Donna drops me in town for a quick explore and says we'll meet for an early lunch at Outfielders Sports Bar & Grill, a couple of doors down from Jason's. If Donna says that's the plan, then that's the plan.

Downtown Kosciusko has a square rather than a traditional main street. A grand red-brick courthouse with four white columns and a clocktower commands the square's centre, with various stores, restaurants and businesses occupying each of the four sides. It feels like a place where the community still comes together in a traditional small-town setting, a throwback to an America before mega-malls. The patties in the burgers at Outfielders Sports Bar & Grill are charred on the outside, pink on the inside and there's just the right amount of pickle. The place is owned and run by a Black woman, who apparently just sold it to another Black woman, and there are plenty of white customers, which makes you think that race relations aren't too bad in this town. You come to Mississippi and the first thing you think about is race or, perhaps more accurately, racism. The state is synonymous with toxic race relations in the popular imagination, from the 1964 Mississippi Burning murders to the 1988 film of the same name, to you name it.

It is hardly an unfair rap for an outsider visiting Mississippi for the first time to frame their idea of the state this way. Mississippi was one of the Southern states that turned Reconstruction on its head, drawing up a constitution which actively made life tough for newly freed African American people and their descendants. Mississippi had more lynchings than any other southern state, even though it had one of the smallest populations of any southern state, and Attala County, where Kosciusko is the county seat, had its fair share. 'We Speak Your Names! Remembering those lynched in my home town of Kosciusko, Mississippi, Attala County,' Oprah Winfrey posted on Instagram in 2018 alongside an image of a plaque at the National Memorial for Peace and Justice in Montgomery, Alabama, with the names of five Black men known to have been lynched in Attala County – James Mitchell, Daniel Gladney, Jim Gaston, Monroe Hallum and Dud Car. Winfrey was born in 1954. Her family lived through segregation in Mississippi but left for greener pastures further north before the Civil Rights Act was passed. You don't have to be that old to have seen dark times in this part of America.

And now?

'I think for the most part everybody gets along,' says Pati Edwards, operations manager of local community body the Kosciusko Attala Partnership. It's a big weekend for the town and especially for Pati. She's one of the key people behind the Natchez Trace Festival, which has well and truly kicked off with food stalls dotting the closed-off streets, a vintage car show, rides and plenty more. Right now, Pati is taking five in her office, dipping fingers of blooming onion into ranch dressing – and if you didn't know that onions bloomed, that's because you never cut the top off an onion, peeled it, placed it cut side down, made vertical incisions around the onion stopping near the bottom to stop the 'petals' breaking off, battered it then threw it in the deep-fryer.

Outside, there's plenty more to eat, most of it even more deeply fried. It's tempting to know what gator balls taste like, but there are times for a humble corn dog and this is one of them. A giant pickle bought for a dollar is a great accompaniment, and there is surely no finer Polish contribution to American life – the life and legacy of Tadeusz Kosciuszko aside – than the pickle.

The town is alive this Friday. Black folk and white folk share the streets and the mood is upbeat and convivial. No-one is expecting an Australian accent but people are more than happy to talk when they get past their surprise. Seventeen-year-old D'Naylah Williams is finishing high school soon. She's looking forward to living on campus at community college and whatever else lies ahead. Maybe she'll fulfil her dream of playing basketball overseas, maybe she'll settle for Plan B and work as a trainer. 'I really wanna get away from here, and I'm not saying it's a bad place but I wanna do better, I wanna be better and when I have that money, I wanna come back down here and build a gym for my school,' she says.

Oprah Winfrey left Kosciusko as a young child and much later in life funded a local Boys & Girls Club, a facility providing after-school programs for young people. It's doubtful that D'Naylah will achieve Oprah's riches or fame but hearing her express similar dreams of going out into the world and coming back to contribute is a sweet note of optimism.

Not so sweet are the notes sung by some of the performers in the street karaoke contest. Cowboy dude in the orange-checked shirt should probably go sing to his cattle and hope it doesn't sour their milk. One guy butchers 'House of the Rising Sun'. Another destroys 'Sweet Child o' Mine'. A Black female gospel singer steals the show and is the eventual winner. A white guy watches on wearing a grey T-shirt that says *Freedom*, a privilege he and his forebears were likely never denied.

'We're all different, that's the good thing about the world,' says the woman emceeing the karaoke contest, and as another Mississippi sunset slowly squeezes the blue out of the sky, you could be excused for feeling that all is indeed good in this town, in this county, in this state, in this country.

Saturday is action day, especially for Donna. We buy fresh fruit for Charlie Musselwhite and his band at the market stalls on the edge of town. We pick up the pre-ordered platter of sandwiches and cold cuts from Walmart. We make the midday sound check at the Skipworth Performing Arts Center, which is located in the junior high school. There's a small pistol strapped to the steering wheel of Donna's car because of course there is. There's a sign on a secure door between the school's front office and its corridors that says NO FIREARMS OR WEAPONS ALLOWED ON THIS PROPERTY because of course there's that too.

After the sound check, Charlie's off for a rest, Donna's off to do more Donna things, and it's a last chance to explore town. A gentle Mississippi rain sets in but it's not heavy enough to spoil day two of the festival. The life-size bronze Kosciuszko statue is visited. It's located just off the square, and a few quick questions fired at strangers reveal that no-one knows much about him. Whippet t-shirts are found and bought. A shrimp po-boy is eaten. The town's murals are viewed and appreciated. There are worse places in America to spend half a day on foot, although there is no shortage of weird looks from passing motorists on the long walk back to Donna's place to shower and change before the concert. No-one walks anywhere in rural America. The lack of a car stamps you as an outsider, as an unknown.

Beware the townsfolk you think you know.

That's another line from Bentley Brumfield's 'Tylertown'. It really is a hell of a grown-up piece of work. Wonder what the good folk of Mississippi make of the strangers they don't know?

'Not only am I glad to be here, I'm really lucky to be anywhere!' That's 79-year-old Charlie Musselwhite taking a good-natured dig at his own age, and while you sense he uses that line at every concert and that the audience knows it, it's still a great opener. The man is incredible. He's best known as a maestro of the mouth organ, a hero of the harmonica, but he sings too and his voice still packs power as he rattles off a line about the Blues making him drunk even though he never touched a drop of alcohol.

The great thing about Blues music is that you feel like you know a song halfway through hearing it the first time. In a fast-paced, ever-changing world, it's a reassuring thing to sense what's coming before it arrives. Blues is more about the rhythm than the tune. Blues is a train chugging across the Deep South to Meridian, Mississippi. It's the rhythm of the working day before it was endlessly punctuated by pings and notifications. Blues is like a corn dog: no single mouthful is the most delicious thing you've ever eaten yet the whole thing is deeply satisfying.

The Skipworth Performing Arts Center would be a fine facility in any large town, let alone a smallish town of 7400. Recently renovated, it seats more than 500 people and has big portraits of musicians on its walls, one of whom is none other than Charlie Musselwhite. There are also two people pictured on the walls who were not professional musicians, although one had a renowned rhythmic musicality in the way he spoke, while the other composed a waltz and two Polish dances known as Polonaises, traditional Polish folk dance music in triple time. They are of course Martin Luther King and Tadeusz Kosciuszko – two freedom fighters who deserve to be mentioned in the same breath, and it took an entertainment centre attached to a Mississippi junior high school to make it happen.

Charlie Musselwhite onstage is ageless. Backstage, there's a crease for every concert he's played, a bead of sweat for every fan.

Being a friend of Donna's makes you a friend of Charlie's and when he hears the Australian accent, he goes, 'I was down that way once.' He was indeed and it led to great things. This was back around 1990, when Australian band INXS was just about the biggest act in the world. Someone from INXS management approached Charlie and told him they needed a harmonica player on their new album. Old Charlie had never heard of INXS but when they told him the band had sold fifteen million albums worldwide, he went, 'I'm interested!' Have you ever heard 'Suicide Blonde'? Can you recall the famous harmonica riff that holds it together? Yep, that's Charlie.

The blues continues the next morning through the Toyota sound system as we drive north along the Natchez Trace Parkway, a road which absolutely demands an appropriate soundtrack. The Trace ends in America's country music capital, Nashville and passes through Elvis Presley's birth town of Tupelo, Mississippi, where – in inadvertent homage to Elvis's later-life weight issues – we stop to buy several packets of pork rinds. The road even runs past a tiny community called Cypress, Tennessee, which was home to a largely unknown musician called Don Von Tress who wrote the Billy Ray Cyrus mega-hit, 'Achy Breaky Heart'.

The Natchez Trace is achy breakingly beautiful, and that's a fact. It's not beautiful in a grab-you-by-the-shoulders, Rocky Mountains, Yosemite National Park kind of way, but in a rich, soothing, tree-lined way. This was originally a route used by the Natchez, Chickasaw and Choctaw peoples as they travelled through their traditional lands. In 1801, Thomas Jefferson designated it a national post road for mail delivery. Today, the Natchez Trace Parkway is administered by the National Park Service. It's another one of their 425 'units', considerably larger and more visited than the Thaddeus

Kosciuszko National Memorial in Philadelphia, stretching 444 miles across three states.

Travel along the Trace is limited to fifty miles per hour, and it would be an insult to the road to zoom along any faster. The relatively low speed limit is partly to cater for cyclists. There's a rule here that cyclists can ride together in small groups with priority over cars, who have to wait their turn to pull out and overtake. Not that cyclists are completely safe here. Donna lost her husband, Gary, on the Trace, killed by a teenage driver while cycling. That was a decade or more ago, and it came eight years after she lost her son, Matthew, in a motor vehicle accident on another road. Today, Donna is dropping off cycling safety kits at visitor centres along the Trace. As if catering to a house guest and organising the Charlie Musselwhite gig wasn't work enough, she's been flat-out over the past few days assembling the safety kits, with their stickers and reflectors and assorted bits and bobs. It's a labour of love. Or duty. Or both. Anyway, she's just gotta do it, that much she knows.

Moseying around Kosciusko and trying to get a sense of what was what, some people heaped praise upon Donna and all she does for the place. But it's fair to say she's not universally loved. The owner of one business on the town square asked, 'How's that going for ya?' when told she was hosting me at her place. Another prominent local figure said they've had their disagreements. That's small towns for you. The local movers and shakers are always going to move and shake some people the wrong way. Undeniably, Donna means well and does great things for the community. She's a fantastic host, too. Craving the famed Southern hospitality? Then stay at Donna's. And if you're the sort of person who's inclined to consign all Trump-supporting Southern white Republicans to a basket labelled 'Deplorables', ask yourself how many hours you spent this week assembling cycling safety kits at your own expense, and how many hundreds of miles you drove on your day off delivering those kits to visitor centres in three states.

Have you ever sat with a large suitcase and a small backpack at a windswept Tennessee truckstop in a chilly drizzle with a too-thin jacket and an accent that makes people squint, waiting for a guy you've never met to turn up and drive you to a soulless airport hotel before flying to New York City to attend a conference at West Point because the subject of the conference is a guy whose name adorns a mountain that you can't stop dreaming and writing about?

Let's start with the Tennessee truckstop where Donna dropped me before heading off to whatever business she had in the Nashville area. In truth, this is several rungs above a truckstop. This is the Leipers Fork market and gas station. Beside it is the RedByrd Café, whose sign says it's *Serving up coffee & joy from our handcrafted tiny home,* except it isn't serving up anything because it's closed, which is a shame because anything even faintly resembling a decent coffee would go down very well right now. Anyway, you get the idea. This place is more hipster than hillbilly. Leipers Fork is part of Williamson County, the wealthiest county in Tennessee. All the country music celebrities live around here, in the rolling green hills just south of Nashville. Justin Timberlake is a local, or was until recently. Ditto Nicole Kidman and Keith Urban. If a pickup truck towing a horse float stops to fill up, you can bet the next vehicle will be an Audi. And when a beat-up old Honda hatchback pulls into the parking lot, there's a good chance that's my ride. A tall bearded guy, almost larger than his car, climbs out.

'I don't usually pick up guys I've never met,' he says.

'Good to meet you too.'

My chauffeur is Barry Johnson and we're best mates in about two minutes. We met on Twitter, or whatever they call it now, where he goes by the name Wyatt Woodbee, and we've chatted about this and that over the years. When he heard about the Kosciuszko trip, we arranged to meet in Nashville and here we are in the Leipers Fork drizzle, drinking root beer and filling in the blanks. Life's card dealer hasn't dealt Barry too many aces of late. Driving for The Big Impersonal Online Delivery Company pays the bills for now, but Barry is a clever, good-natured guy and you just know that better things lie ahead, or that he won't beat himself up too much if they don't. Barry is determined to show his Aussie guest a good Nashville time, so after dropping my stuff at the hotel, we head straight for downtown Nashville, which is absolutely pumping for a Sunday night. Bar after bar after bar is full and it takes time to find a table in one of them. We drink beer, eat Southern barbecue with okra, listen to country music and banter like we've known each other for life.

Before you know it, it's midnight. Then dawn, then noon, and after a plane and three trains, the cliffs of the Hudson Highlands at West Point are in sight.

CHAPTER 15

THE KEY TO THE CONTINENT

Twenty years ago in New York City, it was the people with mental health issues who walked along the streets barking loudly at unseen voices. Now, it's Wall Street types with wireless headphones. Maybe the two aren't that different.

Apart from that, old NYC hasn't changed that much. It's still expensive, the subway still makes no sense and it's still exciting to arrive and a relief to leave. An hour on the streets of Midtown is enough. Then it's up the Hudson on the train, past Yonkers and Peekskill, and there she is on the opposite bank at an elbow in the river: West Point. From the train line on the eastern side of the river, the US Military Academy looks imposing, with huge monolithic stone buildings mimicking the cliffs around them. We'll get a closer look in a couple of days but today, we're heading further upriver, to Rhinecliff station, where my good mate Alan is waiting with his kid.

Alan's wife is my wife's old schoolmate. She came over to the USA and worked her way up to a big-shot job with a big-shot publishing company and did big-shot things until that all came to a screeching halt. It's hard to know how much to let on here. But you might say that an author had the sort of politically motivated hissy fit which would once have been considered unconscionably self-indulgent, and that the publishing house was accused of being an obstacle to the very inclusivity it bent over backwards to promote, and indeed had been promoting for more than 50 years, long before it was de rigueur to do so.

The American right might have become malevolent in all sorts of ways, but like the breed of spiders whose young eat their mother, the American left has a talent for feasting upon its own.

We're now in Kingston, New York, and a delightful small city it is too. It's pretty like Princeton without the pretension and the students, and with its large population of ex-Manhattanites which swelled during and immediately after the Covid pandemic, Kingston has all the amenities of New York City. The plan is to rest here a day before the conference at West Point, and eat anything but corn dogs and fried chicken, which shouldn't be a problem in this vegetarian household.

Alan takes us on a day trip up to Lake Minnewaska, a beautiful cliff-lined natural basin near the top of the Shawangunk Ridge that seems almost to be hanging in a high hollow. It's not officially swimming season yet but telling that to an Australian is like saying you can't eat Tim Tams on a Tuesday, so obviously a dip in the chilly but not painfully frigid water is taken and enjoyed.

The Shawangunk Ridge rises about 500 metres above the Hudson River. From any of several lookouts up here, you can see how the ribbon of river absolutely defines and commands the landscape, and you get a sense of why George Washington called it the key to the continent:

One thing Redcoats and Continentals could agree on in 1775 was the strategic significance of the Hudson River. Both thought it was the most important geographical feature in North America. They thought so at the outset of the Revolutionary War and they thought so at its end eight years later. From a perspective of two centuries, it is hard to refute their evaluation.

So began an article in the May–June 1976 edition of *The Military Engineer* by Colonel Dave R. Palmer of the United States Army who, in a decorated career, would go on to be a Lieutenant General. He would also become a cherished member of the American Association of the Friends of Kosciuszko at West Point.

Palmer's article described how the Hudson bisected the population of the thirteen colonies and how the river separated the primary sources of food for Washington's army, which meant that key crossing points had to be protected. He also explained how the river itself was an avenue, navigable to ocean-going warships all the way to the city of Albany, about 150 miles north of New York City. According to Palmer, whichever side held the Hudson owned the entry to the interior of the country, and probably the initiative in the war. Washington knew it too, and that he couldn't challenge the superior British fleet on water. That's why Kosciuszko's engineering work along the Hudson was so crucial, even if his stint in the area didn't start so well.

Ticonderoga, Saratoga and West Point. Long after Kosciuszko's three and a half years of service in the Hudson River Valley, those are the three place names that ring through time.

Fort Ticonderoga was an outpost at a key location at the southern end of Lake Champlain, about eighty-five miles north of Albany. The colonials had famously captured the fort in 1775 and the British were converging upon it en route, they hoped, to Albany. Kosciuszko had quickly formed a close working bond and friendship with Major General Gates, the new commander of the Continental Army's Northern Division, who called the Pole 'an able engineer, and one of the best and neatest draughtsmen I ever saw'. The Pole reported that the fortress was vulnerable. It was overlooked by a steep and rocky hill, then called Sugar Loaf and now called Mount Defiance. Kosciuszko wanted a battery of guns mounted at the top of the unprotected hill and Gates agreed. But Gates had to return temporarily to Philadelphia, and Kosciuszko was overruled by those who remained in command, his superiors deciding that it would be too tough lugging heavy guns to the top of the hill. Besides, no engineer of any nationality had ever previously suggested such a preposterous thing.

Along came the British, led by General John Burgoyne. They saw the hill, they put cannons on it and they took the initiative and the fort. The colonials had no choice but to run for it. They were pursued through the forest by the British and members of the Iroquois nations who were fighting alongside them. The Iroquois terrorised the colonials, picking them off one by one with knives and tomahawks.

Colonel Kosciuszko was working furiously, and constructively, even in defeat. He designed and helped build a floating log bridge to enable his comrades to escape across a narrow neck of Lake Champlain. He ordered soldiers under his command to block roads by felling trees, to destroy bridges and even to reroute creeks and streams in order to flood roads. The progress of the pursuing British forces slowed to a crawl, allowing the colonials to regroup near Albany.

Kosciuszko had proved that he could think on the run. He also proved himself a soldier's soldier, not ratting on his comrades. Major General Arthur St Clair, who had been temporarily in command of the fort in the absence of Gates, was court-martialled over his decision to abandon it. In Kosciuszko's testimony, the Pole said nothing about Sugar Loaf or his suggestion to fortify it and St Clair was duly exonerated.

That was in the midsummer of 1777. By early autumn, the Continental Army were facing the British at Saratoga, about halfway between Fort Ticonderoga and Albany. This time, with Gates back in charge, Kosciuszko was listened to. Again, Kosciuszko set his sights upon the heights, selecting a position called Bemis Heights for a fortified camp. By the time General Burgoyne's redcoats approached from the north, the defences were ready and because Kosciuszko had selected the encampment so expertly, the British were effectively corralled on approach, hemmed in by the river and hills, and forced to attack the Continental Army in precisely the place where they would be cannon fodder. The British retreated and were surrounded in camp near the village of Saratoga where, on 17 October 1777, Burgoyne surrendered the entire British force of 6000 troops.

This was a victory of monumental proportions. It brought France into the war on the side of the revolutionary Americans, and it enhanced the reputation of Gates to the point where some started to believe he should replace Washington as commander-in-chief. Gates himself knew the Saratoga score. In a letter to his friend Doctor Benjamin Rush, who many years later would tend to Kosciuszko's wounds in Philadelphia, Gates wrote, 'The great tacticians of the campaign were hills and forests, which a young Polish Engineer was skilful enough to select for my encampment.'

'We would not have won [the Revolutionary War] without Saratoga, and we would not have won Saratoga without Kosciuszko,' said the late American historian Thaddeus Radzilowski in a 2017 YouTube video on Kosciuszko's legacy entitled 'Tadeusz Kosciuszko – What you may not have known'.

Kosciuszko spent the ensuing months in Albany, where he met and befriended the Marquis de Lafayette, undoubtedly the most famous foreign officer in the Revolutionary War, who ended up forging a relationship with Washington as close as father and son, and who reportedly called Kosciuszko 'the friend of all humanity' at a memorial service after the Pole's death. But no foreigner would prove more versatile and resilient than Kosciuszko, whose finest work lay ahead of him as he reported for duty at West Point in March 1778.

When you've been dead for more than 200 years, you don't often make fresh news. Yet in August 2023, a time capsule was found under the Kosciuszko Monument at West Point, which had been excavated for renovations. The capsule is believed to have been buried by cadets sometime in the 1820s, and its contents included a handful of coins and an Erie Canal commemorative medal, none of which were too valuable. But any buried treasure–type story is news, and reporters obviously had to explain who this Kosciuszko fella on the statue was, so West Point helpfully provided the following brief blurb in a media release:

> Andrzej Tadeusz Bonaventura Kosciuszko (1746–1817), more commonly known as Thaddeus Kosciuszko, was a Polish general, military engineer and revolutionary. He fought in the American Revolutionary War, as well as an uprising in his home country. He was known for his bravery, kindness, patriotism, likeability and unwavering strength of character.

It's fascinating that the US Military Academy West Point chose to list Kosciuszko's kindness and likeability alongside the requisite military attributes like bravery and patriotism. Today, the American Association of the Friends of Kosciuszko at West

Point exists to keep all aspects of Kosciuszko's legacy alive. This year's conference is in West Point's Thayer Hotel, in a room large enough for 100 or so. The room is about half full. There's no danger of running out of muffins or coffee, and not just because the coffee tastes like Hudson River water. Most heads are balding or greying. The exception is four current West Point cadets with names like every army or police unit in every war movie or cop show you've ever watched: Drake, Arnold, Zuchowksi, Milanesa.

The conference packs a lot into a day. There are experts on Ukraine, on Lithuania, on the state of the statue repairs and, of course, on Kosciuszko himself. There are two superstar speakers. One is James Pula, the Polish American historian and author of *Thaddeus Kosciuszko: The Purest Son of Liberty*. The other is Stephen Olejasz, a West Virginian retired military officer and historian who serves as emcee but who also chimes in with great insights from time to time.

After Kosciuszko arrived at West Point, it didn't take him long to prove himself vastly superior in ability and imagination to the resident French engineers, who acted like they knew what they were doing but largely didn't. Those who subscribe to the stereotype of the arrogant Frenchman, or who believe that all French males in the eighteenth century were called Louis, will find little to change their mind in the names or conduct at West Point of Louis Lebègue Duportail and Louis de la Radiere. The over-confident Frenchmen put Washington in a pickle; he couldn't afford to promote Kosciuszko over them, as France was providing much-needed funds for the Patriots. Soon enough, the French engineers were deployed elsewhere and Kosciuszko was put in charge.

At the crucial location of West Point – the first major bend in fifty miles as you travel upriver from New York City –

Kosciuszko was forced to think on his feet, adapting what he had previously learned to the new military circumstances and the geography of the area. Forts in Europe at the time were huge and monolithic; West Point needed something different because the enemy could approach from virtually all sides, as well as from the river. Thus did Kosciuszko construct a series of interdependent defences, each effectively a link in a chain. He even constructed an actual chain, all sixty-five tonnes and 550 yards of it, floating on a wooden boom and stretching from West Point across the river to Constitution Island. The chain was a defence against British ships sailing north from New York City and was never broken.

James Pula explains:

> While Kosciuszko learned a lot about military engineering from the French in Paris, some people can learn things and memorise them and apply them to new situations which maybe they haven't studied. They kind of just understand what's going on and I think Kosciuszko was one of those ...
>
> He understood what it was to be a military officer and to look at terrain, but he also understood the engineering aspects of how to construct things and how to use different materials. We're all acquainted with people who have so-called book learning, but he had book learning plus a practical approach to things. Like, here's the principle. Now, how can I apply it to this different situation? So I think the real key to his success was not focusing on how he was taught, but how he could take the principles of what he was taught and apply them to entirely different situations.

Walking the spotless grounds of West Point with Stephen Olejasz is a privilege well worth the hours it takes to get security clearance to enter the academy. The campus is so large, it has a 38,000-seat stadium for American football and even its own ski hill, complete with chairlift. As an alumnus of West Point and a former Assistant Professor of History there, Olejasz knows every tree, every cliff, every redoubt, every spot of historical significance. And like James Pula, he understands why Kosciuszko made a difference here.

> This was a transition period in military engineering. There was this old idea in Europe that you had fixed fortifications, but how could they do that here? How would these guys move the rock, make the mortar? Where would they get the money? The French were probably telling General Washington that they needed more money, more horses, more timber, more rock, and Washington would have been like, 'Holy crap, I want to defend a river but I can't go broke doing it'. So that's why Kosciuszko builds these interlocking smaller redoubts, he does the batteries, he builds the chain.

Olejasz believes that Kosciuszko's engineering ingenuity reflects the person that he was. That's a really interesting idea. Does emotional intelligence and empathy make you better at your job? Do these attributes make you not just a nicer, more collegiate person, but improve your productivity and creativity? In Kosciuszko's case that would appear to have been true. The man inspired by Enlightenment thinkers had some enlightened ideas at this outpost on the Hudson River, and the British never came close to overrunning it. Indeed Kosciuszko's defences were so good that they never tried.

From West Point, it's an hour back up to Kingston, New York. From there, it's just over an hour to Stockbridge Massachusetts, home of Kosciuszko's loyal orderly Agrippa Hull.

The free Black man lived until he was eighty-nine and became a landholder, husband, parent, grandparent and much-loved town leader. He lived in many ways an ordinary American life, except that it was pretty extraordinary in his day for a Black man to be such a rock of a largely white community. One man won't let Hull's memory die and is doing everything he can to unearth fragments of his life. His name is Rick Wilcox and he's a retired local police chief. We meet in the Stockbridge Library along with the curator of the library and its archives, India Spartz, and assistant curator and genealogist, Joshua Hall. Rick shares a 121-page document that he has painstakingly compiled, featuring aspects of Hull's life ranging from his local landholdings to the fact that he walked 600 miles to the Southern theatre of war while Kosciuszko rode on horseback. Hull's shoes didn't come close to making the distance before they fell apart.

Rick drives us around the town of 2000 residents in a cold May rain. Stockbridge might be the prettiest town yet encountered on this trip and even the fickle Berkshires weather can't hide it. We stop at Hull's grave. There is one gravestone for the whole family, slightly cracked, with the letters starting to fade with the wear and tear of the years. It reads (and never mind the typos):

Agrippa Hull
Died
May 21, 1848
Jane D.
His wife
There son's
James, Joseph
Margaret
His 2nd wife

Rick Wilcox is a tough old cookie but he looks a little frail standing beside Hull's grave. Turns out he's been fighting cancer. Lord, give him strength. A Vietnam veteran, Wilcox joined the police force in 1971. As a boy, he once sat for a Norman Rockwell painting. The famous artist had his studio here and was a familiar face as he rode his bike around town. But after Rockwell's death in 1978, it's safe to say that Wilcox became the heart and soul of this place. 'He's the most visible face in town,' local paper *The Berkshire Eagle* reported in a 2011 article celebrating Wilcox's forty years on the force. And now, the man who was once the town's most visible face is helping to remove the cloak of invisibility that hangs over a long-dead free Black man who himself was once a pillar of this community.

There are good people doing good things in America – Republicans, Democrats and everyone in between, from Donna handing out cycling safety kits in Mississippi to Rick Wilcox, retired white Massachusetts cop, spending his twilight years telling people that a Black life from two centuries ago mattered. When you look at people from small towns performing small acts which are big in spirit, you feel like America might not be in such bad shape after all.

Maybe all those self-help books have got it wrong. Maybe looking outside of yourself and serving those around you is the true path to fulfilment. Maybe that idea was implicit all along in the phrase 'life, liberty and the pursuit of happiness', but you had to read between the lines to get it. It's certainly right there in the face of every American in the phrase 'We the people'.

Kosciuszko believed that a life of service was a life well lived, a life spent meaningfully on Earth. With the exception of moments when coffee was lacking, it was never about him. If more Americans knew his story and took a leaf out of it, the echoes of his selfless life would surely reverberate from sea to shining sea.

Section Two

Poland: 'I don't want to, but I have to'

CHAPTER 16

A HERO STILL NEEDED?

Preparing to visit Poland for the first time with a view to researching a major historical figure and his legacy, you obviously want to immerse yourself in as much contemporary Polish culture as possible beforehand to get a sense of the place. What is this country now? How might Poland be understood through the stories it tells about itself? So when a Polish movie that was a co-winner of the Jury Prize at the 2022 Cannes Film Festival was showing at a cinema in Sydney, it was too good an opportunity to waste.

The movie was called *EO* and it was bleak beyond words. It's about a donkey called EO, and in the same way that multiple kangaroos fulfilled the role of 'Skippy' in the old Australian TV show of that name, six donkeys played EO, each more adorable and ultimately miserable than the last. Poor old EO starts out as a circus donkey but when the circus goes bust, he's shunted around from place to place in ever-worsening situations, much like Black Beauty in the famous English novel, and also just like Balthazar, the titular donkey in French director Robert Bresson's 1966 classic *Au Hasard Balthazar*, to which the movie *EO* pays obvious homage.

EO is savagely beaten by football hooligans, shot at by hunters and is witness to all manner of human cruelty, including murder and a seedy attempt to buy a homeless woman a meal in exchange for sex. Without giving too much more away, it gets even worse. This is not a redemption story. EO does not live happily ever after, nor do most of the people he encounters, which makes a strong statement about animal cruelty with a clear subtext that there's no hope for humanity if we keep treating animals so terribly. But was Polish director Jerzy Skolimowski trying to tell us something more beyond all that? Were those big, brown, heartbreaking eyes that always seemed to be awash with donkey tears conveying a deeper message?

Online reviews were unhelpful in this matter. Respected movie review site RogerEbert.com called it a 'a nihilist spin-off of Winnie-the-Pooh and its shy donkey hero, Eeyore', which at least helped explain the donkey's name and movie title for those who missed it. Australia's ABC ran a review with the headline, 'Wondrous donkey adventure *EO* decentres the human perspective in pursuit of a new way of seeing' which was a fancy way of saying, 'eighty-eight minutes of donkey cam' and not much else. America's ultra-conservative *National Review* is surely nobody's first stop for movie reviews, but its headline, '*EO*, a Fable of the Great Reset', was amusing for its reference to one of the nuttier conspiracy theories, while the review itself contained at least two gratuitous Joe Biden references, because apparently any bad or depressing thing equals Biden.

What no review from a source reputable or otherwise seemed to consider is that *EO* might have been a great big allegory for Poland itself. Perhaps the director had absolutely no such intention but if you believe that all art is subjective, the idea is irresistible. Which country has been kicked around from owner to owner, endlessly abused and exploited by those who come into contact with it? That would be Poland. Which country has rarely been able to enjoy life safe and secure in its own protected space, given the respect, dignity and carrots it deserves? Poland again, give or take the carrots.

All history is turbulent, or at least it's told that way, distilled to moments of turmoil and conquest rather than the in-between times when not much happens. Poland has had precious few in-between times down the years, enduring more than its fair share of disruption and tumult. Sitting at the crossroads of eastern and western Europe, Poland has been invaded more than any other European nation, and while all nations' borders tend to be fluid over time, Poland's have washed in and out like the tide. But since 1990, when the shackles of communism were broken, Poland has been free. Indeed, it is currently enjoying its longest period of unencumbered liberty and stability in centuries. So, who are its heroes?

Flying across the Atlantic to Poland with the reverential tones of the American Association of the Friends of Kosciuszko at West Point conference still ringing in my ears, it feels like Kosciuszko's legacy will loom as large to Poles as the legacy of any Founding Father to an American. But after a couple of days walking the streets of the sprawling capital, Warsaw, I soon wonder if he's remembered at all. 'Kosciuszko – a Hero Still Needed' is the title of a permanent exhibition at the Tadeusz Kosciuszko Museum in Krakow. But is he?

Warsaw doesn't look like many European cities west of it, and perhaps none of them. Pop out of Centralna Station in bright sunshine on a mild May morning and you don't lose the sun when you cross the road as you would in the claustrophobic inner parts of Paris or London, where tightly packed buildings of a near-ubiquitous height shrink your world. Warsaw of course once looked like these cities, and indeed was regarded as one of the architectural gems of Europe in the period between the two world wars. The Luftwaffe and German artillery and demolition teams pressed the delete button on that, levelling more than eighty per cent of the city. Post-World War II, large parts of Warsaw were rebuilt in communist style, with streets so wide and straight you could land a plane on them, to the point where parts of central Warsaw now feel like Moscow or Beijing. As with many cities built or reconstructed in the communist era, the architecture is demoralisingly bland in some places, declaratively bold in others. Directly across from Centralna rises the Palace of Culture and Science, a towering clocktower-topped art-deco monolith which looks like the lovechild of Big Ben and the Empire State Building. The building was the Soviet Union's 'gift' to Poland, a Mafia offer they couldn't refuse. Originally named for Joseph Stalin upon completion in 1955, his name has since been ditched, along with most Polish vestiges of the despised communist era.

As if to pay a tourist's tribute to the demise of the communist era and all the scarcity and drabness it entailed, the next twenty-four hours turn into a feeding frenzy. This is easy to do in Warsaw, which reveals itself to be a top-shelf food city. We ditch our bags at the hotel and of course start with pierogi. 'We' includes my daughter, Stella, who has flown over from Lyon, France, where she's studying. It's a joy to see her. She has transformed into a terrific little European citizen who instinctively knows how the trains and trams work even though Poland is new territory to her too. Stella loves being with Dad because Dad is awesome, or perhaps it's that Dad pays for everything. Not that pierogi are expensive. They're a mere hip pocket hiccup, and delicious too. Like good Chinese dumplings, the wrapping is silky, not heavy and doughy, and there's a generous filling. We go for the classic cheese and the classic meat, both scattered with fried onions and crispy bacon pieces. Veggies can wait till another day. Give our share to the mistreated donkeys.

We walk northward along the major thoroughfare of Marszalkowska to Ogrod Saski, or Saxon Garden, where flowers have exploded to life, and not just in flowerbeds but au naturel on the unkempt lawns, which are not mown in springtime to promote pollination. This practice has recently become commonplace in other European parks and is part of a movement called No Mow May. Just as colourful as the lawns of the park is the grassy patch where Marszalkowska splits in two. This island in a busy road is pulsating with poppies and, to be frank, it's more striking than the Kosciuszko Monument on the other side of Marszalkowska outside the Lubomirski Palace, which was the purpose of this post-pierogi perambulation. If the name Lubomirski rings a faint bell, it's because Kosciuszko's sweetheart, Ludwika, was betrothed to Prince Lubomirski. As for the statue, it was completed in 2010 and is an exact replica of the one in Lafayette Square. Like the statue in Washington, DC, this one also copped graffiti during the global Black Lives Matter protests. A key figure behind the statue's installation was Doctor Leszek Marek Krzesniak, President of Poland's Kosciuszko Foundation. It's time to pay him a visit.

Doctor Krzesniak is a natural therapist whose central Warsaw clinic also serves as the Kosciuszko Foundation HQ. His office is decorated with a mix of biological diagrams and images of Kosciuszko. There's Classic Koz in military regalia, there's Horseback Koz in battle, and there's even Hot Koz, where his upturned nose is downplayed, his expression brooding, his hair darkened and swept over his forehead in the manner of an anime character.

The good doctor welcomes us warmly and says he once visited Australia and climbed Mt Kosciuszko. He then presents us with a herbal tincture and sweet cherry cheesecake which balance each other out surprisingly well. Doctor Krzesniak grew up in Maciejowice, the small village just south of Warsaw which was the scene of Kosciuszko's near-fatal wounding in October 1794. If that explains his original interest in Kosciuszko, his lifelong fascination with the man centres on two main points.

First, Kosciuszko promised Poles equality and freedom, which no-one had ever done before. 'Kosciuszko took from America the idea of freedom and took it to Poland,' he says. 'This happen nowhere else in Europe, France a little bit, France was trying with its revolution. Britain? No. But Poland was open to the idea of freedom for all. People wanted to fight for Kosciuszko.'

Second, Kosciuszko's character was beyond reproach. 'Kosciuszko was impossible to corrupt,' he enthuses. 'Today, you look at Putin, you look at the world, there is a lot of corruption.'

It's telling that Doctor Krzesniak mentions Putin and corruption. Poles continue to glance over their shoulder at Russia with fear and distrust, and given the history between the two nations, why wouldn't they? Ukraine and Belarus provide a physical buffer against Russia along Poland's eastern border, but not much of a psychological buffer. Belarus has strong pro-Russian sympathies, while Ukraine remains at war with Russia after the 2022 invasion. The war in Ukraine is a daily reminder to Poles of Russian belligerence. Poland even shares a land border with the Russian exclave of Kaliningrad to its north. With Russia in its neighbourhood one way or another, Poles can never quite relax.

Nor could they take their eye off the Russian bear in Kosciuszko's day. Few people outside Poland know that on 3 May 1791, the Polish–Lithuanian Commonwealth famously adopted Europe's first modern constitution and the second in the world, after America's. Incredibly progressive for its time, with strong Enlightenment influences, the constitution's political, economic and social reforms positioned Poland to become a powerhouse in its region. Catherine the Great wasn't copping that. In May 1792, the Imperial Russian Army invaded and installed in power a group of Polish magnates called the Targowica Confederation, whose self-interest had led them to side with the Russians and oppose the constitution's 'contagion of democratic ideas'. To this day in Poland, the word 'Targowica' is an insult slung at traitors and politicians seen to be operating against the country's interests. Also to this day, 3 May remains a Polish public holiday called Constitution Day, even though the 1791 constitution lasted less than fifteen months.

The demise of the constitution led to a war against Russia in which Kosciuszko's leadership proved indispensable, and eventually to the 1794 Kosciuszko Uprising. We'll fill in the blanks in this key period in Polish history and in Kosciuszko's life as a reformer and military leader when we meet Piotr Hapanowicz, Poland's foremost contemporary Kosciuszko scholar, in Krakow. But for now, the point is that Russia thwarted Poland's noblest ambitions in the late 1700s, and has done so more than once since then. So when you meet the head of Poland's Kosciuszko Foundation and he tells you that Kosciuszko is his guy because he was incorruptible and stood for freedom, and when he mentions Putin and Russia and corruption in the same breath, a whole lot of puzzle pieces come together.

People should give Warsaw a break. It's actually a great city to visit. It's clean, it feels safe and you can zip around on trams and change neighbourhoods on a whim. The Old Town was almost totally destroyed in World War II but has been totally reconstructed in the original Gothic and Late Renaissance styles, in places with the original bricks. Mood-lit in the evening, it's a tiny bit too twee and touristy but still lovely. In an understated restaurant serving traditional Polish food, we share a zurek, Poland's famous creamy sour rye soup served in a hollowed-out loaf of crusty bread which you eat when the soup is gone in the unlikely event you've still got room in your belly. The soup is full of egg and white sausage and, like all food in Warsaw, it is absolutely delicious. But is it more than that?

On a project like this, it's tempting to look for analogies everywhere, seeking to fuse culture and meaning in every movie about a donkey or in every bowl of soup. Can we find symbolism in soup served in its own edible tureen? Perhaps the soup represents the essence of Poland while the soup-infused bread bowl consumed towards the end of the meal stands for Poland's historically porous borders. Maybe the legend of the soup's origin holds hidden meaning. They say a traveller once bet an innkeeper a chest of gold in return for his inn if he could finish a bowl of the worst soup the innkeeper could cook. The innkeeper duly threw in a bunch of seemingly mismatched ingredients with fermented rye but accidentally made a soup so delicious, the traveller ate two bowls and won the bet. Is the lesson that you just can't kill Poland? That no matter how much bad stuff you throw at it, Poland still boils down to something beautiful? Maybe it was just a really good bowl of zurek and that's enough.

It's late. The restaurant is closing and the souvenir stalls in the Old Town Market Place are packing up their Poland caps and rolls of toilet paper with Putin's face and the Cyrillic words 'путин, иди, на хуй' which mean, 'Putin, go fuck yourself'.

*

Warsaw's Hotel Gromada Centrum was a swish bastion of western decadence when it opened in the 1960s and is now a ho-hum three-star hotel as Warsaw has modernised around it. The breakfast is still to die for, and possibly to die from if we don't stop shovelling it in. The people from the Big Overpriced Chain Hotel in Charlottesville, Virginia, really should visit this place and feast their eyes and mouths upon the beautifully cooked bacon and scrambled eggs, the fresh fruit and delectable pastries, the array of cold cuts artfully displayed like little meaty carpet samples. The highlight is the salads. Anytime is a good time for cucumber salad with a side of kielbasa, breakfast no less than any other. The same for egg salad. My dear departed maternal grandmother was born in Minsk, which was then a city in Russia and is now the capital of Belarus, about two hours from Kosciuszko's birthplace. She used to lay out breakfast salads with cold cuts. The Gromada breakfast is the taste of my distant childhood. It's sad to think that such abundance vanished during communism. Today in Warsaw, on a busy corner directly above a KFC, the Museum of Life Under Communism documents that dark time from the post-war period through to 1989.

This is not one of Poland's big famous museums, although it deserves to be. It's the work of husband-and-wife team Marta and Rafal Patla, who started taking visitors to Warsaw on tours of significant landmarks of the communist era, then built an exhibition at home. With the help of donated memorabilia, they then assembled the exhibits of the museum, which now occupies several rooms. The museum hits just the right note, blending bleak history with a sprinkling of retro chic, like the room decked out in the style of a typical Polish apartment of the 1950s, or the wall of hair dryers. Who knew there were so many types of hair dryers at a time when even the most basic household item was hard to come by? The point of these displays is not to fetishise the objects and accoutrements of the time. It's to say that freedom paused but people lived on, with all their resourcefulness and simple desires.

There is no making light of some of Poland's darkest history, like the fact that the despised secret police introduced a penal code containing twenty-three offences that were punishable by death, which pretty much licensed authorities to do away with thousands of innocent people who, for one reason or another, were 'inconvenient'. But the museum treats some aspects of daily life with humour, as perhaps it must. Quoting directly from the Polish novelist Leopold Tyrmand, there's the tale told in almost Seinfeldian tones on a large white panel about a guy who sees a beautiful fresh pink ham being sliced for customers in a store. Naturally there is a long queue but the guy joins the line. Will any ham be left by the time he reaches the front? The lean pink meat is becoming fattier but the guy doesn't mind. Any ham will be good ham. Soon, it's mostly fat but still he waits. And then, just as he reaches the counter, there's none left. But then he spies another ham! Another beautiful fresh pink ham! 'Ah, that's tomorrow's ham,' the store owner says, stowing it under the counter. Dismayed, the guy leaves the store. But in a store just down the road, a large fresh block of cheese is beginning to be sliced. He joins the queue and you can guess what happens as he reaches the counter ...

When you think of those four decades when Poland's very soul was strangled by communism, and how communism came straight after Warsaw and numerous other cities were reduced to rubble in World War II, you can understand how the traumas of the twentieth century have reduced the relevance of an eighteenth-century revolutionary like Kosciuszko in the minds of most Polish people. Poland has new heroes, foremost among them Lech Walesa, the shipyard electrician who led the Solidarity trade union and movement of the same name, winning the Nobel Prize for Peace in 1983 and eventually being democratically elected as Poland's president in 1990 after the fall of communism. His campaign slogan was 'I don't want to, but I have to'. If only all politicians were as upfront. The first part of the slogan likely spoke to a deep sense of exhaustion after he had led a workers' movement, which was outlawed for many years despite overwhelming international support, even from right-wing figures like Margaret Thatcher and Ronald Reagan. But the second part of the slogan surely spoke above all to Walesa's unwavering sense of civic duty.

'Now when I'm talking with you, I realise that we don't talk a lot about Kosciuszko,' Marta admits over a coffee in the museum cafe. 'We only focus on the second war or on what happened after that, but Kosciuszko, if I want to be honest, I don't know like nothing. I mean, I know the name, I know what happened, what he did ... oh my god, now you got me interested and I have to read more about Kosciuszko!'

'Do children know about Kosciuszko? We spoke to the head of the Kosciuszko Foundation and he said, "Yes of course!" What's the real answer?'

'The real answer is no.'

'Really?'

'I think, okay we talk about it, but it's very short story. It's like they don't focus too much about it. We have the Warsaw Uprising Museum, we have the National Museum, other national museums. But I have to think if there is Kosciuszko Museum. There's a museum in Wroclaw, the Panorama Raclawicka. Once, maybe in school, you go for a tour to Wroclaw to see Panorama Raclawicka, and then you never think of it again. It's not like it was the Second World War.'

The Panorama Raclawicka, in Poland's fourth-largest city, is a spectacular circular display offering various perspectives of the first major battle of the Kosciuszko Uprising. In that April 1794 battle outside the village of Raclawice, Kosciuszko led a bayonet charge and his peasant warriors successfully captured Russian artillery, winning a pronounced victory which lives on as a symbolic historical moment of Polish resistance. Though the victory would prove to be of limited tactical significance, news spread quickly and spawned skirmishes across the country. A month later, on 7 May 1794, Kosciuszko issued the Proclamation of Polaniec, a landmark document which gave peasants property rights to the land they cultivated. The proclamation never became law but after the 24 March Act of Uprising in Krakow and 4 April victory at Raclawice, the Proclamation of Polaniec was another key moment that rallied peasants to the cause, ensconcing Kosciuszko as the hero and hope of Poland.

Doctor Krzesniak wants the Kosciuszko Foundation to build a similar panoramic display at Maciejowice, where Kosciuszko fell five months after Raclawice, in the largest single battle on Polish soil in the eighteenth century. Maybe he'll garner the support he needs, maybe he won't. Installing Kosciuszko as the hero and hope of Poland in young Polish minds is not an easy task.

It's time to eat again because it's always time to eat in Warsaw. Around the corner from the Museum of Life Under Communism, there's a long queue for a restaurant which snakes out into the street. This seems like a hell of a coincidence but here we are. A city full of cafes and restaurants that you can walk straight into and people are actually choosing to queue like they did in the communist era. But for what? Turns out the line is for exactly the sort of food which was served in communist Poland. There are five choices only: mashed potato, purple pickled cabbage, a pea and carrot medley, something unidentifiable and kotlet schabowy (literally pork chop), a brined pork schnitzel which was a staple of state-owned restaurants in the communist era. The crowd is a mixture of young hipsters and older Poles, which reflects the cultural status of the kotlet schabowy. Popular Polish culture website culture.pl says the kotlet schabowy is a symbol of 'culinary backwardness' which explains the hipsters because anything uncool is obviously extremely cool. As for the older kotleciarze (cutlet lovers), their presence in this restaurant represents not so much an anti-elitist statement as a hankering for simple, hearty, traditional Polish fare.

As Poles move on from the traumatic upheavals of the mid-twentieth century, you might wonder how a freedom fighter of an increasingly distant yesteryear fits into the modern picture of Polish identity. The good news is that Kosciuszko's legacy hasn't entirely faded, and there's one place in Warsaw that demonstrates that in an incredibly poignant way.

CHAPTER 17

THE PARADISE OF THE JEWS

For almost 2000 years between Biblical times and the establishment of the modern state of Israel, the Jews had no land they could call home. Not in Europe, not in the Middle East, not anywhere. Have you ever heard of a people who were stateless for the best part of two millennia? Over the entire course of human history, has any ethnoreligious group ever spent so long without a homeland? Have any people ever been so consistently marginalised, disenfranchised and vilified in the lands in which they were forced to settle? Has any group ever been rounded up and hounded out of so many lands, century after century after century? Has any group ever had so many vile, persistent cultural stereotypes created about them? Did not these offensive characterisations create the social and political licence for the 'pogroms' in Europe – a word of Russian origin which referred to violent attacks on Jews in Russia and beyond, often on a community-wide scale? Was not the slaughter of six million Jews in plain sight during the Holocaust a pogrom on an industrial scale? These, of course, are rhetorical questions.

The Jews came to Poland around the year 1000. Christians beat them to it but not by much. Christianity's arrival in Poland in the year 966 was relatively late in the European context, and while the majority of Poles today identify as Roman Catholic, Catholicism took centuries to gain a dominant foothold. In the period from the founding of the Kingdom of Poland in 1025 until the formation of the Polish–Lithuanian Commonwealth in 1569, thousands of persecuted people enjoyed a haven in Poland – Jews, Protestants, Muslim Tatars, even pagans. In these years, the Jews endured periods of persecution and upheaval interspersed with times of security, tolerance, enhanced rights and prosperity. One high point was the Statute of Kalisz, a general charter of Jewish rights enacted in 1264 by Duke Boleslaw the Pious, which gave Jews the freedom of travel, the right to worship and a range of legal rights, including the right to defend themselves against charges of blood libel, a fabricated slander whereby Jews were accused of murdering Christians to use their blood for ritual purposes.

When Poland's King Sigismund II Augustus died without an heir in 1572, the nobility introduced elections as the new method of choosing the king. Fearful of religious wars that could destabilise the commonwealth, the nobility passed the 1573 Act of Warsaw Confederation. Among other things, the Act ruled that 'the peace be kept between people of different faith and liturgy'. In other words, religious tolerance was now written into law in the Polish–Lithuanian Commonwealth – a first in European history. Granted the freedom to practise their religion, the Jews flourished. Synagogues and Jewish schools were established, Jewish books were printed and the Jews even had their own judicial and administrative bodies.

A popular seventeenth-century Polish proverb held that Poland was 'the heaven of the nobility, purgatory of the burghers, hell of the peasants and paradise of the Jews'. The proverb contains a whiff of anti-Semitism, as Jews were still legally and politically inferior citizens who were barred from owning land, voting, holding office, ascending to the nobility or even living in certain places, so life was hardly all tulips and poppies in a traffic island. Many anti-Semitic tropes gained traction during this period in Poland and elsewhere. At the turn of the seventeenth century, Shakespeare's *The Merchant of Venice* appeared, featuring the contemptible Venetian Jewish moneylender Shylock who, despite his sympathetic 'Hath not a Jew eyes' soliloquy, is still cast as the play's villain. Characters like Shylock date back to the twelfth and thirteenth centuries, when the Church thrust the role of moneylender upon Jews because it considered the practice of charging interest unchristian. Jews were also well-suited to unpopular professions like tax collection and moneylending because they were predominantly urban dwellers, forbidden from owning land.

Despite limited rights and an undercurrent of anti-Semitism which occasionally flared up into violence, the phrase that Poland was 'paradise for the Jews' was true in a relative sense. Jews really did have things better in the Polish–Lithuanian Commonwealth than in any other country on Earth for a good two centuries. By the period just before the three partitions of Poland in 1772, 1793 and 1795, the Jews had become Poland's largest minority group with a population of around three-quarters of a million people, or by most estimates between about seven per cent and ten per cent of Poland's total population. No country in the world had more Jewish people at the time.

Leave it to Kosciuszko to kick the can of liberty down the street and treat the Jews not as a subclass of citizen but as Poles. This he accomplished by encouraging them to take part in his

1794 insurrection. Poland's Jews had rarely taken up arms in their nation's defence, but not for the reasons many believed. Some Poles thought that Jews were cowards with no stomach for a fight, a hateful myth which originated from Jews being unable to enlist because they were forbidden from fighting on the Sabbath and unable to eat the non-Kosher army rations. Polish Jews even paid extra taxes to fund the military because of their inability to serve in it. Yet still they were cast as aloof, spineless and unpatriotic.

All of this went out the window in the Kosciuszko Uprising. When Kosciuszko proclaimed his Act of Insurrection in Krakow's Market Square on 24 March 1794, he began by saying, 'In defence of my Fatherland, equality will prosper in my eyes, and that is why Jews, peasants, aristocrats, priests, and burghers have equal respect from me …'

That came just before the pronouncement mentioned earlier, where he said, 'I pledge not to use these powers to oppress any person, but to defend the integrity of the borders of Poland, regain the independence of the nation, and to strengthen universal liberties.' For Kosciuszko, universal liberties could not be strengthened without including the Jews.

In the days after announcing the uprising, Kosciuszko walked into the Old Synagogue in Krakow's Kazimierz district and formally asked the Jews for help. In Krakow today, a plaque in the restored synagogue recalls the occasion:

> HERE IN THE OLD SYNAGOGUE IN THE DAYS OF THE INSURRECTION OF 1794, TADEUSZ KOSCIUSZKO CALLED THE JEWS TO ARMS IN THE FIGHT FOR THE LIBERATION OF THE COUNTRY.

On the same plaque is a quote attributed to Kosciuszko:

> 'THE JEWS PROVED TO THE WORLD, THAT WHENEVER HUMANITY CAN GAIN THEY WOULD NOT SPARE THEIR LIVES.'

This was true. The Jews would not, and did not, spare their lives in the Kosciuszko Uprising. A Jewish Light Cavalry Regiment consisting of 500 volunteers formed under the command of Berek Joselewicz, a Jewish merchant and trading agent whose work took him across Europe including to France where, just like Kosciuszko, his revolutionary ideals were shaped through exposure to Enlightenment thinking and French revolutionary fervour. Joselewicz issued an emotive appeal to his fellow Polish Jews in Yiddish. Blending language found in traditional Jewish prayers with phrases like 'The Fatherland', meaning Poland, he hit a sweet spot, demonstrating that Polish Jews saw themselves as part of the Polish state even as they maintained a separate cultural identity.

Joselewicz had approached Kosciuszko for permission to form his unit, requesting that the Jewish soldiers be allowed to maintain customs like not fighting on the Sabbath where possible, and being allowed to maintain their beards. Kosciuszko assented and the force soon became known as the 'Beardlings'. Sadly, it was wiped out in the Battle of Praga on the banks of Warsaw's Vistula River in November 1794, in the dying days of the uprising. Joselewicz survived and went on to forge a celebrated military career, eventually dying on the battlefield in 1809 in service of Poland against the Austrian empire. But he is best remembered for leading what is widely believed to be the first all-Jewish fighting unit since the Judean Simon Bar Kokhba led a revolt against the Romans in the year 132.

Jews had of course taken up arms in countless armies in countries as far afield as China, Spain and Yemen in the thousand-plus years between antiquity and the Industrial Revolution but never as a self-contained, wholly Jewish military unit. It took the great social reformer Kosciuszko to enable that, and while it ended in carnage, it still represented a high point for Polish Jews, who found acceptance as they fought in the spirit of brotherhood with their fellow citizens, Jews and gentiles alike.

'Nothing can convince more the far away nations about the holiness of our cause and the justness of the present revolution than that, though separated from us by their religion and customs, they [the Jews] sacrifice their own lives of their own free will in order to support the uprising,' Kosciuszko is said to have written in a statement about the regiment.

Things would get worse for Polish Jews in the immediate aftermath of the failed Kosciuszko Uprising and the Third Partition of Poland in 1795. Darker days of the nineteenth and twentieth centuries culminated in the eradication of almost the entire population of more than three million Polish Jews during the Holocaust.

There are two main institutions you can visit in modern Poland to learn more about the life and times of Polish Jews. An hour west of Krakow is Auschwitz, officially Auschwitz-Birkenau, the site of the largest of the Nazi concentration camps, where well over a million Jews were starved, tortured, subjected to macabre medical experiments and put to death. Then there's Warsaw's POLIN Museum of the History of Polish Jews, situated in the heart of the former Warsaw Ghetto. If you're more interested in how the Jews lived in Poland than how they were slaughtered en masse, POLIN is your best bet. Polin means 'Poland' in Hebrew. The word is composed of two parts: 'Po' meaning 'here' and 'lin' meaning 'rest'. There's an old tale that birds uttered the words 'rest here' to Jews who arrived in a tranquil Polish forest, having fled persecution in western Europe.

The Jews did indeed rest here in Poland for many centuries. POLIN tells that story in a wonderful way with reconstructed villages, interactive displays, the whole potato latke. There's almost too much to take in. What lingers after a visit are scenes, snippets, phrases, emotions.

There's the map of Jewish settlements within the Polish–Lithuanian Commonwealth, so numerous they look like constellations in the night sky. There's the quote from the book *Notes from the Warsaw Ghetto* by historian Emmanuel Ringelblum, who lived in the ghetto during World War II before his family escaped, was betrayed and killed in a nearby neighbourhood: 'One is left with the tragic dilemma: are we to dole out spoonfuls to everyone, the result being that no one will survive? Or are we to give full measure to a few – with only a handful having enough to survive?'

There's the poem 'Jewboy' by Julian Tuwim, a poet who felt both a Polish and Jewish sense of identity, yet who was never quite Polish enough for the Poles or Jewish enough for Jewish nationalists. A middle stanza of that poem captures those feelings:

Where has life brought us? We who are seen by most
As alien, unwelcome – where did we get lost?

In the end, the Jews were lost to Poland. After most were killed in the Holocaust, the majority of those who remained left for Israel or the United States, which is why around eighty per cent of American Jews have Polish roots. As for Poland's current Jewish population, it's rebounding a little as some people reclaim a heritage they had suppressed, hidden or did not even know about. But the Institute for Jewish Policy Research puts Poland's 'core Jewish population', as in people who self-identify as Jewish, at just 4500. The nation which once held the world's largest Jewish population is now number thirty-three on the list.

Talking to Poles today, it's clear that most lament the loss of the Jewish people and culture in their country. There's even a sense of shame that more could not be done to prevent the starvation in the Warsaw Ghetto and the slaughter at concentration camps.

'It's still a very sensitive subject,' Marta Patla from the Museum of Life Under Communism noted on our visit to that institution. 'It was the biggest Jewish population in the world … what happened? We were so open and what happened?'

That said, sympathy for the Jews has tempered to a degree in Poland, as it has worldwide, since Israeli Prime Minister Benjamin Netanyahu's response to the October 7 attacks when more Jews were killed than on any single day since the Holocaust. There is of course a marked difference between anti-Israel sentiment and outright anti-Semitism, but the line is not always clear.

If you ever happen to visit the POLIN museum, and here we enter TripAdvisor mode: eat there! Eat everything on the menu and go back the next day and eat the stuff you couldn't fit in the first time. Jewish food from around the globe is on offer, from classics like latkes and gefilte fish to North African tagine with couscous and Middle Eastern staples done the Jewish way. Is it disrespectful to gorge on such plentiful Jewish cuisine on the site of a ghetto where once the Jews were starved? Absolutely not. The very fact you're here makes it quite the opposite.

As for dinner on the last night in Warsaw for two Australian travellers for whom POLIN was quite the emotional belly punch, comfort food is required. The answer is Vietnamese pho, which is on offer at numerous spots around town. We want pho partly because we're pierogied out, partly out of curiosity to see if it's any good in these parts and partly because it has become one of Australia's de facto national dishes, which means we absolutely crave it. The pho is top-notch. The broth is fragrant and piping hot, there's loads of fresh chilli, mint and bean sprouts, and there's plenty of hoisin and sriracha for dipping on the side.

Vietnamese people came to Poland in two waves, the first in educational exchanges between people of communist nations in the 1960s, the second, larger wave after the fall of communism with people expert in textiles and the food and restaurant trade. Today there are around 50,000 Vietnamese people in Poland, which means there are roughly ten times as many as Jews. The world changes. Communities come and go. Everyone has a right to live in dignity and peace wherever they end up, whether in their homeland or far from it.

Were he alive today, would Kosciuszko feel the Palestinians deserve anything less than a dignified existence in their own defined state? Would he sympathise with Israel over the brutality and horrors of 7 October 2023 at the hands of Hamas – a group designated as terrorists by the European Union and several democratic nations – while still viewing the response of the Israel Defense Forces as an unconscionable over-reaction? As he looked upon the ruins of Gaza, would Kosciuszko unavoidably be reminded of the German destruction of Polish cities in World War II? These, too, are rhetorical questions.

CHAPTER 18

A DELICATE CONSTITUTION

The train from Warsaw to Krakow is swift and smooth with only a few stops, plenty of legroom and a carriage only about half full. These are cheap second-class seats. What could first-class travel possibly entail? Artisanal kielbasa on demand? A serenade on a grand piano by a young virtuoso playing the music of Frederic Chopin? A lecture from an eminent contemporary Polish scientist on the heliocentrism of Copernicus and Marie Curie's discovery of the radioactive elements radium and polonium?

Copernicus, Curie and Chopin were all, of course, Poles whose names have been Anglicised, Latinised or even Frenchified to varying degrees. Indeed, Curie discovered and named polonium in 1898 while Poland was still partitioned, in what was unmistakably a raised middle finger to Poland's longstanding antagonists, Russia, Prussia and Austria. But the three giants of Polish arts and science raise an interesting idea. Curie was born Maria Salomea Sklodowska, and added the 'Curie' upon marriage. What if Kosciuszko's name had been made easier for non-Poles? What if he had gone down in history as 'Kozzie', the name by which most Australians know the mountain named after him? Would he have become a better known, more widely celebrated figure?

As fields of golden canola flash by, it's time to hit the books and address bigger questions. Polish historian Piotr Hapanowicz awaits in Krakow, and a quick revision of key chapters of Polish history is required. The key questions: what happened after Kosciuszko returned from America in 1784? How did Poland move toward its landmark constitution of 1791? When Russia in cahoots with a group of Polish nobles overthrew the constitution in 1792, what was Kosciuszko's role and what then were the steps that led to the 1794 Kosciuszko Uprising? And one more biggie: though noble in intent, was the insurrection named after Kosciuszko itself doomed to failure from the start? This train is not one of Europe's super-fast railway journeys but it's quick enough, and with three hours until Krakow, we'll be there before we know it. Clickety-clack, let's go way back.

After eight years in America, Kosciuszko sailed from New York City in July 1784 under favourable breezes and disembarked in the French port of Lorient less than four weeks later. His first stop was Paris, where he connected with leading figures of the Enlightenment as well as with veterans of America's Revolutionary War who were now in France, many working to strengthen the two nations' mutual interests. Kosciuszko then went home to Poland, where he visited his old benefactor King Stanislaw in Warsaw to ask for a post in the military. No dice. Money still spoke loudest when it came to attaining military rank, and even his highly distinguished service in America could not sway the Polish monarch. So Kosciuszko returned to his modest family estate which was now based at Siechnowicze, and which was now in the hands of his sister, Anna, and her husband, Peter, who had paid off the debts incurred by Kosciuszko's financially incompetent brother, Jozef.

'The one tranquil span of Kosciuszko's life' is how English writer and aficionado of all things Polish Monica Mary Gardner described the ensuing four-year period in her 1920 work *Kosciuszko: A Biography*. Her passage describing Kosciuszko the mud-encrusted farmer is a lovely insight into the everyday side of the man:

> Soldierly simplicity was the note of Kosciuszko's rustic country home. The living-room was set out with a plain old table, a few wooden seats and an ancient store cupboard. The furniture of the small sleeping apartment consisted of a bed and by its side a table on which lay Kosciuszko's papers and books, conspicuous among the latter being the political writings of the great contemporary Polish reformers—Staszyc and Kołłontaj—which to the Pole of Kosciuszko's temperament were bound to be fraught with burning interest. His coffee was served in a cup made by his own hand; the simple dishes and plates that composed his household stock were also his work, for the arts and crafts were always his favourite hobbies. An old cousin looked after the housekeeping. A coachman and manservant were the only other members of the family. There was a garden well stocked with fruit-trees that was the delight of Kosciuszko's heart. On a hillock covered with hazels he laid out walks, put up arbours and arranged a maze that wound so craftily among the thicket that the visitor who entered it found no easy exit. The maze may still be seen, together with the avenue of trees that was

planted by Kosciuszko himself. His interest in his domain was unfailing. When far away from home, in the midst of his military preoccupations, while commanding in the Polish army, he wrote minute directions to his sister on the importation of fresh trees, the sowing of different grains on the farm.

It's sweet to think of Kosciuszko with his fruit trees and his hedge maze, his handmade coffee mug resting on his 'plain old table', and to remember that George Washington had only recently inducted him into the Society of the Cincinnati, named for the Roman statesman Cincinnatus, who was as comfortable on the battlefield as in a wheatfield. It's equally endearing to picture Kosciuszko at the end of his four-year stint at Siechnowicze when, having at last secured a military command in service of his homeland, he still found time to send instructions to his sister on which seeds to plant. In Kosciuszko's attention to agrarian detail, there are echoes of Jefferson's lists and inventories at Monticello. When the two weren't discussing such trivialities as republicanism and liberty, perhaps Kosciuszko and Jefferson bonded over the finer points of eighteenth-century agribusiness – two farm nerds steered by fate and a sense of duty into lives as statesmen.

Of course, the enduring difference between Kosciuszko and Jefferson is that Kosciuszko was never anything less than disgusted by slavery or indentured servitude. The peasants at Siechnowicze lived in small cottages on the estate and while they held more rights than enslaved Americans – such as being able to own property, albeit not the land itself – they were nonetheless vassals. Kosciuszko was desperate to free his serfs but his hands were tied. To draw another similarity between Kosciuszko and Jefferson, the Pole couldn't free his serfs because there were bills to pay. Complicating matters, the interest accruing on his unclaimed Revolutionary War pay never arrived. However, unlike Jefferson, Kosciuszko would take meaningful steps in due course.

Meanwhile the winds of change were gusting through Polish politics, fanned by Hugo Kollataj and Stanislaw Staszic, the two reformers whose writings Kosciuszko hungrily consumed, as highlighted by Gardner. The Polish–Lithuanian Commonwealth was trying to modernise. With Enlightenment thought and the Industrial Revolution sweeping across Europe, the Commonwealth remained socially and technologically backward. It was primarily an agrarian society with a rigid class system where rights and privileges were held by only the top ten per cent of the social strata. This weakened not just the power of the lower classes but of the nation itself. Even the military was primitive, with the majority of the self-serving nobility unwilling to fund it or to undertake meaningful service beyond parade drills.

There were also institutional roadblocks to the Commonwealth's prosperity. The big one was the liberum veto, or free vote, a rule which allowed any individual representative to block legislation in the sejm, or parliament. The history of the liberum veto is interesting. Introduced in 1652, it was founded on the idea that regional representatives should be able to block decisions that didn't suit their local constituents. So, in a sense, it was rooted in ideals of democracy and equality. But because the liberum veto was applied frequently, it backfired, miring the Commonwealth in a near-permanent state of legislative gridlock as it only took one dissenting voice to block the passage of legislation.

Russia and other nearby powers loved the way the liberum veto thwarted progress and reform. Poland's wealthiest magnates also welcomed the liberum veto, as any impediment to reform kept wealth and power ensconced in their hands.

In 1785, the priest and philosopher Stanislaw Staszic called for the abolition of the liberum veto among reforms including a hereditary monarchy to replace the elected monarchy, industrial development, the expansion of the army and the abolition of serfdom. Hugo Kollataj, who was a priest as well as a reformer, wrote a series of anonymous letters calling for similar measures, arguing that Poland needed a democratic constitution and an end to the class system. More than once in the letters, Kollataj referenced America's struggle for Independence in the context of Poland's need for change. He also argued for a strengthening of the military. Kosciuszko consumed their writings hungrily, and met Kollataj on a trip to Warsaw during this period. They became friends, and Kollataj would later write the first draft of Kosciuszko's proclamation in Krakow's Main Square on 24 March 1794, heralding the start of the uprising. He also penned the famous Proclamation of Polaniec that followed. But that was still six years away.

The year was 1788 and things were coming to a head in Warsaw, with the gathering of the Great Sejm – a sitting of the sejm that would last until 1792. The timing was good for Poland. Russia was involved in a war with Turkey which had started in 1787 over competing claims to Crimea, the strategically located Black Sea promontory which Russia would annex in 2014 when it was part of Ukraine in a prelude to its larger 2022 invasion. With Russia's attention on the Turks, the Poles felt emboldened to take steps toward greater self-determination in defiance of their meddling, belligerent neighbour which had occupied parts of the Commonwealth since the first partition of Poland back in 1772 when Kosciuszko was a student in Paris.

What transpired from the Great Sejm was the famous constitution of 3 May 1791, the world's second written constitution, a remarkable fact which today is little-known outside of Poland, although it was greatly celebrated in both European and American newspapers of the time. George Washington, by then serving as the first American president, praised Poland's King Stanislaw Augustus for the constitution. The king had helped draft it, with significant help from the silky pen of Kollataj and others, including Kosciuszko's soon-to-be aide-de-camp, the writer Julian Niemcewicz.

Poland's constitution arrived exactly four months before the French Constitution, in which the famous Declaration of the Rights of Man and of the Citizen – which had been penned two years earlier – served as the preamble. But unlike France's constitution, Poland's came into being without violence. A peaceful revolution was underway, even if the revolution didn't entirely overthrow the status quo. The 3 May constitution was not as radical a document as the American or French constitutions. But with its mix of the pragmatic and the progressive, it was still a huge step forward and its authors had plans for future reforms that would go much further.

The new constitution did not abolish serfdom but it did give new powers to serfs, including the right to take legal action against abusive masters. It did not specifically diminish the rights of the nobility but it did bestow new powers upon burghers, the townsfolk who sat below the nobility but above the peasants on the societal pecking order. The liberum veto was scrapped. The monarchy became hereditary, a measure designed to prevented the election of monarchs who could become pawns of foreign powers. Separate executive, legislative and judicial arms of government were enshrined in law. Roman Catholicism was acknowledged as the official religion but tolerance was promised to the Jews and those of other faiths.

Part of the preamble stated:

> Despite obstacles that may cause passions in us, we do for the general welfare, for the establishment of liberty, for the preservation of our country and its borders, with the utmost constancy of spirit ordain this Constitution and declare it to be entirely sacred and inviolable until the people, at the time by law prescribed, by their clear will recognize a need to alter any of its articles.

Sadly, the constitution would not prove 'sacred and inviolable'. Indeed, it lasted little more than a year, ultimately blotted out by the very king whose pen had helped write it.

Meanwhile as Poland manoeuvred its way toward its new constitution, Kosciuszko was at last manoeuvring his way back into military service — this time for his homeland. In 1789, during the second year of the Great Sejm, his old flame Ludwika Sosnowska, now Princess Lubormiska, wrote to tell him that the sejm was about to commission officers for the army. *The Peasant Prince* author Alex Storozynski argues that she risked her marriage writing this letter. If the letter itself was risky, its language in places was risqué: 'As your best girlfriend, I advise you to be in Warsaw ...' she began. Storozynski then details how Kosciuszko heeded Ludwika's advice and journeyed to Warsaw, where he had a chance meeting with the Princess which ended with no words spoken and the two in tears in separate corners of a room.

But the trip was a success in other ways. On 1 October 1789, Kosciuszko became Major General Kosciuszko. Though he was by far the most seasoned and adept officer, Kosciuszko was not made the supreme commander of the military. In a continuation of old nepotistic ways which had never served Poland well, that role fell to the king's nephew, Prince Jozef Poniatowski. In the period after the passing of the constitution, Kosciuszko busied himself by moving around Poland, training troops. It was during this period that he met and fell in love with Tekla Zurowska. It was his second doomed romance. Rejection by her father was painful but, as ever, the call of duty took precedence over the pangs of personal happiness. After the constitution was passed, it was not long before rumours started to spread of powerful magnates colluding with the Russians in opposition to the constitution. Kosciuszko was in charge of protecting the Russian border. His goal was to build an army capable of liberating Poland, an army similar to the one he had served with in America, comprised of citizen soldiers willing to sacrifice all in defence of their country and its constitution. Kosciuszko fell immediately back into his Revolutionary War ways, refusing food when rations were scarce and the men were wanting, and even at times sleeping on bare earth. His popularity grew. The great general of America was becoming a beloved Polish military figure. His engineering, military and motivational skills would soon be needed.

In April 1792, a group of Polish magnates whose powers had been diminished by the new constitution met Catherine the Great in St Petersburg. This was the Targowica Confederation, so-named for the village in Poland where they vowed to overthrow the new constitution shortly after meeting in the Russian capital, thus ensuring that the village's name would forever be synonymous with treason. Within a week, more than 100,000 Russian troops invaded. The Polish–Russian War of 1792, known in Poland as the War in Defence of the Constitution, was a short-lived affair, with the Polish–Lithuanian

Commonwealth losing within ten weeks, a defeat that led to the Second Partition of Poland when in 1793 Prussia to the west and Russia to the east both seized large chunks of Polish territory, shrinking its size by around two-thirds. Defeat also killed the constitution.

For the Poles, as for Kosciuszko, the high point of the war was the Battle of Dubienka at a small village on the Bug River, which today forms the border between Poland and its eastern neighbours Ukraine and Belarus. With the Russians bearing down, the Poles were hopelessly outgunned and outnumbered, with a force of 5300 while the Russians had five times that many. But the Poles had Kosciuszko, who went into Saratoga mode, cleverly using the terrain to advantage. Kosciuszko rode along the river to seek a key point to engage the enemy that made use of the natural protection of swamps and forest. He burnt a bridge over the river so the Russians could not cross with their artillery, then set underwater traps to thwart crossing by other means. His men dug trenches on his side of the river, set up artillery batteries and constructed palisades on the high ground that would slow a Russian advance. By the time General Kakhovsky appeared with his huge army, Kosciuszko's men were ready. In a bloody conflict that lasted five hours, the Polish position was too well protected to breach. Four thousand Russians were killed, with 900 Polish casualties.

Eventually, Kosciuszko ordered a retreat, as the Russian forces were just too numerous and he knew they would eventually encircle the Poles. With supplies low, a siege would be a slow suicide. Some officers who were envious of Kosciuszko's growing popularity tried to paint the retreat as a failure, but the Polish people got it. Kosciuszko had humiliated the Russians, who dug mass graves to hide the magnitude of the slaughter.

General Kakhovsky got it too. 'After a month of action with the Polish armies, this is the first time that I have stood against an adversary working in great unison with such a passionate plan to repulse our attacks and stubbornly defend themselves,' the Russian wrote in his battle report.

King Stanislaw also got it. Upon the former student who had been a favourite at the Corps of Cadets a quarter of a century earlier, the king bestowed the Virtuti Militari, Poland's highest military decoration. He also promoted Kosciuszko to Lieutenant General. But these honours meant little to Kosciuszko as they came after the war was lost. Despite the patriotic shot-in-the-arm of Dubienka, the king had considered defeat inevitable and negotiated a ceasefire. Catherine the Great's response was to make him join the Targowica Confederation. The monarch who on the passing of the constitution had publicly proclaimed, 'I swear before God that I won't regret it!' apparently now regretted it very much and annulled the constitution.

As people expressed outrage at the king's actions, Kosciuszko was now the hero of the nation. At last, Poles had grasped what Americans had long since known. They understood how well he had chosen the battleground at Dubienka, and how expertly the men under his command had constructed defences. They appreciated how many lives he had saved with his strategic retreat. They lapped up stories of his fearlessness in battle and his care for the wounded. But after attending the ceasefire meeting, Kosciuszko left in tears then resigned from the military. What remained to fight for?

King Stanislaw tried to talk him out of it, and the story goes that he sent a bevy of attractive women to try to sweet talk him but Kosciuszko's decision was made. As things turned out, he couldn't have stuck around even if he'd wanted to.

Threatened by his popularity, Catherine the Great had a warrant issued for Kosciuszko's arrest. He had to leave Poland.

Where would he go and what would he do? America was an option. So was France, where he had just been made an honorary citizen along with several American Founding Fathers and other Patriots. Meanwhile, there was the matter of his estate at Siechnowicze, which he left in the hands of his sister, Anna. Having lost the war, Kosciuszko's dream of meaningful changes to the feudal system on a nationwide scale was thwarted – for now. He still had the power to change lives on his own estate, and he duly reduced the weekly forced labour of male peasants by around half, while completely abolishing the forced labour of the female peasants.

'His personal loss was considerable,' Gardner wrote.

But Poland's loss was worse.

CHAPTER 19

TOO GENTLE FOR A REVOLUTIONIST

If there's a finer town square in Europe than Krakow's Rynek Glowny, or Main Market Square, then this Australian traveller hasn't seen it. London's Trafalgar Square is a glorified traffic island. Venice's St Mark's Square is a tourist hell covered in pigeon shit and smelling of rancid seaweed. There's something forbidding about Moscow's Red Square with the red wall of the Kremlin along its western flank, a mood even the cheerfully spectacular onion-domed Saint Basil's Cathedral can't lift. The Grand-Place in Brussels is death by ornateness and twee. But Krakow's Main Square is perfection. Immediately upon entering it, you feel like you love the entire city – and where has it been all your life?

The square is surrounded by historic townhouses painted in cheerful but not gaudy shades. Think the colours of gelato, with lemon, boysenberry, hazelnut and pistachio. Dotted around the square's perimeter are bars, museums and cafes serving excellent coffee of which Kosciuszko would approve. A few small broad-leaf trees growing out of pots add just a touch of greenery, augmenting the built aesthetic without obscuring it. In the centre of the square stands the old Cloth Hall, a Renaissance masterpiece which was once the hub of trade in Krakow and now tactfully conceals bustling souvenir stalls within. Beside it rises the seventy-metre tower of the old Town Hall, which features in a famous painting of Kosciuszko reading his oath on the morning he declared the 1794 uprising. These structures form islands which make the largest medieval plaza in Europe feel surprisingly intimate, or as intimate as any place can be with loud British people populating the restaurants and cafes. The Brits have well and truly invaded Krakow. Budget carrier Ryanair has a base here, operating more than 200 flights a week during the peak summer season. But such is the Main Square's charm that not even an inebriation of lager louts can ruin it.

At the northwest corner of the square is the Krzysztofory Palace, an old Baroque mansion which today houses the main part of the Historical Museum of the City of Krakow. The director of the museum is Doctor Piotr Hapanowicz and he has kindly agreed to meet us with his wife, who is serving as translator. Before our meeting, Hapanowicz emailed a 2022 article that he wrote for the quarterly American journal *The Polish Review* entitled, 'Tadeusz Kosciuszko and Liberty'. In it, he casts Kosciuszko not just as a great military leader but as a leading light of Polish Enlightenment thinking who didn't just call out injustice and inequality but had the will and fortitude to do something about it.

The Hapanowiczes are warm and welcoming. We start with a quick tour of the museum, then move up to a beautiful room with an immaculate parquetry floor and fine stuccos on the ceiling. Portraits adorn the walls, their frames lined with gold. Windows overlook the square. This is a fine setting in which to discuss one of Poland's finest sons. But who was Kosciuszko?

We're starting with a question as wide as the frame on the largest portrait, with the aim of narrowing the answer down to the point of light in the subject's eye.

'Kosciuszko was thinking about the freedom not only for his nation but for all nations, for all people on Earth,' Hapanowicz replies. 'Other great thinkers were thinking about freedom theoretically, but he was thinking pragmatically.'

'So he was a pragmatist?'

'He was also a radical, but not too much.'

Kosciuszko the radical and Kosciuszko the pragmatist: these seemingly contradictory characteristics are a persistent theme in Hapanowicz's writing. Most revolutionaries tend to lean heavily toward one trait or the other – but therein lies the essence of the man. 'Riding the highest mountains and the smallest valleys taught me that it is best to stick to the middle road, if you can find it,' Kosciuszko wrote from Switzerland in his twilight years to Prince Czartoryski, the cousin of King Stanislaw who helped get the young Kosciuszko into the Corps of Cadets. You can feel the internal tug-of-war in Kosciuszko's mind – the rocket-fuelled rush of idealism and the gravitational pull of moderation – in the way he carried out the 1794 Kosciuszko Uprising, the plans for which were hatched outside Poland.

Leaving his homeland late in 1792 to avoid being arrested, on the premise that he was going to America to claim his war pay, Kosciuszko travelled under the pseudonym Mr Bieda – which means 'Mr Misery' – a name which reveals all you need to know about his mindset. He ended up in Saxony, the region which today lies in the eastern part of Germany bordering south-west Poland. In the city of Leipzig, Hugo Kollataj and other Polish exiles were busy plotting their next move. Kosciuszko joined them in January 1793 and was chosen as the emissary to go abroad to drum up support for a Polish insurrection against Russia.

Kosciuszko arrived in Paris the day King Louis XVI was beheaded. France was in turmoil, yet the Polish hero managed to meet with many key figures of the French Revolution including Maximilien Robespierre, the leader of the violent Jacobin group which later that year would unleash the infamous Reign of Terror. Kosciuszko also met French Minister of Foreign Affairs Pierre Lebrun-Tondu and handed him documents he had written which advocated for the abolition of the monarchy, the end of serfdom and equal rights for all within the Polish–Lithuanian Commonwealth. Kosciuszko felt that the French would surely support his vision of a true republic that could stand as a bulwark against Tsarist Russia but their own revolution was apparently distraction enough.

Kosciuszko then visited Italy, where he lobbied the Vatican for assistance. No help was forthcoming there either and the trip ultimately proved fruitless.

While Kosciuszko was away, his exiled compatriots came to believe that he was the only person who could lead an uprising. On his return to Saxony in September 1793, he met with the conspirators and agreed to lead it. Kosciuszko had no desire to fight two futile wars inside two years against an enemy with a better-equipped, much larger army, but when he heard that the Tsarist occupiers had decided to disband what remained of the Polish army, he knew it was time to act. Poland's very existence was at stake.

> Despite the lack of a chance for a Polish victory in 1794, they had to fight because they were threatened with the complete liquidation of even that fragment of a state dependent on Russia that remained after the second partition.

That's a line from eminent twentieth-century Polish historian Andrzej Zahorski, which Hapanowicz quotes in his article. Kosciuszko's compulsion to do what's right irrespective of the cost brings to mind Lech Walesa's presidential campaign slogan: 'I don't want to, but I have to'. The other obvious similarity between Walesa and Kosciuszko is that their legacies are defined by their advocacy not just for Poland itself but for its ordinary citizens. The Solidarity union which Walesa led in the 1980s amassed ten million members at its popular peak. Kosciuszko too knew that Poland's power lay in its common people: his uprising would be a people's uprising.

On 23 March 1794, after spending the previous night sleeping in a barn, Kosciuszko snuck into Krakow, arriving incognito, leading a horse and wagon. He stayed at the house of General Jozef Wodzicki, where they were joined by a band of revolutionaries. Here, final plans for the uprising were hatched.

> The wretched state in which Poland finds itself is known to the universe; the indignities of two neighbouring powers, and the crimes of traitors to their country have sunk this nation into an abyss of misery …

So began the proclamation read by a representative of the sejm at 10 am the next morning in unseasonably warm early spring weather in Krakow's Main Square. Then Kosciuszko took over, now effectively the Polish–Lithuanian Commonwealth's benevolent dictator with supreme powers. He announced:

> I pledge not to use these powers to oppress any person, but to defend the integrity of the borders of Poland, regain the independence of the nation, and to strengthen

universal liberties. So help me God and the innocent passion of His Son.

Wild applause and chants of 'Long live Poland! Long live Kosciuszko!' immediately followed. Kosciuszko then set about preparing his people for war.

One male member of every fifth house was required to report to duty equipped with a carbine, pike or axe. All able-bodied males in Krakow aged between eighteen and twenty-eight years of age had to enlist. Kosciuszko reached out to women too, asking them to make bandages and contribute in any way possible. He made his appeal to the Jews. He entreated the nobility for money to fund the insurrection and the zlotys soon came flowing in. So did the Russians. On hearing news of the revolt, Catherine the Great dispatched General Fyodor Denisov with 5000 troops toward Krakow. Kosciuszko realised his forces would be stronger if they joined up with a pair of Polish generals who were already in the field, one of whom had refused to disband his regiment in defiance of Catherine the Great's orders.

The opposing Russian and Polish armies clashed at the village of Raclawice, about forty kilometres north-east of Krakow.

Thus began the Battle of Raclawice, the battle celebrated in the circular panorama in the city of Wroclaw. The hero of the battle was a peasant called Wojciech Bartosz, who charged toward a Russian cannon and prevented it from firing by snuffing out the fuse with his hat. Kosciuszko's scythemen were heroic too, and brutal. In hand-to-hand combat, even hardened Russian soldiers were no match for peasants who wielded their agricultural tools as though the Russian army was a wheat crop. Surrounded Russian soldiers begged for mercy and received none. Those who fled were quite literally cut down. By the end of the battle, 800 Russians had been killed, roughly four times the number of Polish casualties. In triumph, Kosciuszko removed his uniform and donned the sukmana, the sheep's wool peasant robe that he would wear for much of the ensuing campaign. The symbolism was unmistakable. It was the ultimate sign of respect for those from the lowest class of society who had joined the uprising. Centuries before the age of 'inclusivity' Kosciuszko's army was truly inclusive.

Though of limited strategic significance, Raclawice was the morale boost that Poland needed. Alex Storozynski makes the great point that a ragtag assortment of Polish farmers had done at Raclawice to the Russian army what American famers had done to the British in the American Revolution. In recognition of the peasants, and in accordance with his dream of a homeland that was not just free of invaders but truly free for all, on 7 May, Kosciuszko issued his famous Proclamation of Polaniec in the small town of Polaniec, about 120 kilometres north-east of Krakow. Though the proclamation didn't abolish serfdom, it gave peasants a raft of significant new rights including the right to own their own land and the promise of freedom after the revolution to all peasant conscripts.

On the same day, Kosciuszko delivered an appeal to religious figures, urging them to 'join your hearts with the Poles, who defend our freedom and yours'. The phrase 'our freedom and yours' caught on and became the motto of the uprising, although it was soon transposed to read 'For your freedom and ours'. The motto lives on in Poland today and has surfaced throughout its military history. Polish fighter pilots in World War II formed a squadron called the Kosciuszko Squadron (officially 303 Squadron) and their battle cry was 'For your freedom and ours'. The squadron downed 126 German planes in the famous Battle of Britain, considerably more than any other Allied aerial squadron.

Not everyone responded positively to the Proclamation of Polaniec. The nobility did not approve, and neither did the Church. Both groups had opened their pockets for the revolution but both feared for their future income as even the Church kept serfs.

If the Proclamation of Polaniec was Kosciuszko at his most radical, and radical Koz didn't please everyone, then pragmatic Koz had his detractors too. As the revolution progressed, a Jacobin fervour took hold in Warsaw, where members of the Targowica Confederation were hanged. Even the king feared becoming Poland's Louis XVI, although Kosciuszko spared him. In June, when several Russian collaborators were hanged in a Warsaw public square having been given no trial, Kosciuszko was infuriated. Away from the battlefield, he had no taste for blood, demanding that even the most despised traitors should be tried in accordance with the law.

'French historian Jules Michelet seems to have been right in his opinion when he acknowledged that the Chief of the Insurrection was too gentle for a revolutionist,' wrote Hapanowicz in his *Polish Review* article.

'Too gentle for a revolutionist' is an interesting turn of phrase and, as Hapanowicz explains, it's definitely not a put-down. Indeed, he argues that Poland desperately needed a leader who was a symbol of national unity and solidarity rather than a rabble-rouser. Kosciuszko's character played a huge role in that.

In the end, the Kosciuszko Uprising was quashed. The turning point was the entry of a huge Prussian army, estimated to be 25,000-strong, which had made its way east without Kosciuszko's knowledge. Meanwhile, the Austrians moved in on Krakow.

Battles were won and battles were lost but the writing was on the wall after Kosciuszko fell at Maciejowice on 10 October, and the letters were painted in blood. Fierce fighting continued in Warsaw until thousands of its citizens were slaughtered and by November 1794 it was all over. In October 1795, Prussia, Russia and Austria negotiated the terms of the Third Partition of Poland as the Polish–Lithuanian Commonwealth dissolved. King Stanislaw abdicated and spent his final years in captivity in St Petersburg. He was Poland's last king.

> The 1794 Kosciuszko Insurrection had no chance of succeeding. The agreement between two and eventually three partitioning powers constituted the world's greatest military might of that day and exceeded Kosciuszko's actual and potential forces many times over …

That was the conclusion of historian Lukasz Kadziela in his 1994 article in *The Polish Review*. But as he went on to argue, some failures are much more valuable than others:

> The final collapse of the Polish state without at least an attempt at armed resistance would have sent a most depressing signal to the Poles. But an unsuccessful insurrection inspired them to launch successive attempts to regain their independence and thus their own state. These attempts comprised much of the substance of Polish history throughout the nineteenth century and, in 1918, after 123 years of foreign occupation, they finally succeeded.

Historian Andrzej Zahorski also made this point in the book *Three National Uprisings*:

Although Kosciuszko suffered defeat, he showed the path to fight for freedom through the collective effort of the entire nation, and this became his political testament. Kosciuszko's ideological and political thought will be taken up by Poles, who every generation take up the fight to rebuild the country.

As for Piotr Hapanowicz's view, he says simply that Kosciuszko became 'a monument of a person'. While the translation at first might seem a little imperfect, it's clear what he means. Kosciuszko was a symbol not of bloody resistance but of selflessness and humanity. 'He was a good guy, not a warrior,' he says.

Remember the archetypal history teacher who would sneer at a wishy-washy phrase like 'good guy' for a major historical figure? Turns out, it was Kosciuszko's most important attribute.

CHAPTER 20

A TWINGE OF THE HEART

If the Main Square and the surrounding Old Town district are the beating heart of Krakow, its modern-day soul is the neighbourhood of Kazimierz, a web of old cobbled streets, bars and eateries which seamlessly blend the grungy with the upmarket, like a high-end fashion model in ripped jeans. This is the old Jewish quarter, where the Jews moved en masse in the late fifteenth century when it was still a separate village.

Krakow itself was reputedly founded by legendary fourth-century ruler Krakus, who is said to have slayed a resident dragon by feeding it either a cow or sheep stuffed with sulphur, which explains the dragon motifs on every dishcloth, trinket and knick-knack. The city rose to become a centre of trade, science and the arts, serving as Poland's capital from 1038 to 1596. It was ransacked by the Mongols in the thirteenth century, by the Swedes in the seventeenth century, and occupied by the Austrians from the late eighteenth century. At times, Cracovians ravaged their own, which is how most of the Jews ended up in Kazimierz after an outbreak of anti-Jewish violence in 1495. There, they flourished for centuries before they were herded by the Nazis into a ghetto on the other side of the Vistula River. Most were murdered there or in concentration camps, and almost every Krakow Jew who survived the war emigrated to Israel or the United States soon afterward. By the 1970s, Kazimierz had become a virtual ghost town, rundown and unloved.

It could hardly be more different now. On this cool but clear May evening, Kazimierz is alive. Everyone told us to stay in this part of Krakow and it was good advice. We check into our hotel with twilight fading and search for something cheap and cheerful to eat. This is easily achieved. Behind the hotel is the unapologetically shabby Plac Nowy, or New Square, at the centre of which is a circular building with a dozen stalls selling something called zapiekanka, or zapiekanki in plural form, which is a sort of toasted open bread roll with a range of toppings – a bit like pizza with a baguette base. Like kotlet schabowy, zapiekanki have undergone several phases of acceptance in their brief history. Invented in the 1970s, they were a way of turning Polish staples like bread, kielbasa and pickles into a fast food sold from the rudimentary food trucks which were permitted during the communist era. When communism ended, zapiekanki became less ubiquitous, viewed as a cheap and nasty reminder of bad times. They are now enjoying a huge resurgence and are a staple of Polish street food, especially late at night, especially if you're drunk and especially if you're drunk and British, which is to say if you're British and in Krakow.

We order a Zapiekanka Tatrzanska, whose signature ingredient is a smoky, slightly rubbery cheese called oscypek, a delicacy of the Tatra Mountains on the Slovakian border, about an hour south of Krakow. Like every meal or morsel we've sampled in Poland, it is delicious. Even the dill pickle-flavoured instant noodles, bought entirely out of curiosity from a convenience store, turn out to be a terrific late-night snack back at the hotel after a couple of hours walking the lively night streets of Kazimierz. Sleep comes easily. A bunch of Brits are boozily singing 'Don't Look Back in Anger' by Oasis over in Plac Nowy and it's far from the world's worst lullaby.

Morning heralds a big day of homage to Kosciuszko. We must walk to Wawel Cathedral and place on his tomb a special gift which we think he'll really like. At lunchtime, we've got an insider's tour of Rynek Underground, the museum under the Main Square. Afternoon will invert our world and take us to the top of the Kosciuszko Mound, a few kilometres on the other side of the Vistula River. Then this evening, there's a function at the mound with a choral performance by some singers who've come a long, long way to be here.

But first, there's the matter of coffee with Mat Schulz, an Australian who has lived in Poland for about thirty years and who now runs a successful music festival called Unsound, which has spread its wings from Poland to cities around the world, including Adelaide back home in Australia.

'Back in the nineties, few of my friends would come to Kazimierz or even think of living here,' Schulz says. 'After communism, it was quite rough and dangerous. There were everyday stores but there were none of these cafes and none of the buildings were renovated. It was completely different to what it is now until around the early 2000s. There were lots of vacant buildings as well where the ownership was unclear.'

The uncertain proprietorship was mostly due to Jewish people abandoning the area in great haste during and immediately after the war, or being forced to leave. Poland has grappled with property restitution laws, passing a 1997 law on the restitution of Jewish communal property which did not apply to property owned by individuals. Then, in 2021, the government passed a controversial law with set a thirty-year limit on appealing decisions on property, which meant no compensation for people who owned property seized by communists after the war. The Jews felt they'd been dudded or, since President Andrzej Duda was the man who signed it into law, you might say they'd been Duda'd.

Poland's relations with its eastern neighbour Ukraine have also been uneasy of late. After Russia's 2022 invasion, Poland supplied military and humanitarian aid to Ukraine and took in around a million Ukrainian refugees, who were welcomed by the majority of Poles. Schulz says there are as many as 200,000 Ukrainians in Krakow, which correlates pretty closely to official estimates. At least two-thirds of those were displaced by the current war, and Schulz and his friends have done their best to help.

'We had some Ukrainians staying in our apartment while we were in Australia. Other people I know had Ukrainians living with them.'

'Paying rent?'

'No. They were just hosting them. The Ukrainians were traumatised but I think the Poles have been kind of traumatised too. A lot of people felt like Ukraine was just the start and who knows what would happen next with regard to Russia?'

But Schulz says that anti-Ukrainian sentiment is on the rise. Ukrainian attitudes toward Poles have also cooled, and quickly, due mainly to border blockades by Polish truck drivers and farmers protesting cheap Ukrainian imports. An April 2024 poll by Kyiv-based think tank the Razumkov Centre showed that the proportion of Ukrainians with a positive attitude towards Poland plummeted from 92 per cent in early 2023 to just 26 per cent in April 2024. Alliances shift quickly in this part of the world, and perhaps always have.

As for Poland itself, in recent years it has lurched politically between progressive and conservative – a sign of good democratic health, even if some argue that Poland flirted with so-called 'illiberal democracy' under the populist right-wing Law and Justice Party, which was ousted in the October 2023 Polish parliamentary election after eight years in power.

Andrzej Duda has served as Poland's president since 2015, which means he is the official head of state. In December 2023, Duda swore in a new coalition government comprised of a mix of left-wing, centrist and centre-right parties led by Prime Minister Donald Tusk. He can't have enjoyed that, but Duda's hardline policies have well and truly left their mark on Poland's political and social landscape. Ahead of the 2020 presidential election in which he narrowly triumphed despite winning just four of Poland's thirty largest cities, Duda said LGBT rights were 'an ideology more destructive than communism'. In 2017 he enacted laws undermining the impartiality of the judicial system, and brazenly turned state media into a bastion of what Schulz calls 'rabid, pro-government, crazy propaganda that you would only turn on if you wanted to get angry or have a laugh'.

'I don't think Duda's illiberal democracy would be Kosciuszko's version of democracy,' Schulz says.

Yet much of Duda's reactionary handiwork was rapidly unwound after the 2023 election. The management of Polish public television, radio and news agency PAP was dismissed, swiftly unshering in a return of state media impartiality. The new government's swift manoeuvres to restore the independence of the judiciary resulted in over a hundred billion Euros of EU money being unfrozen. Teachers have received a significant pay rise, while mothers who return to work after childbirth receive a monthly benefit.

'Poland is an example of how illiberal democracy can be reversed,' Schulz says, and that is surely something that would have warmed old Kosciuszko's heart.

Kosciuszko's eternal resting place is a crypt deep down inside Wawel Cathedral. The cathedral is part of Wawel Castle, a twenty-minute stroll from our part of Kazimierz, and if Krakow's Main Square is on every list of Europe's finest squares, then Wawel Castle must surely appear on similar lists for fortifications. It sits on a low hill beside a ninety-degree bend of the Vistula River – or maybe it actually *is* the hill – and its architecture consists of Baroque, Gothic, Renaissance, Romanesque, Neoclassical and Neogothic elements, which sounds a bit like a zapiekanka with too many ingredients but the overall effect is both elegant and spectacular.

Visitors entering from its northern entrance are greeted by a dramatic bronze of Kosciuszko on horseback, waving his hat to admirers unseen while his horse paws the ground in its eagerness to gallop onward. The first version cast in 1900 was destroyed by the Nazis, then the monument was replicated in 1960 as a gift from the German city of Dresden.

Kosciuszko was indeed quite the horseman. He led two cavalry units in the final days of the Revolutionary War, while later in life, at the request of his old Revolutionary War comrade General William Richardson Davie, Kosciuszko wrote a manual called *Manoeuvres of Horse Artillery*, which became a textbook used by some of the first West Point cadets.

Inside, Wawel Cathedral is unbelievably crowded. It feels like every school teacher in Poland scheduled a visit on the same sunny spring day, so it takes a while to descend to the crypt to pay our respects to old Koz. Our stop is brief due to the babbling flow of humanity but on top of his white marble tomb, we lay a sprig of alpine mint from the national park in Australia that bears his name. Weeks after being picked from a landscaped bed in the alpine village of Thredbo – an important technicality as it means we didn't violate the rule of not taking naturally growing plants from a national park – the sprig of mint still carries its distinctive menthol aroma. Realising that a cleaner or custodian might remove the sprig in the evening when the throng has dissipated, a quick finger flick pushes it behind the tomb, where with luck it will remain in perpetuity, a small piece of a landscape named after Kosciuszko to honour the great man. It's a surprisingly emotional moment. Doubtless the African American community leader and author Booker T Washington experienced a similar feeling when he visited in 1910 and placed a rose on Kosciuszko's tomb 'in the name of my race'. Washington, who was born into slavery in 1856, had learned about Kosciuszko's role in America's Revolutionary War at school, which is an interesting insight into the degree to which he has fallen from the picture of American history. But as Washington wrote in his 1911 book *My Larger Education*, 'I did not know, however, until my attention was called to it in Krakow, what Kosciuszko had done for the freedom and education of my own people.'

The walk from Wawel Castle to the Main Square via Planty Park is delightful. There are frequent trams but who needs a ride on a morning like this? From a stall in the square, we buy a pair of deliciously chewy poppyseed bagels – the famous boiled, then baked, bread rings invented by Polish Jews. Then it's time for our next rendezvous. We're meeting Mieczyslaw Bielawski – Mietek for short – creative director of a company called ART FM which designs and builds multimedia exhibitions. Mietek is a friend of our Aussie mate Mat Schulz and has kindly agreed to give us the insider tour of one of his finest works – the Rynek Underground, a reconstruction of life in Krakow toward the end of the Middle Ages, complete with holograms and other multimedia tools depicting scenes of daily life and commerce.

Some cities like Pompeii disappear underground because they are instantaneously covered in a pall of volcanic ash. Other cities sink beneath the surface a lot more slowly. The exhibits under Krakow's Main Square are reconstructed scenes that originally existed at ground level but, over centuries, the city grew on top of its old self due to a combination of dust, silt from Vistula River floods, buildings built upon the ruins of others (because it was too expensive and cumbersome to remove old building materials) and even compacted sand which was routinely brought up to cover human waste and other refuse. Then, in the 1950s, workers digging a tunnel for a new sanitation pipe discovered the ruins and work was halted. The tunnel they dug created the space for today's museum.

As we sip good strong coffee in a ridiculously cool restaurant/bar/cafe called Aries on the south-west corner of the square, we chat about Kosciuszko the man and Kosciuszko the Australian mountain. Mietek says he's been to Australia, seen the poverty of Aboriginal communities in the outback and is fascinated to learn that a choir of Ngarigo people – traditional owners of the country around Mt Kosciuszko – awaits us this evening at the Kosciuszko Mound, one stop in a trip organised by a Polish Australian couple to educate them on the man and Polish culture in general. Mietek instinctively grasps the dilemma of a great humanist and liberator like Kosciuszko having his name on a mountain that belonged to other people for tens of thousands of years. Does the name 'Mt Kosciuszko' pave over history, just as Krakow's modern-day Main Square sits atop former medieval market stalls, workshops and dwellings? Do Australians, too, need to dig deeper to understand their past?

The tram to the Kosciuszko Mound leaves you a kilometre or two short, after which you steadily ascend the Blessed Bronislawa hill along a tree-lined road. The mound sits atop the hill, sharply rising thirty-four metres behind a red-brick fort built by the Austrians in the 1850s, in which the Kosciuszko Museum is located. Completed in 1823 after three years of work, the mound was fashioned from local soil. Buried within the earth are urns of soil from Kosciuszko's American and Polish battlefields. A snaking path winds to the top around perilously steep grassy flanks. The summit has Polish and Ukrainian flags flying in unison and a large grey stone that says KOSCIUSZCE – meaning 'To Kosciuszko'. A pleasant spring day among the birch and oak has become a chilly, windswept afternoon up here, with snow clearly visible on the summits of the Tatra Mountains to the south. Spring, like freedom, is a fickle creature in Poland.

The Kosciuszko Museum does a fine job of telling the great man's story for newcomers through its permanent exhibition, 'Kosciuszko – a Hero Still Needed'. Its most striking exhibit is a collection of scythes respresenting those used by many peasants who joined the Kosciuszko Uprising. The elongated agricultural implements are suspended in mid-air by almost-invisible cords and illuminated by red light, as though to create the impression of bloodied scythes being thrust in all directions in the fury of battle. Earlier today, Mietek talked about designing installations that use imagination and emotion to convey substantive content. This particular museum is not his work but his principles apply. The swarm of flying scythes is an incredibly effective piece of visual storytelling, history brought to life through creativity. You could even call it art.

There's a graphic novel of Kosciuszko's life on sale in the museum bookstore which does a similar job. More than two centuries after Kosciuszko died, some of Poland's most fertile minds are doing whatever it takes to bring his story to life.

Song is another artform that can tell history, and not always in ways you expect. When the Djinama Yilaga choir takes the stage in the performance space which is part of the Kosciuszko Museum complex, it's a surprise to be told by choir leader Cheryl Davison that they had to learn the Dhurga language in which their songs are sung. That's because the parents and grandparents of the older choir members were forbidden from speaking or passing down their language, and the Dhurga language – like many other Australian Aboriginal languages – became all but extinct. Dhurga is the language of the Yuin people of the south coast of New South Wales, an area where most of the Ngarigo people of the Kosciuszko area now live, having been forced out of the mountains. The choir's singers have a mix of Yuin, Ngarigo and other blood.

Their music is haunting and powerful. It's a hell of a thing to sit in a room above a city first settled in the fourth century listening to songs with lyrics dating back tens of thousands of years. The words are unintelligible to the Poles in the audience but Australian ears can occasionally detect a familiar place name or two, especially in one song which seems to be talking about a journey along the south coast of New South Wales through towns including Ulladulla, Moruya and Narooma – all Aboriginal names.

Andrzej and Ernestyna Kozek, the Sydney-based Polish Australian couple who organised the Djinama Yilaga choir tour, see parallels between the plight of Australia's Aboriginal people and the predicament of the Poles at the hands of Russia and other powers down the years: two peoples half a world apart, both robbed of their sovereignty, their agency, their dignity. To the Kozeks, the shared experience of historical subjugation is a reason to keep Kosciuszko's name alive on Australia's highest peak. *We get what happened to you,* they're saying. *It happened to us too.* But does that make a hero of this world the right name for a sacred mountain in their world? The members of the choir and the other Aboriginal people here as part of the delegation to Poland seem to be mulling this over on this trip.

What's clear on this evening at the Kosciuszko Mound is that the visiting Australian Aboriginal people are sold on Kosciuszko the man. They're also genuinely grateful to the Kozeks for taking an interest in their culture, even if a cynic might frame it as an elaborate and expensive public relations exercise designed to garner support for retaining the Kosciuszko name on Australia's highest mountain.

'They've just shown us so much respect,' choir member Michelle Davison says, and she's right. In attendance this evening is Lloyd Brodrick, the Australian ambassador to Poland, Lithuania and the Czech Republic. That's just one of many ways on this visit to Poland that this highly marginalised group of Australians has been told that they're important, that their lives matter – a message they don't always get back home.

After an early evening concert on a windswept Polish hilltop, anyone with a couple of spare seats in their car is a good person to know, so despite extravagant eyerolls from Stella, we hitch an ambassadorial ride down into the city. 'It opens doors,' Ambassador Brodrick says of the general awareness among Poles that Australia's highest peak is Mt Kosciuszko. 'It's a point of common contact and interest.' As to whether the name should be changed, Australia's chief diplomat in these parts is suitably diplomatic, saying it's a matter for the Aboriginal people here and others back home.

Two museums is more than enough in any day of travel but as we walk down the busy street Stradomska toward Kazimierz after a deliciously hearty meal of traditional kharcho beef soup at a little Georgian place, a museum that's still open catches our eye and we simply have to pop in. If, like me, you misspent your youth and plenty of your adulthood chasing high scores on the Indiana Jones pinball machine and similar games, then the Krakow Pinball Museum will be silver ball heaven. The museum's impressive collection includes dozens of machines spanning multiple decades, spread across the cellar of a fifteenth-century building. It's a bit like Rynek Underground, only you can control the action with flipper buttons. The difference, of course, is that pinball machines are not objects of Polish history. Indeed, most of these games would have been unavailable in communist Poland. We typically think of nostalgia as a feeling for a long-gone time or place or person that was once part of our own life. But sometimes, we can have nostalgia for things we never had. 'It's a twinge in your heart far more powerful than memory alone,' fictional ad man Don Draper said of nostalgia in the famous Kodak scene in the TV series *Mad Men*.

You wouldn't say there's a nostalgic Kosciuszko revival taking place across Poland, and maybe that's a good thing, because nostalgia can be weaponised, commodified, twisted into something insidious and evil that distorts history rather than giving it new life. America's Lost Cause mythology is the perfect example of that. Maybe it's a good thing that Kosciuszko is respected and remembered but not quite deified. Certainly he is rarely invoked by nativist Polish politicians as the standard-bearer of all values true and good and Polish, and his essence could potentially be violated if that happened, his words and deeds bastardised beyond recognition. Maybe a twinge in the heart is just about the right level of feeling to hold for an old freedom fighter whose most endearing, and perhaps enduring, characteristic was his gentle soul.

CHAPTER 21

THE DIFFERENCE BETWEEN MUD AND DIRT

Swiss trains are a miracle. You might think the greatest thing about Switzerland is skiing or Toblerone or lakes the colour of Listerine or Roger Federer's single-handed backhand, but it's actually the trains. The national train network map looks just like a city subway or metro system, only it's the map for the entire country. Got eleven hours between connecting flights on the way home from Krakow to Sydney via Zurich and Singapore and need to get 100 kilometres from Zurich Airport to the provincial town of Solothurn in the Jura Mountains, where Kosciuszko died? Just take the escalator down to the platform under the airport terminal and board one train, which takes exactly one hour and eight minutes. It's an absolute breeze in terms of both time and convenience, especially compared to the almost equidistant journey from West Point to Newark International Airport, which was a five-hour marathon involving a twenty-minute lift over the river to Garrison

Station from a very kind retired lieutenant colonel, a slow train along the Hudson and through the Bronx, a subway ride, an eight-block walk through midtown Manhattan, a train out to the airport, then two rides in the impossibly congested Newark Airport AirTrain, a monorail looping the terminals which was not in the least bit airy. 'The rides at Disneyland ain't what they used to be,' some wisecracking Australian remarked as he feared missing his flight to Poland. No-one laughed.

Solothurn is a large regional town in a German-speaking part of Switzerland, sometimes called by its French name, Soleure. It sits at the foot of the Jura Mountains, which are nowhere near as high or jagged as the Alps but still quite impressive, sharply rising a good vertical kilometre above the valley. From the station, you cross the Aare River and walk up into the centre of town, parts of which are vehicle-free. Here, on a part-paved, part-cobbled street called Gurzelngasse, is the Kosciuszko Museum, located in the rooms in which Kosciuszko lived his final two years in an apartment within the home of the Zeltner family. Across the road from the museum is a convenience store with a sign that says *k kiosk*, which looks like yet another mangled spelling of the old fella's name.

Kosciuszko arrived here in October 1815. You wouldn't say he was a broken man as he was not one to mire himself in despondency. But the pragmatist in him was resigned to the fact that he was now powerless to help his homeland, having lobbied for Poland's cause all the way up until the continent-shaping diplomatic meetings of the Congress of Vienna in 1815.

Here's a quick recap of how Kosciuszko's final decades played out. After being captured in the uprising in October 1794, being shipped off to prison in Russia then freed by Tsar Paul I in 1796, he returned to America in 1797, wrote his will with Jefferson and then left America for the final time in 1798. It seems likely that Kosciuszko never seriously considered settling in America as long as there was the faintest hope of restoring Polish sovereignty, but when and under what circumstances he would depart were matters for fate and the four winds.

Kosciuszko's moment arrived in March 1798, when he received a letter inviting him to a meeting with the French Directory – the five-member committee that served as the government of Revolutionary France from 1795 to 1799. The letter was part of a mail package which also included news on General Dabrowski, a key figure in the Kosciuszko Uprising who had founded Polish legions in Italy and had been co-opted into fighting with Napoleon, whose star was rising as he waged war on Austria and its Italian allies. Dabrowski believed that if France could win this war, it would fight for the freedom of Poland. That was enough of a sniff of hope for old Koz.

For various reasons, Kosciuszko needed to keep his departure a secret, so Jefferson arranged a fake passport for him under the name Thomas Kannberg and asked a favour in return. Despite France having supported America in its Revolutionary War that had ended fifteen years earlier, relations between America and France had soured under President John Adams to the point where the two nations stood on the brink of war. Vice President Jefferson asked Kosciuszko to engage in some light diplomacy while he was in France. It was at this point that Kosciuszko gave his friend the sable coat depicted in the Jefferson Memorial.

On 4 May 1798, having concealed his plans from all but Jefferson, Kosciuszko told his compatriot and friend Julian Niemcewicz – who, on Kosciuszko's insistence, had accompanied the national hero all the way from Russia – that he planned to leave for Europe that very evening. Niemcewicz had worked his way into Philadelphia society and in 1800 would marry an American woman before eventually returning to Europe. Niemcewicz felt blindsided and betrayed but Kosciuszko had to go.

Kosciuszko disembarked in Bayonne, France, on 28 June 1798. You'll recall that he had been covertly exercising in his room in Philadelphia, and Storozysnki wrote that he walked down the gangplank in France with a limp but without his crutches. Despite travelling under an alias, the French knew who he was and the Directory sent for him. Their talks achieved little, although Kosciuszko did manage to play a part in easing tensions between France and America during his first year back on European soil. His dealings with Napoleon were considerably less constructive.

Kosciuszko had rented an apartment on the Left Bank of the Seine in Paris, and Napoleon had just blown back into town from his Egyptian campaign. On his way to see the Directory, he dropped by Koz's place, as you do, and the two met for the first time. While on the surface the encounter was cordial enough, Kosciuszko's insincere-o-meter was beeping off the scale. He correctly guessed that Napoleon had no real interest in Poland's emancipation, nor any intention to use the Polish legions for purposes other than fighting his own wars.

Shortly after the meeting, Kosciuszko warned the Directory to watch their backs. That was on 16 October 1799. On 9 November, Napoleon staged his coup, effectively becoming the leader of France. Kosciuszko called him 'the gravedigger of the republic'. A short time later, Kosciuszko was invited to a banquet at the Luxembourg Palace, where an official told him that Napoleon had been talking about him. 'I never speak of him!' Kosciuszko hissed in reply.

Every instinct Kosciuszko had about Napoleon's intentions was right. Napoleon sent the Polish legions all the way across the Atlantic to quell an uprising in Saint-Domingue – the French colony in what today is Haiti – where they were virtually wiped out. Meanwhile, Napoleon made it clear in dealings with Tsar Paul I that he had no interest in an independent Polish state.

The Polish historian Jaroslaw Czubaty wrote a piece in 2014 in *The Polish Review* entitled 'A Republican in a Changing World: The Political Position and Attitudes of Tadeusz Kosciuszko, 1798–1817' which contained a memorable line about Kosciuszko's behaviour toward Napoleon during this period: 'He chose to exert moral authority rather than pursue the role of an active politician.'

By any reasonable measure, this has to be read as a compliment. When has the world needed another politician? Not in Kosciuszko's day, and not now. Kosciuszko was coming to understand that even the deftest political manoeuvring would likely not restore Polish independence, so why play the game? Kosciuszko was willing throughout his life to get his hands bloody and muddy on the battlefield but the older he got, the less taste he had for the grubby nature of politics.

This attitude was also evident in his rejection of the funds Tsar Paul I had put in a London bank for him back in 1796. On his return to Europe in 1798, Kosciuszko attempted to return the money, telling the Tsar in a letter that he had only accepted it so that Polish prisoners in Russia could be freed. The Tsar returned serve, writing that he would accept nothing from a traitor, as the duo's LinkedIn-style insincerity of 1796 morphed into the open hostility of a Facebook spat.

More than a decade later, Kosciuszko displayed similar bluntness with Tsar Alexander I, the successor to Tsar Paul I, who was assassinated in 1801 by officers from his own army. Napoleon's army had been defeated in Leipzig in 1813, leading to the French emperor's abdication and leaving the door ever-so-slightly ajar for the restoration of Poland's borders. Kosciuszko attended the Congress of Vienna, where Europe's powers met to iron out the new European power balance. The partitions of Poland were officially sanctioned at the Congress and old Koz gave Tsar Alexander a piece of his mind, calling the situation a 'joke'. He then declared that he would take refuge in Switzerland as he could no longer be of service to his country.

Sometimes, a man just runs out of patience.

Meanwhile, in the period between 1801 and 1815, Kosciuszko took up residence in Berville, a small village near the larger town of Fontainebleau about fifty kilometres south of Paris. There he lived with the family of Peter Zeltner, a Swiss diplomat he had met and befriended in Paris. He helped with tutoring the Zeltner children and became close to his wife, Angelique (some say too close). He was visited by many women during this time, and while he loved their company, he never could abide obsequiousness. The memoirs of Polish general Stanislaw Fiszer, who visited Kosciuszko during this time, contain a passage detailing a visit from French writer Germaine de Staël, who a little too fawningly asked Kosciuszko to tell stories of the uprising. 'I was a soldier and I fought,' he harrumphed.

After the Congress of Vienna, Peter Zeltner's brother, Francis Xavier Zeltner, invited Kosciuszko to stay in Solothurn. With France in post-Napoleon turmoil, Switzerland was becoming a better option for Kosciuszko and he gratefully accepted the offer.

Kosciuszko was by now an elderly man. The museum has a portrait of him by the Polish artist Walery Radzikowski with his grey hair thinning, his face wrinkled. There's also a painting of Kosciuszko on his deathbed by the Swiss artist Heinrich Rieter. There are also portraits of the younger man as well as artefacts galore, including Kosciuszko's favourite pistol and the saddle on which he rode around town each day on his black pony Dobry, handing out food and money to the poor. The focal point of the museum is the bedchamber in which he breathed his last breath, an alcove in the main room. The bedspread is burgundy, with a bold white eagle symbolising Polish sovereignty. It feels surreal standing here in the pinprick of the universe where Kosciuszko's star faded. What do you do in such a place? What should you feel? And why are so few people here pondering the same questions?

The Kosciuszko Museum in Solothurn has existed since 1936 and today is run as a labour of love by local Polish expat Teresa Ackermann. It sees just 800 visitors per year, plus a few school groups, and Ackermann has opened it specially today for her Australian visitor plus a group of London-based Poles. In a three-way, four-language conversation over strong black tea and the famous Polish caramel fudge called Krowki (little cows), we stutter our way through a conversation containing a mixture of English, Polish, German, and French about the legacy of Kosciuszko, the source of my interest in the man, the mountain in Australia, and the fact that Australia's Aboriginal people have formally tried in the past to change the mountain's name and likely will again. It's time to go and meet those people, the traditional owners of the land around Mt Kosciuszko – and not in Poland where they were in guest mode, but in their own country.

Section Three

Australia: The learning walk

CHAPTER 22

PEAKY BLINDNESS

On the summit of Mt Kosciuszko, at the very highest point of Australia, there is a lie. In fact, there are several lies. Most of them are benign and open to historical interpretation. But one is as large as the mountain itself and flows downward like the rivers, spreading across the ranges, valleys, tablelands, plains, forests, deserts, bays and beaches of the world's only island continent.

Around 100,000 people climb Mt Kosciuszko each year. Most do it in summer, when it's snow-free except for a few large drifts that persist into the New Year on the mountain's eastern flank, remnants of wild winter blizzards that pummel the mountain from the west, blowing huge quantities of snow to the lee side of the mountain, where it piles up deep enough to bury a stack of buses and takes many months to melt. Walkers usually tackle the mountain from the ski resorts of Thredbo or Charlotte Pass. Thredbo is a little closer, especially if you start at the top of the Kosciuszko Chairlift. The chairlift runs all year, serving skiers and snowboarders in winter and hikers and mountain bikers in summer. It does all the hard work, taking barely ten minutes to ascend two linear kilometres and more than 500 vertical metres from the bottom of the steep, V-shaped valley of the Thredbo River. At the top station, hikers are deposited on a high plateau above the tree line, just six kilometres from the apex of Australia.

The thirteen-kilometre return hike over undulating terrain is far from challenging and achievable by kids not much older than pre-schoolers. Within half an hour, Kosciuszko appears, an unimposing rounded hump atop the range. At 2228 metres, Mt Kosciuszko is higher than any mountain in America's Appalachian chain and indeed any point east of the Mississippi River. But in raw statistical terms, that's about the biggest rap you can give it. Kosciuszko is dwarfed by the world's great peaks. The knoll at the crest of a continent stands only half as high as the loftiest summits of America's Rockies or Europe's Alps, a third the height of Aconcagua, the highest peak of the Andes, and only a quarter the altitude of Mt Everest's 8848 metres. Indeed, every other continent's high point is at least twice the height of Kosciuszko. But Australia's highest mountain has something none of them will ever have. While the upper reaches of the world's great mountain ranges are forbidding, craggy, icy and barren, Kosciuszko is alive.

Mt Kosciuszko caps the uninspiringly named Main Range in the unimaginatively titled Snowy Mountains in a wider region officially known as the Australian Alps, colloquially called the High Country, in the south-east corner of the blandly named state of New South Wales. Don't let the drab nomenclature fool you. In both winter and summer, the Australian High Country is a place of incredible complexity and beauty, unlike anywhere else on the world's hottest, flattest, driest continent and indeed unique in the world. In places, the High Country is bold and dramatic. A sharp peak here, a sheer mountain flank there. But like Australia's most celebrated ecological marvel, the Great Barrier Reef, the true majesty of this landscape is on the micro-scale.

The path from the top of Thredbo starts as paved stone but soon becomes a steel mesh walkway rusted a deep russet brown raised about shin height off the ground. The walkway is designed to let light through and to protect the fragile alpine vegetation from trampling. The rust is actually deliberate or, at least, unavoidable. In the mid-twentieth century, ecologists undertook an extensive conservation program on the highest peaks of the range to repair soil stability and vegetation cover after the area had been devastated by sheep and cattle grazing. The ecologists installed galvanised wire mesh to hold entire slopes together but the wire's rust-proofing zinc leached into the soil, proving toxic to native plants and animals. Countless mistakes have been made in this country since colonisation, sometimes even in the name of caring for it.

The mesh walkway is wide enough to carry two or three hikers abreast and does its job well, as the vegetation beneath could be easily damaged, especially the sphagnum moss. Sphagnum is the miracle of the mountains, a lemon- and lime-coloured bog species that grows in giant cushions and holds water like a sponge, filtering it and releasing it drip by drip, drop by drop, so that alpine creeks run clear and true in even the driest summer. Candle heath, also known as dragon bush, flourishes among the sphagnum bogs, its protruding rods of creamy flowers protected by a web of coarse, pineappley foliage. Like the abatis, or outward-facing sharpened logs, that Kosciuszko employed to defend his redoubts on the Delaware River in Philadelphia, those ankle-slashing leaves are the perfect defence against intruders. The walkway stops people finding out the hard way.

At every step, there is the sound of trickling water, tiny creeks that are the headwaters of the legendary Snowy River.

The music here is strings and triangles but soon turns to brass and drums just a few kilometres downstream. In the babbling shallows beneath the walkway, finger-length Kosciuszko galaxias flit and dart in search of larvae or a bug fallen from an overhanging bush. The galaxias are the only Australian fish that subsists below a blanket of snow in winter.

Clouds up here are the landscape's ever-changing wardrobe, not a lid to the sky. They sweep up and over Kosciuszko's long south-west ridge, vanishing as quickly as they arrive. Nestled below the ridge, Lake Cootapatamba soon comes into view. This is Australia's highest lake, a boulder-encircled alpine tarn whose greeny-blue waters deliver instant brain freeze to anyone mad enough to swim, even in midsummer. Cootapatamba is one of five small glacial lakes in the shadow of Kosciuszko, each a tiny teardrop lamenting the passing of the Ice Age some 10,000 or more years ago, when glaciers carved cirques, or high shallow valleys shaped like the hollow left behind by an ice cream scoop, that filled with water when a warmer climate returned. All five lakes freeze firm over the whole winter, the only sizeable natural water bodies on mainland Australia to do so. The largest is Blue Lake, a sixteen-hectare basin of cobalt blue which is four times the size of the Melbourne Cricket Ground – the sports stadium which serves as the ubiquitous base measurement of surface area in modern Australian life.

Shortly after Cootapatamba, you reach Rawson Pass, in the saddle between Mt Kosciuszko and Australia's fifth-highest peak, Mt Etheridge. Here, where the Thredbo trail meets the Charlotte Pass trail, you'll find Australia's highest toilet block, and if you think a public amenity facility on a high mountain pass can't be a masterpiece of modern architecture, you've never seen the way the Rawson Pass toilet block melds into the mountainside, its only giveway a queue of hikers and the smell if you stray too close.

The steel mesh walkway returns to paved stone and continues upward, encircling the mountain like the lead strand of a ball of string. Most summers, the snow drifts have receded above the path but after particularly snowy winters, they still cover it, making the going precarious for anyone who didn't bring hiking poles to this treeless, stickless alpine landscape. If you're lucky enough to score a clear day, the landscape multiplies a millionfold as you wind toward the summit. To the east are the high, dry, yellowy-brown plains of the Monaro. To the west, endless blue forested ranges stretch to the horizon. To the south, you can see the terrain you've covered and far beyond the Thredbo Valley to the hazy wilderness of the lower Snowy River. To the north, Australia's second-highest peak, Mt Townsend, and the other peaks of the Main Range loom large in the foreground, while the crouching lion of Mt Jagungal – the region's most significant peak with an Aboriginal name – rises in the middle distance. You can even make out the Brindabella Range far to the north, just outside the national capital, Canberra. In the National Gallery of Australia in Canberra hangs an 1863 painting titled *North-east view from the northern top of Mount Kosciusko* by Austrian-born colonial artist Eugene von Guerard. Painted in a dreamy Romantic style, it tells its own little lie: the view is clearly from Mt Townsend.

The scene on the summit of Kosciuszko is like a picnic in the park this fine summer day, with people queueing to take an Instagrammable photo on or beside the summit plinth before settling in for lunch among the snowgrass tussocks and small granite boulders. Some wander down the mountain's steep eastern flank to play in the snow, greeted by vast flocks of little ravens cawing in glee as they feast upon insects immobilised by cold after they landed on the drifts. It's interesting being here, on the best-known site celebrating Kosciuszko outside of Poland, and perhaps the best-known in the world, having stood atop this mountain a dozen or more times in all seasons and in every type of weather, yet never having seriously pondered who Kosciuszko was, what he stood for, or why the mountain was named after him. A small plaque on a shard of granite a few metres from the plinth explains the history of the mountain's name, with a quote from Pawel Strzelecki:

> The particular configuration of this eminence struck me so forcibly by the similarity it bears to a tumulus elevated in Krakow over the tomb of the patriot Kosciuszko, that, although in a foreign country, on foreign ground, but amongst a free people, who appreciate freedom and its votaries, I could not refrain from giving it the name of Mount Kosciuszko.

It sounds like a reasonable story. Polish explorer climbs foreign mountain. Experiences surprise and delight when its shape and texture irresistibly bring to mind the grass-flanked mound built to honour Kosciuszko in Krakow. He stands triumphant in the twilight, in an age when European explorers routinely name New World geographical features after important Europeans. How could he refrain from immortalising the name of Kosciuszko, when this peak so strongly resembled the earthen mound built to honour Poland's hero?

Alas, the story is probably not true. There's an argument that the mountain could have looked like a plate of pickled herring and Strzelecki would still have named it Kosciuszko. It all depends how you interpret the diary of James Macarthur, who accompanied Strzelecki as far as Mt Townsend, which they both believed was the highest peak before they spotted the slightly higher Kosciuszko just a few kilometres to the north, which had been obscured for most of the ascent:

> Before leaving the Count told me of his intention of recording his visit to the highest point of Australia by associating the name of Kosciuszko with our successful ascent. I could not but respect and feel deep sympathy with my friend when with his hat off he named the Patriot of his Country.

That's part of an entry from Macarthur's diary dated 12 March 1840, and it captures the moment when the two men parted at the summit of Townsend, Macarthur retreating to camp as Strzelecki declared his intention to attain what they now realised was the highest point. But what exactly did Macarthur's diary entry mean? That Strzelecki decided on the spur of the moment to name Australia's highest point Mt Kosciuszko, or that he'd long had the idea in mind and only just thought to tell Macarthur? Was the baby's name chosen long before it popped out? Was the resemblance to the Kosciuszko Mound in Krakow just a happy coincidence? That was absolutely the opinion of Helen Heney, an Australian writer who spent years working as a translator in Poland. 'He had the name in mind for some time and planned to give it to the highest point when he reached it,' Heney argued in her 1961 book *In a Dark Glass: The Story of Paul Edmond Strzelecki*.

There are other ambiguous or misleading facts on the summit plaque. For example, the date of the ascent is stated as 15 February 1840, when Macarthur recorded it as 12 March. The plaque also mentions the similarity the mountain bears to a tumulus elevated in Krakow over the tomb of the patriot Kosciuszko, when of course Kosciuszko's tomb is a few kilometres away in the depths of Wawel Cathedral. There's even a sliver of doubt as to whether Strzelecki climbed the mountain at all. Certainly there's no proof beyond his word, since Macarthur did not accompany him. Strzelecki's footsteps have been forensically dissected over the years, and we'll follow them a bit later. But in the big scheme, these are trifling matters.

The big lie on the summit of Mt Kosciuszko is not anything Strzelecki said, did or claimed to have done. The big lie is the name 'Mt Kosciuszko' itself, because for tens of thousands of years before Strzelecki came along, the mountain had other names.

CHAPTER 23

'YOU PROSPER ON OUR NATIVE SOIL AND WE ARE FAMISHING!'

> Byamee, the creator of the land, created the highest point, Kunama Namadgi. From there, he sent all the rivers across country and when he sent the rivers, he sent the law and the stories with them. The rivers divided the country and isolated people who became custodians of the different nations.

That's Aunty Rhonda Casey telling her nation's creation story. Aunty Rhonda is an Elder of the Monero-Ngarigo Mob. There are more than 500 Indigenous Nations in Australia, each with their own creation stories and languages, which have been passed down for up to 65,000 years. The University of Melbourne's Indigenous Knowledge Institute explains that, 'These stories often blend science and historical events, such as how things came to be, with cultural norms and important lessons for living.' Aunty Rhonda's creation story of Byamee does exactly that. She continues:

> Every year Byamee comes back to the mountain. We know he's coming because the mist tells us. The mist announces his arrival and his departure, and he is there while the snow falls. So in law, you shouldn't go to the mountain when the snow is falling there. It's when the ancestors are coming back, a sacred time and if you go to the mountain at that time, you'll be punished. He'll take your fingers and toes. You have to wait for the wildflowers before you go to the mountains.

Kunama Namadgi, Aunty Rhonda's name for Mt Kosciuszko, roughly translates as 'Snow Mountain'. But that is far from its only name. The Ngarigo Nation is broken into several clans, or family groups, each of whom traditionally occupied different parts of the mountains or nearby foothills, valleys and high plains. Aunty Rhonda's clan hails from the Monaro plains east of the mountains.

In 2000, George Martin, then the mayor of the town of Tumbarumba on the western slopes of the mountains, stood atop Mt Kosciuszko with the then Australian Deputy Prime Minister Tim Fischer – who was on his annual 'Tumbatrek' bushwalk through the mountains – and announced to media that the name should be changed to 'something more Australian'. That was the first publicly aired informal proposal to rename the mountain.

Monero-Ngarigo Elder Iris White doesn't see eye to eye with other groups on the subject. She says it's not her business to share her preferred name, although she does say that her interpretation of the word 'Kunama' in 'Kunama Namadgi' is 'faeces'.

A fascinating, passionate and potentially bitter battle looms over the renaming of the mountain, and not just among the

Ngarigo. Neighbouring Nations also have their own name for the mountain, which could make any move to change it all the more fraught. No formal proposal exists at present but the rumblings will undoubtedly surface again, and sooner rather than later.

The mountain actually had a formal name change in 1997. After Strzelecki named it Kosciuszko, it soon became bastardised as Mt 'Kosciusko' on maps and even on the official register of the Geographical Names Board of NSW. For around a century and a half, the mountain was spelled like the town of Kosciusko, Mississippi. That all changed in 1997 and there's a fair chance it happened with the help of people in higher places than any mountain on Earth.

Gough Whitlam, the most progressive prime minister in Australia's history, who was in office from 1972 until 1975, had long been annoyed by the missing z and was an early agitator for change. Sir Ninian Stephen, who served as Australia's Governor-General from 1982 to 1989, was also on the case, stating, 'If we are proud to be a multicultural nation, we should at least get our spelling right.' The missing z particularly annoyed a Polish-born Queenslander called Marian Szuszkiewicz-Landis, who in 1993 formed a group called Australians Calling for the Correct Spelling of Mount Kosciuszko.

The bandwagon grew. Soon it included future High Court Justice Michael Kirby and the renowned Australian author Thomas Keneally (whose novel *Schindler's Ark* would become the basis for the Spielberg film *Schindler's List*, and whose 1972 novel *The Chant of Jimmie Blacksmith* was one of the first major works to tackle the tension between Aboriginal people and European colonial settlers). Prominent Poles also got involved. The Polish ambassador to Australia and the Polish Consul-General in

Sydney joined the movement, the latter declaring the spelling change a key issue in Polish–Australian relations. Eventually 200 petitions were sent to the Geographical Names Board of New South Wales, including one from the then Polish President Aleksander Kwasniewski.

But it was none other than the Polish Pope, His Holiness Pope John Paul II, who got the campaign over the line, or so the story goes. The petitioners took their cause all the way to the Holy See and, according to journalist Martin Daly, who in 1997 wrote about the story behind the name change for Melbourne's *The Age* newspaper, the pontiff said that the petition had been 'carefully noted' and that 'His Holiness will remember you in his prayers'. Did it really go all the way to the top? Did a papal prayer or perhaps even a secret edict make the difference? Whatever the case, the z was duly added.

You have to wonder if it will take the nearest thing to divine intervention to get the name changed again.

First, the Nations will need to settle their linguistic and personal differences and come up with a new (old) name that pleases all. If that happens, the first step might be dual name status. So it might, for example, become Kunama Namadgi–Kosciuszko or Tar-Gan-Gil–Kosciuszko. (Tar-Gan-Gil is another Indigenous name sometimes put forward, although some claim that it's the original name for Mt Townsend.) The name Kosciuszko might then disappear over time, intentionally or otherwise.

This is what has happened with Uluru, the giant red sandstone monolith in the heart of Australia. Officially changed from Ayers Rock to Uluru/Ayers Rock in 1993, it's now ubiquitously known as Uluru, or colloquially as The Rock. Few Australians lament the passing of the interim name, which lasted just 120 years after surveyor William

Gosse named it after South Australian politician Sir Henry Ayers. Not to belittle Ayers but hardly anyone knows anything about him, and the man himself never even saw the monolith which bears his name – much as Britain's Surveyor General of India George Everest never saw the world's highest peak, and indeed left India long before it was confirmed as such. Tadeusz Kosciuszko never saw his mountain either, so you might imagine that his name would drop off the end of a dual-titled mountain as naturally as an alpine copperhead snake sheds its skin.

But there's a key difference between the names 'Mt Kosciuszko' and 'Ayers Rock', which is that Australians have a fondness for the name Kosciuszko. Were it to be altered or removed entirely, many would rage against the change. Rightly or wrongly, justly or unjustly, Kosciuszko has become a much-loved, magnificently quirky Australian place name. It's a word celebrated in Australian poetry and song. It's a word whose pronunciation has taken on a unique Aussie twang far removed from the correct Polish pronunciation, to the point where it almost sounds like an Aboriginal word. Woolloomooloo, Indooroopilly, Onkaparinga, Maribyrnong, Joondalup, Kosciuszko: the first five are suburbs with Aboriginal names, one in each of Australia's largest cities. The sixth is a mountain named after a long-dead Polish freedom fighter. To many Australians, they're all equally endearing, equally evocative, equally valid, equally Australian names.

The word 'Kosciuszko' has even come to mean more than the mountain itself. Kosciuszko National Park is the largest national park in Australia's most populous state of New South Wales. Longer than it is wide, the park stretches 150 kilometres from north to south, totalling almost 7000 square kilometres, which makes it larger than the American state of Delaware. The park contains Australia's largest contiguous area of snow-covered country in winter, and has become synonymous with snow. As America's Yellowstone and Yosemite National Parks are simply called Yosemite or Yellowstone, Kosciuszko National Park is simply 'Kosciuszko', or 'Kozzie' – and an abbreviated nickname has long been the surest sign of acceptance in Australian life.

But no matter how attached Australians have become to the name Kosciuszko, there's no escaping that humans lived here for tens of thousands of years before the mountain and the land around it was known as such. Many people discount that ancient history. One person in particular should have known a whole lot better.

Alan EJ Andrews was an accomplished back country skier, walker and the author of the 1991 book *Kosciuszko: The Mountain in History*. He died in 2014. In 2005, amid talk of a dual name in the draft version of the national park's 2006 Plan of Management, Andrews penned an article for the autumn bulletin of the Polish Community Council of Australia and New Zealand. It contained this comment:

> A name was given to our highest mountain on the occasion when that fact was realized. To change that name to some meaningless sound, albeit Aboriginal, would achieve nothing. Historic names – the names of our heritage – should not be changed.

Where to begin unpacking that? Do you start with the deeply objectionable line that Aboriginal words are 'meaningless sounds' – as if all foreign languages are not exactly that to those who don't speak them? And what about the call to protect 'our' heritage? Who is the implied 'us' here? White folk who've been in the mountains for the merest clock-tick of geological time? What about the Aboriginal heritage stretching back to the era of ice sheets and megafauna? It is baffling beyond words that the author of a book on the mountain could have such a flagrant disregard for anything that happened before Strzelecki. And that's putting it extremely politely.

Then there was this doozy:

> Our highest mountain is tied to two important figures of the eighteenth and nineteenth centuries and it is tied to Freedom. It is not tied to any Aboriginal connection.

Again, how could anyone, let alone a scholar of the mountain, possibly discount Australia's Aboriginal heritage by arguing that the mountain 'is not tied to any Aboriginal connection'? Australia's highest point had no plaque, plinth or proper noun that was universally agreed upon but that didn't make it unknown, unvisited, unnamed or anything less than sacred. The creation story related by Aunty Rhonda Casey proves the mountain's importance to her people. Indeed, she says it's the most significant site on Ngarigo country and one of the most important sites in Australia.

A blend of sheer ignorance, wilful indifference and even outright hostility to Aboriginal culture has long been a feature of Australian life. But there's a twist in this tale because Strzelecki himself was no racist. Indeed, the man who was twenty years old when Kosciuszko died, and forty-three when he named the mountain, was a humanist straight out of the Kosciuszko school who deeply respected Aboriginal culture and lamented its breakdown under colonialism.

Strzelecki is an interesting if somewhat contradictory character. He is listed in the Australian National University's *Australian Dictionary of Biography* as a 'capable and thorough scientist and excellent administrator', which makes him sound about as exciting as a suburban accountant, but he lived quite the colourful life. His body of work is impressive. His geology and exploration took him from South America to the Caribbean to the Pacific and beyond. Like Kosciuszko, he became a staunch opponent of the slave trade. Later in life, he was credited with helping save tens of thousands of lives through his work coordinating efforts to feed starving children in the Great Famine in Ireland. He was even knighted. Strzelecki was a scientist, a humanist, a philanthropist and several other worthy types of 'ist'.

Yet Strzelecki was also the classic unreliable narrator. In his will, he left instructions to burn all his 'papers, manuscripts, extracts, scraps, notes, memoranda, journals and letters'. Who does that? What did he not want the world to know? In his travels abroad, he often went by 'Count Strzelecki', an honorific to which he would have been entitled had his family in Poland applied for it, but which he technically never held. Strzelecki lost the diary of his trip to Mt Kosciuszko, which was understandable given the hardship and near-starvation endured by his party later in that trip, when they were forced to eat wombat and koala in the area he named Gippsland, after Sir George Gipps, then governor of New South Wales. All the same, when did you hear of a scientist losing their field book?

In 1845, working largely on memory due to his lost diary, Strzelecki finally completed his *Physical Description of New South Wales and Van Diemen's Land*, the account of his travels through south-eastern Australia and Tasmania. No less a giant of science than Charles Darwin praised it. 'I congratulate you on having completed a work which must have cost you so much labour and I am astonished at the number of deep subjects which you discuss,' the Father of Evolution wrote in a letter to Strzelecki, now held in the Yale University Library.

Strzelecki was living in England when he wrote the report, half a world and half a decade removed from his Australian journey. That, plus the absence of his diary, accounts for the muddled dates and some other sketchy details. Strzelecki could be scatty for a man of science. But say this for our absent-minded adventurer: he got the important stuff right.

On the nation-shaping, morality-defining subject of Australia's Aboriginal people, Strzelecki showed insight, thoughtfulness and kindness, where the majority of British colonists cultivated ignorance, dogma, cruelty and murderous violence. Where most British saw savagery, Strzelecki recognised an impressive civilisation. Set aside for a moment that he named Mt Kosciuszko after his esteemed compatriot without politely inquiring whether it already had a name; such was the presumptuous and paternalistic way of his age. But the inquisitive Pole travelled with open eyes and wrote with an open heart. His chapter entitled 'The Aborigines' in his *Physical Description of New South Wales and Van Diemen's Land* contains perceptive and sympathetic insights into Aboriginal culture, traditions and language. At one point, he even adopted a despairing first-person Aboriginal voice, a powerful stylistic device which flipped the narrative on just about every word ever written by early European colonists about Australia's first people.

'Our fields and forests, which once furnished us with abundance of vegetable and animal food, now yield us no more; they and their produce are yours,' Strzelecki wrote at the close of the chapter.

'You prosper on our native soil and we are famishing!'

CHAPTER 24

OF MOTHS AND MYTHS

Strzelecki had plenty in common with Kosciuszko besides his broad humanism and sympathy for the enslaved, the downtrodden and the dispossessed. Like his idol, he also fell in love with a young woman whom he met while tutoring and was considered unsuitable by the young lady's father. Like Kosciuszko, rather than dwell in lovestruck misery in his homeland, he set off to make his name abroad. And like Kosciuszko, Strzelecki never quite fell out of love as the years passed, even from afar. The object of Strzelecki's infatuation was Adyna Turno, whom he'd met aged twenty-three when she was just sixteen. Twenty years later, he picked her a flower from Mt Kosciuszko or whichever peak he actually climbed, and enclosed it in a letter:

> Here is a flower from Mt Kosciuszko – the highest peak of the continent – the first in the New World bearing a Polish name. I believe you will be the first and perhaps the only Polish woman to have a flower from that mountain. Let it remind you ever of freedom, patriotism and love.

The type of flower Strzelecki sent is unknown, but in some accounts it's called a daisy, so the smart money would be on the silver snow daisy, which has large white petals and tall, pale green stems tinged silver by thousands of tiny plant hairs called trichomes. On mild summer afternoons, the combination of white daisy petals and silver stems swaying in the breeze create the illusion of a thick unseasonable frost.

Then again, he might have chosen any of 200 flowers unique to the area. Few alpine regions in the world have a summer wildflower display as brilliant as the Australian High Country. Blessed with rich soil a metre deep extending to all but a few bouldery summits, this land nurtures carpets of colour that would shame your average rainbow.

Perhaps Strzelecki sent his beloved a billy button, a long-stemmed bright yellow orb composed of hundreds of tightly packed tiny flower heads. To venture off-track down Kosciuszko's southern flank and walk through crowds of billy buttons is to experience the delightful sensation of having your shins and knees thrummed by a thousand soft-topped xylophone sticks.

There's a chance Strzelecki went for something more delicate, like the anemone buttercup, a shy creamy flower which huddles below summer snow patches, sustained by their meltwater. This quite literally is a plant reliant on Australian summer snow to survive, which seems about as likely as a group of Greenland's Inuit people who live on fresh mangoes, but the Australian High Country is that kind of magical place.

Walking off-track on a different route back toward Thredbo, the trick is to carry a compass in case the clouds close in, and to stick where possible to the dry ridges so you dodge the sphagnum moss on boggy ground. But even the wind-battered ridges of the Main Range have botanical wonders that must be avoided. Feldmark is an incredibly rare type of plant community which exists only on the very highest parts of the range. The Australian High Country occupies only about a sixth of one per cent of the entire Australian landmass, and the feldmark vegetation – which is reminiscent of tundra plant communities – occupies a tiny portion of the highest parts. It is a pinprick within a speck within a dot and it's as delicate as a spider's web. There are two types of feldmark communities: snow patch feldmark, of which the aforementioned anemone buttercup is a member, and windswept feldmark, which comprises a variety of dwarf shrubs, cushion plants and herbs. Windswept feldmark is like a natural bonsai garden situated on ridges and slopes so scoured by the elements they hold almost no snow in even the snowiest winter.

Even sticking to the snowgrass has its perils. The grass is springy underfoot and pleasant to walk on but you must stay ever-cautious of the ankle-spraining hollows between tufts, which are hidden by overlapping strands of grass. Snowgrass is also surprisingly slippery. On steeper slopes, the carpet of slick green strands becomes so glassy and smooth you can slide downhill using your pants as a toboggan. Far below in the valleys, the snowgrass forms coarse brown tussocks, some of them large enough to perch upon as a stool, each strand of grass sharp enough to grate your skin like cheese.

A few kilometres south of Mt Kosciuszko in the general direction of Thredbo lies Australia's fourth-highest peak, Mt Rams Head, its summit a dishevelled pile of dark, rounded granite tors, each perched atop the next in apparent defiance of gravity. Countless nearby peaks look the same. There's South Rams Head, North Rams Head and numerous minor summits collectively known as the Rams Heads. This is a confusing part of the mountains. Even lifelong visitors to this part of the range can become disorientated in fine weather, let alone during a blizzard. The Rams Heads can be deadly in winter. But in summer, they are life.

This is bogong moth country. Bogongs might just be the most important creature in these mountains, and if you think that's a bold claim for a plain-looking brown moth that flaps madly into walls and windows like a blindfolded drunk, then you need to understand their place in the alpine ecosystem. Bogongs breed in hotter, drier areas of Australia before maturing and making an annual pilgrimage of up to 1000 kilometres to the mountains. They come from southern Queensland, northern and western New South Wales and western Victoria, flying at night, navigating by constellations and by an internal compass attuned to the Earth's magnetic field. Each moth makes the trek once only, meaning they have no guide. Yet for who knows how many years, they have completed their annual pilgrimage. North America's monarch butterflies are famous for a similarly epic journey which ends with them roosting en masse in tall trees in southern California and the mountains of central Mexico. Bogongs nestle not in tall timber but in the cool cracks and crevices of granite boulders on the rocky outcrops of the Rams Heads and other High Country summits. There they stay cool through summer, assembling themselves tightly on rock faces side by side, moth by moth, a natural tapestry of lepidoptera.

Bogongs are a crucial food source for birds and animals and, back in the day, they were just as important to humans. British explorers William Hovell and Hamilton Hume skirted the mountains on their 1824 expedition – which traversed much of the route now covered by the Hume Highway between Sydney and Melbourne – and had no idea about the moths.

Hovell wrote in his journal:

Whatever place we have been in, whether on the top of the highest mountain, or in any of the deepest ravines, we always find evident marks that the natives occasionally resort to them, although there does not appear to be any inducement for them to visit those secluded places.

The bogongs were of course one of the inducements.

Aboriginal people would trek to the mountains to gorge on the nutrient-rich flutterers, smoking them out with a fire set with green bushes, then singeing off their wings before cooking them in the coals and either eating them on the spot or grinding their bodies into a nutty-tasting paste which could be baked into transportable cakes. Nations from well beyond the Ngarigo lands would travel long distances each summer to join the feast. People from the Wolgalu, the Wiradjuri, the Ngunnawal and many other Nations were welcomed by the Ngarigo people as the summer gathering was an opportunity for trade, ceremony, marriages, social events and the settlement of differences between Nations and clans.

Some moth hunters would camp near Jindabyne east of the mountains, or at Wollondibby, about halfway between Jindabyne and Thredbo, before making their way up to the high peaks from Dead Horse Gap, about four kilometres up the valley from Thredbo.

The aim on this sweet summer day is to walk down to Dead Horse Gap, then back along the river to Thredbo to collect the car, then drive to a place called Geehi Flats at the western foot of the mountains. That's where Strzelecki commenced his ascent of the Main Range via a much longer, tougher and steeper route than the tracks from Thredbo or Charlotte Pass – and we'll have a crack at climbing from there.

As you drop from the Rams Heads, the snowgrass gradually disappears, replaced by thick, heathy bushes, none more beautiful or fragrant than the alpine mint, with its tightly bunched leaf clusters and tiny white flowers. This is challenging off-track walking. Never, ever attempt this terrain without long pants for protection, hiking poles for stability, a keen eye for the sphagnum and the energy and will to detour around it. There's no real way to weave between the bushes, so you carefully tread atop them, hoping they'll bear your weight. One step, the combined mass of thin branches provides a sturdy platform. The next, you crash through, sometimes landing on rock, sometimes earth. Who knows how many venomous red-bellied black snakes lurk below? How many deadly funnel web spiders? They named a ski run over the hill at Thredbo 'Funnel Web' on account of all the spiders that plagued the crew who cleared it.

Soon the ground becomes both boggy with sphagnum and spiky with shin-pricking candle heath. Then at last, the tree line is reached. Now we are among the snow gums, a hardy variant of Australia's near-ubiquitous eucalypts. At their highest reaches, the snow gums are gnarled, stunted, tortured survivors of a thousand winter storms, the smooth bark on their thick trunks rippled with streaks of blood orange, mustard yellow and olive green that turn all the more gaudy when wet. Nothing beats skiing through snow gums, especially at these upper elevations where soft snow collects between stands of trees. The snow gums are like gates on a slalom course, encouraging a natural rhythm as you weave in and out of glade and clump, and in winter this long slope from the Rams Heads down to Dead Horse Gap just outside the

Thredbo resort boundary is one of the best places to ski them. Lower down, they become slender, white-limbed dancers as tall as chairlift towers, often but not always too tightly packed to ski through. This is far from the toughest backcountry ski run in Australia but few runs are longer, more beautiful or more exhilarating. There is power in this place, whether walking or skiing.

Dead Horse Gap is a natural mountain pass between the western and eastern side of the mountains. Descend westward from here on the Alpine Way toward the valley of the upper Murray River and as you plummet in elevation the snow gums soon disappear, replaced by much taller trees. There are alpine ash, towering straight-trunked forest giants known in some parts of the mountains as woollybutts on account of their fibrous, stringy bark. Lower down in wet gullies are the mountain ash, the mightiest of which can grow to 100 metres, the world's tallest flowering plant, only a few metres shorter than the world's tallest tree, the Californian redwood. Lower still, in gullies on the southern and western flanks of the mountains, are small patches of temperate rainforest with giant ferns. There is literally rainforest and tundra-style vegetation within a few linear kilometres in these mountains.

The High Country fauna is no less remarkable or exotic than the flora. In the sphagnum bogs live corroboree frogs, startling black-and-yellow speckled amphibians so named because their markings resemble the paint worn during Aboriginal tribal dances, so small you can fit several in a matchbox. The pygmy possum is a similarly tiny, equally elusive marsupial that is one of the few Australian animals that hibernates. The broad-toothed rat is a shy cuddly furball that scurries through tunnels beneath the snowgrass tussocks, the matted thatch the perfect defence against avian predators. Much more easily spotted in the valleys and plains are wallabies, kangaroos, emus and wombats.

The mountains are also one of the favoured habitats of the world's only two monotremes, or egg-laying mammals. One is the echidna, a spiky ball of ant-eating purposefulness. Then there's the platypus, a flippered, venomous, semiaquatic freak of nature that looks like a type of Pokémon that never quite caught on with the kids. Walking from Dead Horse Gap back to the car in Thredbo at twilight on the muddy, mossy path along the Thredbo River, there's every chance of spotting one.

You've never heard mournfulness until your ears have been pierced by the wail of the yellow-tailed black cockatoo on a calm winter morning, its cry said to portend an oncoming storm. You never winced at a squeaky gate more in need of oil than when a pair of gang-gang cockatoos call to each other from their perches in the woollybutts, the female charcoal grey, the male desperate to impress with its wispy helmet of magenta. You've never truly appreciated the pure whiteness of snow until you've seen blue and blood-red crimson rosellas flitting among the snow gum branches in a blizzard. These are all parrots, a type of bird you'd normally associate with tropical climes but, like the black swans of Western Australia that so astonished seventeenth-century Dutch seafarers, the animals of the Australian High Country defy European textbooks and expectations.

Even the insects are interesting. The chameleon grasshopper changes colour from blue to green to black depending on the air temperature. High Country march flies have crazy green eyes and will drill through the thickest hiking pants with their proboscis. The 'marchies' win huge bonus points for weirdness, although they lose plenty for annoyance.

And then there are those bogong moths. Aunty Rhonda Casey has a story about them too.

> Once upon a time Mrs Bogong was beautiful. She wasn't grey or brown, but was every colour of the rainbow. She lived in the flat country where she would look out to the mountains and see this white stuff covering them. Her husband, Mr Bogong, would say, 'That's far too dangerous, you're not allowed to go there.'
>
> But one day, when he had gone off hunting, she flew off toward the mountains. As she was flying, she noticed the air was getting colder, and she was very tired. Then it started snowing and her wings were weighed down and she was pinned to the ground and entombed there.
>
> But when the spring came and the snow melted, she was freed. And as she hovered above the landscape, she saw wildflowers everywhere and thought, This is so beautiful!
>
> And then she flew home, but no one recognised her when she got there because all the colours had leached from her wings and she was no longer a beautiful matriarch but was just like everyone else. And from that day onwards, all the bogong moths were grey and brown.

Like all stories, this one is open to interpretation. You could take it as a curiosity-killed-the-cat type tale, reminding us that it's sometimes better to stick to what you know. For Aunty Rhonda, the story goes deeper. To her, the colourful moth giving her colours to the mountains and remaining ever after drab and brown is a parable of personal sacrifice. She says it's about leaving a place in better shape than you found it.

But that lesson has not been heeded. Like the Indigenous societies that once flourished in the shadow of the mountain that bears Kosciuszko's name, the landscape of the Australian High Country has been ravaged. The assault started when Europeans arrived in the early nineteenth century and continues to the present day despite the best efforts of conservationists and National Parks and Wildlife Service staff after the establishment of Kosciuszko National Park in 1967 and ten other alpine national parks or reserves across the Australian Alps in ensuing years.

Australians are in danger of losing everything that is precious and unique about the High Country, just like that. As if to prove the point, in 2019 the bogong moths stopped coming.

CHAPTER 25

TALES OF THE GARDEN OF KOSCIUSZKO

Kosciuszko built a garden at West Point on a natural ledge on a cliff overlooking the Hudson River. Today, it's a popular attraction for visitors to the campus of the military academy and is located directly under the West Point Club where, if you miss Taco Tuesdays or Wing Wednesdays, you can still enjoy a range of international cuisine any day of the week, Polish included in a respectful culinary nod to Kosciuszko.

The garden was Kosciuszko's sanctuary in his three years at West Point, a refuge from the close quarters of military life. Kosciuszko sought no help from soldiers, civilians or prisoners of war to sculpt and beautify the rocky plot. He cleared the vegetation himself and lowered soil with rope and bucket down the cliff face so he didn't have to carry it down the perilously steep path. Kosciuszko cultivated flowers and other plants in his garden. He even channelled a natural trickle to make a fountain.

> The Garden is about thirty feet in length, and in width, in its utmost extent, not more than twenty feet, and in

some parts much less. Near the centre of the garden there is a beautiful basin, near whose bottom, through a small perforation, flows upward a spring of sweet water, which is carried off by overflowing on the east side of the basin toward the River, the surface of which is some eighty feet below the garden ... It was here, when in its rude state, the Polish soldier and patriot sat in deep contemplation on the loves of his youth, and the ills his country had to suffer. It would be a grateful sight to him if he could visit it now, and find that a band of youthful soldiers had, as it were, consecrated the whole military grounds to his fame.

So wrote the American author and lawyer Samuel Lorenzo Knapp in the introduction to his popular 1834 short story collection *Tales of the Garden of Kosciuszko*. Knapp's visit to the garden inspired the book, serving as a metaphor for the state of mental repose required to create great art. Kosciuszko's garden was an artwork in its own right, with its flowerbeds and fountain. It may also have been a reminder of his agrarian upbringing, where young Tadeusz played in the fields and had a favourite boulder upon which he'd clamber to survey the land. When you've grown up with soil under your fingernails, it becomes strangely addictive.

Kosciuszko would have loved the rich soil and earthy beauty of the Australian mountain named after him and the national park that encompasses it. But Kosciuszko would no doubt despair at the current state of the park and indeed the entire Australian High Country. Environmentalism wasn't an 'ism' that existed in his day but it's not hard to imagine him championing its cause, viewing it as a key pillar of human wellbeing and liberty. That was certainly the view of Doctor Janus Rygielski, former president of the Polish Community

Council of Australia and New Zealand, as expressed in the inaugural issue of the council's magazine: 'In the 18th century, Kosciuszko was one of the greatest soldiers. If he were alive today, it is certain that he would be counted among the great conservationists.'

The first thing Kosciuszko and even the most disengaged sightseer would notice today is the state of the forests. On virtually every mountain slope and ridge, dead trees stand like whalebones washed up on an ancient tide. Snow gums are dying en masse, partly because of an infestation of a native wood borer called the longicorn beetle but mostly because of fires which are coming more frequently and burning more fiercely than at any time since the landscape took its current form after the Ice Age.

Most of Australia's eucalyptus forests can handle fires; indeed, they depend on them for regeneration as fires release seeds from their woody seed capsules. Most eucalypts also re-sprout after fire thanks to dormant buds underneath their thick bark. But snow gum bark is thin, and the unusually intense fires of recent years have burned the buds and killed trees outright. Snow gums have a Plan B: a large woody swelling at their base called a lignotuber stores energy and protects dormant buds. But after two or three fires in quick succession, the lignotubers die too. In the Victorian High Country, south of Kosciuszko, there have been five huge, fierce fires in the first two decades of the twenty-first century compared to just one mega-blaze in the entire twentieth century. The snow gums simply can't cope. Without the buzz of a chainsaw or the rumble of a bulldozer, one of the world's most exotic tree species is being wiped out.

The tall alpine ash trees on lower slopes are doing no better. Young ash grow for fifteen years before they first flower, then take another five years to produce seed for the next generation. In other words, they need a minimum of twenty undisturbed years to reproduce. Massive, extremely hot fires swept through northern Kosciuszko National Park in 2003 and 2020, killing trees en masse. That seventeen-year gap was just a few years too short for the next generation to mature and produce seed. Huge swathes of alpine ash forests of northern Kosciuszko are now dead, probably destined to become ecologically barren scrubland. Nineteenth-century sawmillers did their best to destroy the ash forests; now climate change is doing the job just as ruthlessly.

Even the highest parts of the mountains have started to cop it. The windswept feldmark burned in the 2003 fires. Not all of it, but then, there's not much of it to burn. The fire started in the valley grasslands and roared its way up through the mountain ash, the alpine ash, the snow gum, the heathy bushes and upward, ever upward, its appetite so voracious it burned lichen off rocks en route to the miniature feldmark shrubs, most of which still haven't recovered. Never in recorded history had a fire burned so high on the Main Range, except of course for the fires deliberately lit by European cattlemen with wax matches to promote grass growth, a lowland land management trick borrowed from Aboriginal people which was devastatingly inappropriate in the alpine area where growback is infinitely slower and erosion of bare earth exponentially more rapid.

Climate change is also decimating the winter snowpack. They used to have a ski race at the top of Thredbo the day after Christmas. Now there's a small patch or two at best near the top station of the chairlift. Strzelecki wrote of a 'region of perpetual snows' when he visited the Main Range in March 1840. These days, the last stubborn snow patch has usually melted by February. Already, one of Australia's nine mainland downhill ski resorts – Mt Buffalo in Victoria – has closed due to diminishing snow cover. In January 2020, fire swept through Selwyn Snow Resort in New South Wales, destroying all of its buildings. It reopened to great fanfare in 2023, only to close in midwinter due to lack of snow.

Snow loss is just as devastating for hibernating mountain pygmy possums, which rely on snow as an insulating blanket. It's never colder than zero degrees Celsius under the snow, but air temperatures just above ground have dropped as low as minus 23 Celsius in the pygmy possum stronghold of Charlotte Pass. If that frigid air starts seeping through a patchy snowpack, it's like replacing a camper's winter-rated sleeping bag with a light summer bag. And as much as pygmy possums need snow for warmth, they need bogong moths for food. Bogongs are not the nocturnal omnivore's only food source but they're a staple part of their diet and any sudden change in diet typically affects an animal's wellbeing and, in turn, its fertility. With only 2000 pygmy possums remaining in the wild, every protein-filled moth counts.

Why did the moths vanish? That, too, is a climate story. The year 2019 was Australia's warmest and driest on record and was the third year of severe drought across huge parts of the country. Bogong numbers were already dropping before the drought due to habitat destruction and agricultural pesticides in their breeding grounds but their numbers plummeted by 99.5 per cent over the course of the drought. Then, in the Black Summer of 2019/20, they didn't show up in the mountains. Nobody had ever seen that happen, or not happen, more accurately. For the first time, bogongs were placed on the endangered species register. Their numbers have since recovered after wetter years fuelled by the La Niña climate pattern, but what happens in the next severe drought? What happens when 99.5 per cent becomes 99.9 per cent and then 100 per cent?

If the indirect effects of climate change are like a slow drawn-out death by smoking, the direct human imprint on this landscape since colonisation has been like violent self-harm. Ski resorts, roads and other types of tourist infrastructure inevitably scar a landscape but at least they are managed and limited to certain areas. But the High Country was decimated on a landscape-wide scale by the early European arrivals, primarily through the practice of grazing sheep and cattle.

Graziers in the mid-nineteenth century couldn't believe their luck when they found evergreen pastures in the mountains in high summer, when the plains either side lay parched and devoid of feed. There is even a suggestion that one or two of them may have climbed the Main Range and Mt Kosciuszko before Strzelecki but kept schtum, not wanting to broadcast the existence of such bounteous pastures. Access to the mountains was unregulated for years until a system of leases came into effect, which legally enshrined the enviro-vandalism. The main issue with grazing in the High Country is that Australia has no native ungulates – large mammals with hooves. Prior to colonisation, the feldmark, the snowgrass and the sphagnum had known only lightweight animals with soft, padded feet. European grazing animals were like ploughs. In a twinkling, grassy mountain slopes festooned with wildflowers became stony wastelands. Wetlands were churned to mud. Valleys were chewed bare like cricket pitches. There's a shocking old black-and-white photo of a herd of cattle grazing on the shores of Club Lake – one of Kosciuszko's five glacial lakes – during the Federation Drought of 1900, which at the time was Australia's worst recorded drought. A small snow patch in the background is the only sign it's a Kosciuszko landscape.

Dozens, perhaps hundreds, of cattle dot the denuded slopes around the lake. Two horses, with men atop them, drink from the lake. The lake's waters are turbid rather than their natural clear state. The whole scene is the environmental equivalent of a paintball game in the Louvre.

According to Ngarigo Elder Uncle Rod Mason, things were no better over at Blue Lake, which must have seriously angered Dyillagamberra, whose camp is there. Every region across Australia has a rainmaker and the rainmaker of the southern Snowy Mountains and the Monaro plains and south coast to the east is called Dyillagamberra by the Ngarigo people. From his camp at Blue Lake, Dyillagamberra is responsible for the water that all plants, animals and people need. If people walk to the rainmaker's favourite waterhole, throw in three pebbles and say his name three times, the rainmaker will keep the rivers, creeks and waterholes full while the people travel around Country. There is no Aboriginal traditional story that describes what happens if some of the highest, most beautiful waterholes are despoiled, because they had no way of imagining that anyone would commit such a crime.

The first committees examining soil erosion caused by grazing were established in New South Wales in 1933 and Victoria in 1941. As the extent of the problem became clear, grazing was eventually banned on the highest parts of the Main Range in the 1950s. It took decades to repair the damage. The phase-out continued across lower parts of the mountains in ensuing years, although it wasn't completely banned in parts of the Victorian High Country until as late as 2015. Even today, cattle families whose forebears once held leases in the mountains rage against their exclusion. In towns around the mountains, you'll see bumper stickers that say, *Mountain cattlemen care for the High Country* and people actually believe it. Former mountain cattlemen and their descendants are so hurt by the loss of their annual economic windfall that they are blinded to the land's ecological health. Another popular bumper sticker says, *Grazing prevents blazing*, as in cattle prevent bushfires in the mountains by chomping their way through flammable vegetation. They believe that too. Indeed 'Grazing prevents blazing' is a rallying cry for the return of grazing to the mountains, and a simplistic idea the average Australian is ill-equipped to dismiss. Who wouldn't believe that a landscape becomes less fire-prone when you reduce the fuel load?

But 'grazing prevents blazing' is one-dimensional gobbledygook. First of all, cattle selectively graze the sweet leaves of wildflowers like the anemone buttercup, so they're a huge threat to biodiversity. But the main point is that the grasses and herbs that the cattle favour are a fraction of the fuel load. It's mostly the shrubby bushes that carry fires into the crowns of trees, turning small fires into large ones, and those bushes are unpalatable to cattle. And here's the kicker: by eating the grass cover to the ground, cattle promote the takeover of the landscape by the very shrubby bushes that burn so fiercely. In other words, cattle actually increase the High Country's susceptibility to fire. Grazing doesn't prevent blazing: it encourages it. These are the irrefutable facts.

> The long, drawn-out argument about domestic stock grazing in the mountains provides a key example of how a way of thinking, an experience of use, can be intractable in the face of evidence to the contrary.

Those wise words come from Deirdre Slattery and the late Graeme L Worboys, scientists and authors of the indispensable 2020 tome *Kosciuszko: A Great National Park*. They illustrate their point with a great example of a cattleman called Ted Taylor who, even in 2001, was still banging on about the land going to ruin since cattle were removed. Old Ted lamented the demise of an open creek on a particular plain in northern Kosciuszko where his cattle used to drink. After the landscape had begun to recover, all he saw was a worthless swamp that you couldn't even ride a horse through.

But the boggy ground was the land's natural state. The wetland was the water's natural filter and the natural regulator of run-off, storing water for dry times, protecting against raging torrents in times of heavy rain and snowmelt. The clearly defined creek line favoured by Taylor had been carved by the hard hooves of cattle accessing water far more regularly than kangaroos and other native animals, which generally don't drink daily and which don't damage wetlands with their soft, padded feet. In a blink, cattle had reduced a rich ecosystem formed over millennia to the equivalent of an urban stormwater drain. And old Ted wanted it that way.

To this day, some of the loudest voices in and around the mountains continue to promote junk land management information around bushfire mitigation, waterway wellbeing and more. In some cases, these people are driven by ideological opposition to the very existence of national parks. Sometimes they are motivated by greed. In all cases, they are slaves to their own ignorance. And these days, all that ignorance, self-interest and resentment is funnelled into the protection of brumbies.

Brumbies are raggedy, fly-ridden feral horses which inhabit the park, descendants of escaped white-settler horses from yesteryear. With their hard hooves and their daily need to drink, brumbies are pests turning pristine wetlands and waterways into ecologically worthless mudheaps, and grasslands into scoured bare earth. The brumbies themselves are hardly in a better state than the land. They live short, miserable, vermin-infested lives and die horrible slow deaths in times of drought, spending their last days as ribcages on legs. Any animal activist worth their salt would call for their complete eradication. Instead, they fight for their protection. So too do many former High Country cattle families from their farms in the lowland valleys flanking the mountains, who put forward specious, infantile arguments that brumbies somehow nourish an environment that evolved over millennia without them.

The cattle families see brumbies as an avatar for the lost High Country grazing life. Many Australians beyond the mountains romanticise brumbies because of their presence in popular stories like the iconic Australian poem 'The Man from Snowy River' and the *Silver Brumby* series of children's books. More broadly, horses have long featured in Australian mythology from colonial times through to the Light Horse brigades in wars of yesteryear, through to the ongoing annual madness of the Melbourne Cup, a public holiday in Victoria which encourages people to indulge in government-sanctioned binge-drinking and betting. More broadly, who doesn't love the universal symbol of horses running free and wild?

Kosciuszko National Park rangers first realised they had a growing brumby problem in the late 1990s, when there were barely a thousand of them. Various brumby management plans were cobbled together but most ended up as confetti, the planning process thwarted by brumby advocates who wouldn't compromise. Brumby numbers kept growing through to the mid-2010s, and just when ecologists thought the problem couldn't possibly worsen, they were blindsided by the most insane political act any of them had ever seen.

In 2016, John Barilaro, then deputy premier of New South Wales and the local member for the Monaro electorate which lies in and around the mountains, cleverly leveraged pro-brumby sentiment and pushed the *Kosciuszko Wild Horse Heritage Act* through the New South Wales Parliament. Never had an Australian politician so brazenly declared war on the environment. Never had ecologists witnessed a 'heritage' feral animal protected at the expense of native species. By the end of 2022, more than 20,000 brumbies were estimated to be galloping around Kosciuszko National Park. Don't ask how the corroboree frogs were doing in their sphagnum bogs.

High up in the Brindabella Range of the Australian Capital Territory, there's a wonderful pristine sphagnum bog called Ginini Flats Wetland where you can still find a frog or two because Parks ACT has a no-horse policy and humanely dispatches them on sight. But over the border in Kosciuszko National Park in New South Wales, every bedraggled brumby was a 'heritage horse' and just about every corroboree frog was dead. A type of fungal infection had already devastated corroboree frogs, while climate change has been degrading their sphagnum bog habitats. Brumbies were the final straw. The only confirmed population in New South Wales now is in Sydney's Taronga Zoo. As for the broad-toothed rat, how do you think it's faring against birds of prey when the matted snowgrass that it relies on for tunnels has been devoured to the roots by equine eating machines?

After a change of state government in 2023, New South Wales Environment Minister Penny Sharpe lifted the restriction on aerial culling of brumbies, the only effective form of control. You can imagine the furious response of pro-brumby folk. The culture war rages on and, like all culture wars, it's about more than the issue itself. It's about people and the symbols that are important to them. It's also an information war. Brumby advocates say the count is wrong, that the number is overstated, that every brumby culled could be the last survivor of a bloodline that took our soldiers to war, even though only one Australian horse ever returned from war and it belonged to a high-ranking officer who didn't set it loose to breed in Kosciuszko National Park. As for the disputed tally, let's just say that Felicity from Facebook doesn't know better than scientists who count feral animals for a living.

Brumbies are not the only feral species in Kosciuszko. Like the rest of Australia, the High Country has numerous introduced invasive species, from goats to rabbits to pigs to cats to dogs to increasing numbers of deer. Even trout have played a part in changing the natural balance. Trout fishing is a tourism drawcard but these introduced fish have virtually wiped out the Kosciuszko galaxias. Those swift translucent little fish underneath the Mt Kosciuszko track now cling to a perilous existence in those few tiny creeks and nowhere else. In northern Kosciuszko, a different species of galaxias – the stocky galaxias – now occupies just one section of one gurgling creek above a waterfall where the trout can't get to them. But the brumbies are encroaching on that area. If they trample the banks of that stream and muddy the clear waters that the galaxias need to survive, it's all over.

The 200-year assault on the Australian High Country is an ongoing national tragedy that is rarely framed in such blatant terms. How we got here is part of a much bigger Australian story that the nation also hates to talk about. Leave it to Slattery and Worboys to speak the truth. Their book *Kosciuszko: A Great National Park* is not only an invaluable ecological and historical resource but a treasure trove of straight-shooting truisms:

> The British way of thinking was applied to alien conditions and in ignorance of the land's capacity for use. Long-

established Aboriginal methods of balancing resource availability with human needs were not seriously observed.

In ecological terms, the 'British way of thinking' has been devastating to the High Country, as elsewhere in Australia.

And for more than 200 years, the British way of thinking was underpinned by yet another lie.

CHAPTER 26

'AND THE EARTH ITSELF TO NOBODY'

In 1755, Kosciuszko's father sent his nine-year-old son to a school in Lubieszow, a town which you'll find on contemporary maps as Lyubeshiv in north-western Ukraine. The school was run by the Catholic Piarist Fathers, an order dedicated to children's education. The school's founder, Father Stanislaw Konarski, was a fascinating figure. The Roman Catholic priest was an educator and reformer who instilled a progressive curriculum at schools dotted across the Polish–Lithuanian Commonwealth that taught the works of key Enlightenment figures in addition to traditional school subjects. British scholar Professor William Rose wrote in a 1925 issue of British journal *The Slavonic Review*:

> He transformed the attitude of his fellow-countrymen to public questions, making them see things as they were, and consider persons in their relation to the body politic ... The Piarist School at Lubieszow can claim its share in fitting for his lifework that brightest flower of Polish chivalry and national service – Tadeusz Kosciuszko.

Kosciuszko was introduced to British philosopher John Locke's theory of a social contract in which people submit to the authority of a ruler or government in exchange for social order. Kosciuszko's friend Thomas Jefferson would also be strongly influenced by Locke's ideas and indeed many of Locke's phrases are dotted throughout the Declaration of Independence.

Kosciuszko lasted only a few years at the school before his father died and he had to return home to the family estate to help out his mother, Tekla, and three siblings. But the Enlightenment seeds sown by Father Konarski had taken root. As a young man studying in Paris, Kosciuszko read Jean-Jacques Rousseau, whose *Discourse on Inequality* had been published in 1755, the same year Kosciuszko started school. The opening paragraph of its 'Second Part' is famous because of the provocative idea that property ownership is a construct rather than part of the natural order of the universe, and doubtless also because of its scathing, almost comical tone:

> The first man who, having enclosed a piece of ground, bethought himself of saying This is mine, and found people simple enough to believe him, was the real founder of civil society. From how many crimes, wars and murders, from how many horrors and misfortunes might not any one have saved mankind, by pulling up the stakes, or filling up the ditch, and crying to his fellows, 'Beware of listening to this impostor; you are undone if you once forget that the fruits of the earth belong to us all, and the earth itself to nobody.'

You can disappear down an intellectual wombat burrow for days when you start reading Locke and Rousseau and comparing their ideas about property. The point here is that

Kosciuszko engaged with ideas around land, wealth and justice from an early age. Remember that he was a fan of French physiocrat François Quesnay, who believed that land – and especially the agriculture practised upon it – was the source of all wealth. Remember that late in life, Kosciuszko arranged to liberate the serfs on his estate. Remember that in May 1794 Kosciuszko issued the Proclamation of Polaniec, which granted peasants significant new rights including property rights to the land they cultivated. Remember that in the original version of his American will, before it was edited by Jefferson, Kosciuszko wrote that the people who had been enslaved at Jefferson's Monticello plantation should not only be freed and educated but given land, tools and cattle. Remember that Kosciuszko told Russia's Tsar Paul I, 'I never grieved for my own fate, but I will never stop grieving the fate of my Fatherland.' Land, and the right to live freely upon it, was everything to Kosciuszko.

Would you like a side of irony with your history and philosophy?

Kosciuszko's name sits on the highest point of a land that was never formally ceded, on the sacred summit of a continent whose original inhabitants were denied their rightful claims to the land by the British, first by ceremony, then by force, then with a cynical swish of the quill.

The British played it very differently across the Tasman Sea in New Zealand. On 6 February 1840, as Strzelecki was commencing his journey to climb and name the highest point on the Australian continent, the Treaty of Waitangi was signed. Regarded as the nation's founding document, the treaty was an agreement between the British Crown and New Zealand's Māori people which made the Māori British subjects while allowing them to retain full ownership rights of their traditional lands, fisheries and other possessions. The finer points of the treaty continue to be debated to this day, sometimes vigorously. Indeed, a major flare-up occurred in early 2024 after Prime Minister Christopher Luxon of the centre-right unwound certain pro-Māori measures enacted by his predecessor, the left-wing Jacinda Ardern. But Waitangi Day continues to be almost universally celebrated across New Zealand each 6 February as the country's national day.

Australia's national day is far from universally celebrated. Australia Day marks the day on 26 January 1788 when a fleet of six convict transport ships, three supply ships and two navy ships landed to found a penal colony on the shores of Port Jackson, better known as Sydney Harbour. Many people now call Australia Day 'Invasion Day' and refuse to recognise it. A growing number of local councils – eighty at last count – have stopped holding citizenship ceremonies on 26 January, believing the date to be disrespectful to Australia's first people.

The founding of the penal colony in Sydney was made possible by Captain James Cook who, eighteen years earlier, was the first European to chart the continent's east coast. Previously, Australia had been visited by Europeans only on its western, southern and northern coastlines. Europeans of that age believed they were legally entitled to appropriate uninhabited land in the name of their country but this land clearly had an Indigenous population. Cook encountered Aboriginal people when landing at Botany Bay, about twelve kilometres south of Port Jackson, and saw further evidence of human habitation as he sailed northward, as the Aboriginal people lit signal fires to alert nearby clans and Nations to the unusual vessel.

Cook was under explicit instructions from the Admiralty not to claim any part of the land without the 'consent of the natives'. Yet on 22 August 1770, he climbed the highest point of a small island just off the continent's northern tip and took possession of the entire east coast of Australia – a vast stretch of coastline considerably longer than the US east coast from the Florida Keys to the northern tip of Maine. Displaying either a dry sense of humour or no humour at all, Cook named the small island on which he stood 'Possession Island'. Displaying either an extremely vivid imagination or no imagination at all, he named the entire eastern portion of the continent New South Wales. A plaque on a small boulder outcrop on a high point of Possession Island today commemorates Cook's annexation. Like the plaque on the summit of Mt Kosciuszko, it tells a lie.

How could the British Crown possess a land which was already inhabited by others when this was forbidden by law? Why did Cook overlook or overrule the explicit instructions of the Admiralty? What made Australia different? Arguments generally boil down to four main reasons.

First, the local inhabitants seemed at first glance to be few in number. This led Joseph Banks, the botanist aboard Cook's ship the *Endeavour*, to conclude that they would pretty much just scuttle off into the bush if the British settled at Botany Bay or nearby. 'From the experience I have had of the Natives of another part of the same Coast, I am inclined to believe they would speedily abandon the Country to the New Comers', Banks told the House of Commons Committee on Transportation in London in 1785, the body tasked with selecting the location of a new penal colony. Where exactly Banks imagined they would go remains a mystery.

Second, Cook's party was unable to trade with the locals they met at Botany Bay as the Aboriginal people placed no value on any gifts the Europeans gave them. This led Banks and others to conclude that there was no way the land could be purchased, which more or less put negotiations in the too-hard-basket, which accordingly emboldened the British to take the land.

Third, the locals appeared to have no permanent dwellings. In the British mind, this effectively put Australia in a legal grey area between inhabited and uninhabited.

Fourth, the British saw no evidence of agriculture. 'The Natives know nothing of Cultivation,' Cook wrote in his journal after visiting Botany Bay. This key observation set Australia aside from lands like New Zealand and North America. To Europeans, land cultivation and permanent dwellings were the first sign of civilisation. Without them, how could a people claim ownership of land?

The widespread perception that Aboriginal people never built permanent dwellings or cultivated the land persisted for more than 200 years. A big shift in understanding occurred in 2014 with the publication of Bruce Pascoe's book *Dark Emu*, which presented evidence of permanent dwellings and settlements as well as sophisticated agriculture and aquaculture, upending the assumption that Australia's pre-colonial inhabitants were only hunter-gatherers.

Not everyone was convinced by the substance of Pascoe's book and a bitter culture war has since raged. Certain high-profile provocateurs argue that the book's evidence of agriculture and permanent dwellings was partially or entirely fabricated. Even some academics argue that Pascoe's claims are inconclusive, if not overstated. These are murky waters and rather than wading deeper into them, it's best to reframe the debate entirely.

The point is not whether Aboriginal people practised the type of agriculture which looked like agriculture to European eyes. The point is that Aboriginal people managed the land with a view to both conservation and food production in ways that early European visitors didn't recognise as stewardship. A well-known example was 'fire-stick farming', where small patches of land would be burnt with a relatively cool, slow-burning fire so that weeks or months later it would yield palatable young plants and fresh grass which attracted kangaroos for hunting. It's one of countless examples of Aboriginal people preparing the land for future food harvesting, even if the land was not under seed and plough. Captain Cook never got it. Most early colonists didn't get it. Many Australians still don't get it.

But Strzelecki got it. The Polish explorer saw clearly that the majority of British colonists were viewing the relationship of the Aboriginal people to the land through a narrow Old World lens. As he wrote in his report to Governor Gipps:

> Their traditions, language, customs, moral, social and political condition, seem, ever since their discovery, to have been regarded as a subject unworthy of European study. Hence, all the observations contained in the narratives, whether of the early navigators, or of modern travellers, bear more upon what this race is to the colonist than to mankind.

Only once in Australia's colonial history was a treaty negotiated between a white settler and Aboriginal people and when authorities got wind of it, they could barely cancel it quickly enough.

John Batman, the man who negotiated the treaty, was no superhero. Born in 1801 in the small settlement of Rosehill which today is the geographical heart of Sydney, he moved to Tasmania, then known as Van Diemen's Land, where he became a farmer, bushman, explorer and mass murderer. In 1829, Batman participated in a massacre of Aboriginal people.

He 'had much slaughter to account for' wrote George Arthur, then Lieutenant-Governor of Van Diemen's Land. So did many others in Tasmania. The genocide perpetrated upon Tasmanian Aboriginal people by people of European heritage would be an indelible stain on the island's history.

Batman owned a large property on rough country in Van Diemen's Land but he had eyes for Port Phillip, the large bay on the southern coast of the mainland. Journeying up the Yarra River that flowed into the bay in 1835, he declared the land 'Batmania'. The settlement that grew from the spot Batman favoured is today known as Melbourne, and has recently become Australia's most sprawling and populous city. Australia Post will also deliver letters addressed to 'Naarm', the area's name in the Woiwurrung language of the Kulin Nation. The name Batman chose didn't stick, and his treaty didn't last long either.

On 16 June 1835, Batman offered Elders of the local Wurundjeri people of the Kulin Nation forty blankets, thirty axes, 100 knives, fifty pairs of scissors, thirty mirrors, 200 handkerchiefs, 100 pounds of flour and six shirts in exchange for the right to rent their land on an annual basis. The treaty was signed. Historians now argue that it stood on shaky legal and ethical ground as the very notion of a transfer of land was nonsensical to Kulin people because Aboriginal people across Australia saw themselves as belonging to the land, not possessing it. At any rate, it hardly mattered as New South Wales Governor Richard Bourke immediately kyboshed the deal, as well as the possibility of any future treaty, in perhaps the most important proclamation in Australian history.

On 26 August 1835, Bourke issued an untitled proclamation which has come to be known as the Proclamation of Terra Nullius, a phrase which translates from Latin as 'Nobody's

Land'. In 299 words of waffling legal gobbledygook, Bourke formalised that Australia belonged to no-one before the British Crown took possession of it. Here's a sample:

> All Persons who shall be found in possession of any such Lands as aforesaid, without the license or authority of His Majesty's Government, for such purpose, first had and obtained, will be considered as trespassers, and liable to be dealt with in like manner as other intruders upon the vacant Lands of the Crown within the said Colony.

Bottom line: it ain't yours, it never was and we're not paying a cent for it.

Of course, the British had effectively been operating under the principle of Terra Nullius in the huge chunk of eastern Australia that they called New South Wales ever since Cook had claimed it in 1770. Sixty-five years later, though the phrase did not appear in Bourke's proclamation, the doctrine was official.

It's amusing to ponder what Rousseau would have made of all this. When he wrote that 'the fruits of the earth belong to us all, and the earth itself to nobody', Rousseau was imagining a nonplussed response to the first person who came up with the crazy idea of land ownership. When the British, through the blunt instrument of Terra Nullius, said the eastern half of Australia belonged to nobody, what they really meant was it belonged to them.

Terra Nullius stood as a principle in Australian law until the landmark High Court Mabo legal decision of 1992, which invalidated Cook's declaration of possession. 'Native Title' could now be claimed by Aboriginal people in areas where they could show an unbroken connection to the land. Tireless land rights campaigner Eddie Mabo died just months before the decision that bears his name was handed down. Three years later, his grave was painted with swastikas by white supremacists. Australia as a nation still struggles to recognise the deep relationship of its original inhabitants to the land the British stole. It still struggles to recognise its original inhabitants at all. They are not even mentioned in the Constitution.

Aboriginal people were literally written out of law, out of land ownership, out of legal existence. They – and the country as a whole – are much the poorer for it, and nowhere is this better illustrated than down by Kosciuszko.

CHAPTER 27

'AND DOWN BY KOSCIUSKO ...'

When Kosciuszko died in 1817, his organs were buried at Solothurn, except for his heart, which was preserved in an urn. There were instructions to transfer his heart to Poland only when the nation was free. Thus in 1927, a decade after Poland had gained independence near the end of World War I and 110 years after his death, Kosciuszko's heart made its way to Warsaw, where it now rests in a chapel in the Royal Castle. His embalmed body was kept in Switzerland until 1819, when it was repatriated to its final resting place in Krakow's Wawel Cathedral.

Interestingly, an Australian icon received similar treatment. Phar Lap was a champion racehorse of the Depression era of the late 1920s and early 1930s who, after finishing unplaced in eight of his first nine starts, won a Melbourne Cup and thirty-six other races, including a major race in Mexico. He then mysteriously died in California, probably after being poisoned by gangsters working for bookmakers. Today, Phar Lap's preserved heart, all 6.35 kilograms of it, is one of the most popular exhibits at the National Museum of Australia in Canberra. And that's not the only piece of Phar Lap set aside for the eager public. His stuffed hide is by far the most popular exhibit at the Melbourne Museum, while his skeleton holds pride of place in Te Papa Tongarewa, the Museum of New Zealand, the nation where he was foaled (although he never raced there).

Why did the body of an Australian racehorse – or at least a horse adopted by Australians as their own – receive the same reverential treatment after death as a great freedom fighter of two continents? The title of the 1983 feature film says it all: *Phar Lap: Heart of a Nation*. Phar Lap was indeed that. The rich red chestnut gelding was a bright light in dark economic times. You could reliably bet your last pennies on him and feel sure of winning. But he was bigger than the ability to put bread on the table. The enduring legends of Phar Lap and his contemporary, the champion cricketer Don Bradman, speak to the fact that Australia lacks true national heroes. Outside of the sporting realm, it is almost impossible to pick one man or woman who qualifies as a universally known and loved Australian figure.

Poland has Kosciuszko, Lech Walesa, Pope John Paul II and others, each of whom in their own way either embodied or laid out their country's beliefs and dreams. America has too many national heroes to name, but generally they are people who 'made it', who fulfilled the American Dream. Throughout its history, America has laid down mission statements, guidelines to the realisation of that dream, some clear, some loosely defined, but always hopeful and upbeat. There's 'all men are created equal'. There's 'we the people' in the constitution, which is like the beginning of a manifesto which says, 'Hey, we're all in this together.' There's the iconic inscription on the pedestal of the Statue of Liberty, quoting part of Emma

Lazarus's 1883 sonnet 'The New Colossus': 'Give me your tired, your poor, your huddled masses yearning to breathe free.'

Australia has no equivalent of any of these statements, nor any figures like the Founding Fathers whose words and deeds are lionised to this day. In Chapter 24 of his magnum opus *Moby-Dick*, Herman Melville's narrator described Australia as 'That great America on the other side of the sphere', and while Australia is roughly the same size as the USA minus Alaska, the country is much more modest in its stated ambitions. Australians don't have a Dream in the American sense. Indeed, the phrase 'Australian Dream' specifically refers to the dream of home ownership. If the American Dream is to rise to the top, or at least to fulfil your personal potential unencumbered by the government or any other impediment, the Australian Dream is to park yourself on a small patch of the country that you can call your own.

That's why the nearest thing to a national hero to emerge in modern Australian life is Darryl Kerrigan, the fictitious protagonist of Australia's best-loved movie *The Castle*. Shot inside two weeks on a budget of under a million dollars, the sweet self-parodying 1997 comedy tells of a working-class outer-suburban dad who fights the compulsory acquisition of his home to expand the airport over the back fence. Almost every scene is iconic but two stand out. There's Kerrigan on holiday at Bonnie Doon on the fringe of the Victorian High Country, puffing out his chest and rhetorically asking, 'How's the serenity?' which doesn't sound funny but you need to watch it to get it, and it helps if you're Australian. Then there's the first court hearing, where Kerrigan's low-rent hapless suburban lawyer summarises his client's case with the statement: 'It's the Constitution. It's Mabo. It's justice. It's law. It's the vibe and uh … no that's it. It's the vibe. I rest my case.'

Spoiler: a fancy lawyer takes an interest in Kerrigan's predicament, represents him pro bono and wins. Thus is the right to the Australian Dream upheld, and thus does the Aussie everyman triumph. Those right there are the two key ingredients of an Australian hero. You have to be relatable. And ideally, you're the quintessential 'Aussie battler', the type of person who struggles through life with nothing more than a can-do spirit, homegrown smarts and dogged persistence. Big bonus points if you're a battler like Darryl Kerrigan, who takes on the system and beats it, because whether real or fictional, all of Australia's great heroes are outsiders.

Americans also have their outsider heroes but they're more in the antihero mould of Travis Bickle in Martin Scorsese's *Taxi Driver* or Walter White in *Breaking Bad*, or Holden Caulfield, the disaffected schoolkid in JD Salinger's *The Catcher in the Rye*. These characters are champions of their own mini universe, not the nation as a whole. But Australia's antiheroes are often our national heroes too. The real-life bushranger Ned Kelly is a classic example. Born in 1854 of Australian Irish stock and downtrodden by those with wealth and power, he became an outlaw in a trademark suit of armour through either choice, necessity or a mixture of both, depending on your historical reading. Either way, he persists as a folk hero in Australia's popular imagination.

Then there's the whole subgenre of characters penned by the poet AB 'Banjo' Paterson. Born in 1864, Paterson grew up in the bush and spent a lifetime romanticising its hard-bitten mavericks, long after he moved to Sydney and became a lawyer, lawn tennis player and competitive harbour rower. Internationally, Paterson's most famous work is 'Waltzing Matilda', which is widely known because of the song of the same name which has become a de facto national anthem, lustily sung by sporting crowds and other Australians at moments of patriotic effusion.

'Waltzing Matilda' requires translation for non-Australians and perhaps even for modern Australians unacquainted with the bush parlance of yesteryear. To waltz matilda means to carry a swag, which was an old-fashioned backpack or bundle of belongings. A man who carried a swag was a swagman and in the context of the poem, the swagman was a homeless itinerant worker in the 1890s Depression who camped by a billabong – a small waterhole or natural pool which often lies beside a larger creek or river. So the swagman in the poem steals a sheep for food. On being discovered, he drowns himself rather than being taken by the police. This act is both an ode to freedom and a middle finger to authority, and the sympathies of the average Aussie absolutely lie with the swagman, not the cops or the wealthy landowner whose sheep was stolen. Thus are great Australian stories written, fictional and non-fictional. And no story in this tradition is greater than 'The Man from Snowy River'.

A thirteen-stanza masterpiece which proved to be Paterson's breakthrough poem when it was published in 1890, 'The Man from Snowy River' tells the tale of a group that rides off in search of a valuable escaped thoroughbred which has fled its farm below the mountains to join a mob of mountain brumbies. After an exhausting chase, only one member of the pursuing posse is game enough to follow the brumbies down a ravine so steep it's almost a precipice; that of course would be the eponymous Man, who not only survives his terrifying ride but duly rounds up the mob and returns the prize galloper intact. Here's the final stanza in all its iambic pentameter rhythmical glory:

> And down by Kosciusko, where the pine-clad ridges raise
> Their torn and rugged battlements on high,
> Where the air is clear as crystal, and the white stars fairly blaze
> At midnight in the cold and frosty sky,
> And where around the Overflow the reedbeds sweep and sway
> To the breezes, and the rolling plains are wide,
> The man from Snowy River is a household word today,
> And the stockmen tell the story of his ride.

It's not just the stockmen who tell the story of the ride. The quintessential bush yarn resonates throughout Australia to this day, and was even referenced on the biggest international stage imaginable. At the Sydney 2000 Olympics, with the world's undivided attention on Australia, the opening ceremony commenced with a 'Man from Snowy River'-themed group of riders, complete with music from the hit 1982 film which starred Tom Burlinson, who is now an outspoken advocate for keeping brumbies in the High Country. As recently as early 2024, the movie was enjoying a nostalgic revival around the country, playing to packed houses with live orchestral accompaniment in venues including the Sydney Opera House. The Man was everything that Australians of the age admired, and largely still do. He was unheralded but supremely capable. He was courageous but humble. His currency was deeds, not words. He risked it all and triumphed. He was Darryl Kerrigan with stirrups and a whip.

As you'd expect, 'The Man from Snowy River' still dominates High Country iconography. Drive through the Snowy Mountains gateway town of Jindabyne and the first thing you see, right opposite the giant Strzelecki statue in Banjo Paterson

Park on the shore of Lake Jindabyne, is the Banjo Paterson Inn. Half an hour up the Kosciuszko Road at Australia's largest ski resort, Perisher, The Man from Snowy River Hotel sits in the heart of the valley. On the Victorian side of the mountains, the town of Corryong has The Man from Snowy River Museum and holds an annual Man from Snowy River Bush Festival. There is even a High Country removal business amusingly called The Van from Snowy River.

But 'The Man from Snowy River' tells the same lie as Mt Kosciuszko in the way it erases Aboriginal history. Paterson said his poem was a fictional work based on stories recounted to him by mountain cattlemen, including a stockman called Jack Riley in whose rough hut he once stayed. Today, many believe Riley was The Man. But was he? As detailed in my previous book *The Brumby Wars*, there's a huge clue to The Man's identity in the first line of the stanza quoted above which speaks of the 'pine-clad ridges' down by Kosciuszko. Pine trees?! What happened to all those snow gums and alpine ash? Turns out there's an area called the Byadbo Wilderness along the valley of the lower Snowy River which today sits in the south-east corner of Kosciuszko National Park. Due to its comparatively dry climate in the rain shadow of the mountains, Byadbo is dominated by native cypress pines, which thrive in dry zones. Byadbo is also a landscape of precipitously steep rocky slopes, perfect for the setting of the poem. No other section of the Australian High Country looks anything like it, and back in the day, all Byadbo stockmen were Aboriginal. Was The Man based on an Aboriginal rider? Real or mythical, did Banjo paint him white to appease the literary tastes of the time?

To this day, the best-known High Country stories are white folks' stories about white people in the mountains. Make no mistake, they are captivating tales.

Way back in 1861, during the gold rush on the frozen plains of Kiandra in northern Kosciuszko, snowbound miners in need of entertainment and exercise fashioned rudimentary timber skis and formed the world's first ski club, the Kiandra Snow Shoe Club. Australia's unlikely winter sports legacy didn't end there. Elyne Mitchell wrote the *Silver Brumby* series of children's books and numerous other works about the High Country. In 1938, this self-taught skier, who cut her teeth on the steep western faces of the Main Range, won Canada's national downhill championships. In 2011, Australia topped the medal table at the 2011 Snowboarding World Championships. Overall, Australians have won a total of 19 Winter Olympic medals. The most famous came in the final of the 1000-metres short track speed skating at the 2002 Salt Lake City Games, when a totally outclassed Steven Bradbury watched all four rivals crash to the ice nearly half a lap ahead of him in the argy-bargy on the home turn, leaving him to skate across the line in first place, arms aloft, his face a timeless blend of shock and sheer elation. Everything about that story made Bradbury an instant Aussie hero. He was the heroic outsider. He was literally the last man standing. Today, 'Doing a Bradbury' means to pull off an unexpected or unlikely victory from a seemingly hopeless position.

Beyond alpine recreation, stories of colourful mountain characters and their gritty exploits abound. Canberra-based author Klaus Hueneke's books, including *Huts of the High Country* and *Kiandra to Kosciuszko*, document the lives and adventures of those for whom happiness was a ramshackle tin hut and a cup of a hot tea around the fire. To read Hueneke's work is to be transported to a place of warmth and humanity, hope and endurance, even as a frigid south-westerly whistles through the cracks of a hut's walls. Hueneke even tells the story of a timber structure that once stood atop Kosciuszko. In the 1890s, British meteorologist Clement Wragge built an observatory on the summit. His nickname 'Inclement' Wragge would never prove more apt. The observatory eventually burned down. That was after rain flooded it, snow buried it, rats infested it and the wind just about blew it across the Tasman Sea to New Zealand.

Some stories are so big, they literally changed the mountains. The Snowy Mountains Scheme was a hydro-electric and irrigation project which remains Australia's largest engineering feat. Started in 1949 and completed a quarter of a century later, the Snowy Scheme was monumental in both size and ambition, damming mountain rivers and storing and diverting their waters for irrigation and hydro-electric power generation. As many as 100,000 workers toiled on the Snowy Scheme, the majority emigrating from Europe post–World War II. Many became key figures in the cultural life of the mountains and the development of the ski industry.

While Australia benefited economically and socially from the Snowy Scheme, environmentally it was a catastrophe. Dams reduced the Snowy River's flow by as much as 99 per cent, and while campaigning by environmentalists eventually saw its flow restored to around a third of the old average, the huge sand banks far above the waterline on the river's middle reaches tell you the river is still a ghost of its old self.

There has been human tragedy in these mountains too. The first person killed in an Australian avalanche was a young woman called Roslyn Wesche, who was staying in Kunama Hutte, a ski lodge built high up the Main Range in an area where development of any kind is no longer permitted for both safety and environmental reasons. There have since been numerous victims of both avalanches and bad weather, some killed by bad luck, others by a lack of respect for the conditions. On a bad day, the Australian High Country weather is merciless, partly due to rain, snow, ice and low temperatures but also due to the mountains' ancient geography, with the rounded summits providing no barrier against wild gales that roar northward from Antarctic waters.

It was undoubtedly the weather that killed Laurie Seaman and Evan Hayes. The duo set off for Mt Kosciuszko on skis on 14 August 1928, in an age when the first basic hotels had begun to pop up in the mountains, but were never seen alive again after leaving Charlotte Pass, although both bodies were eventually recovered. Film developed from Seaman's camera showed that both men had reached the summit. After that, who knows? The search was the talk of Australia for months but these mountains can keep a secret. Today, the spot where Seaman was found is marked by Seaman's Hut, a sturdy stone shelter resembling the refuges of Europe's Alps. It's a welcome sight for hikers or back country skiers or snowboarders when the Main Range weather turns ugly in any season. A plaque inside tells of the ordeal of Seaman and Hayes. Nowhere are the names William Rutherford or Alex Brindle mentioned. They were the Aboriginal trackers who led the search for Seaman and Hayes and the whole operation would have been impossible without them.

One famous story of tragedy evolved into a story of heroic survival. In 1997, a landslide in the ski village of Thredbo took out two ski lodges and killed eighteen people. Overnight temperatures dropped to minus fourteen degrees as rescuers combed the rubble for survivors. And then, with hope virtually extinguished nearly three days after the slide, they heard a voice.

Stuart Diver, a 27-year-old ski instructor, had miraculously survived more or less unhurt. Tragically his wife, Sally, had died beside him. The dazed look on his face as he surfaced was captured in an immortal news photograph. 'That sky's fantastic,' he reportedly told rescuers as they pulled him out.

Banjo Paterson also wrote about those fantastic Kosciuszko skies in the final stanza of 'The Man from Snowy River' in the lines 'the white stars fairly blaze / At midnight in the cold and frosty sky'. It's an undeniably beautiful piece of poetry. If you're ever around a High Country campfire and a Banjo devotee is reciting the poem, that'll be the moment when their throat reveals a lump. Those blazing white stars might also be read as an unintended play on words. Like the gleaming white snow for which the High Country is famous, the stars of its folklore are all white too.

Among people of European origin, perhaps only the rock band Midnight Oil have told a story linking Kosciuszko with Aboriginal people. Their anthemic song 'Kosciusko' appeared on their 1984 album *Red Sails in the Sunset* and is one of their best. Drummer Rob Hirst penned the lyrics and is well aware of Strzelecki's exploits and Kosciuszko's admirable work in 'lifting the subjugation of enslaved people in the USA', as he puts it. But he's equally mindful of what he calls 'the ancient nature of the mountain's creation which reflects the similar longevity of Australia's First Nations custodians'.

Each verse of the song begins with the phrase 'Older than Kosciusko', followed by lyrics invoking the disruption to ancient ways caused by mining companies in the outback. Even though Kosciuszko is a long way from the outback, the mountain serves as a symbol of an ancient place, a sacred place, the sort of place that can be ruined forever in a blink by exploitative land use. 'The song predicting an imaginary clash between the oldest cultures of our continent and the arrival of mining companies was informed by events such as the 1967 Referendum, the

Wave Hill Walk Off (1966 to 1975) and the commencement of Ranger's uranium mine's operations in the Northern Territory in 1981,' Hirst says.

In their signature song 'Beds are Burning', written three years after 'Kosciusko', Midnight Oil sang that it was time to pay both our rent and our share. You might argue the band was speaking metaphorically rather than literally calling for reparations. Perhaps they just wanted us to pay our share of attention to what's happening in this country. That's the problem with most stories told by white folk about Kosciuszko. They can be heroic and tragic, inspirational and epic but rarely do they address the true state of Country.

That doesn't mean such stories aren't out there. It's time to hear some Aboriginal tales of the mountains, and where better to start than the Snowy River?

CHAPTER 28

THE STONE FROM SNOWY RIVER

The moon took the water from the ocean and travelled to the mountains. When the moon fell asleep in the mountains, the platypus burst the moon's waterbags and the water gushed out. And that, according to Ngarigo Elder Uncle Rod Mason, is how the Snowy River formed.

Aboriginal people tell contemporary tales of the Snowy too. Richard Swain is a Wiradjuri man who grew up on Ngarigo country and guides multi-day paddling trips down the Snowy. The severely diminished flow disturbs him on a personal and spiritual level but it's not his only lament. The landscape used to be a haven for yam daisies and their nutritious tubers, before brumbies got to them. The brumbies even ate the seeds of the giant phragmites reeds along Reedy Creek, a small tributary of the Snowy, during the crippling 2017–20 drought. Now the reeds are gone, all of them, because they couldn't reproduce. Ngarigo Elders Uncle Max Dulumunmun Harrison and Uncle Snappy told Swain the story of a nearby massacre, when the kids hid in the giant reeds. The University of Newcastle's

Centre for 21st Century Humanities has documented the time and location of 416 massacres of Aboriginal people from 1788 to 1930. The massacre near the small tributary of the Snowy is not one of those documented. Some stories survive only through oral history.

If there's one story about the Snowy River that every Australian should read or hear, it's 'The Learning Walk' by Monero-Ngarigo Elder Aunty Rachel Mullett. It tells the tale of a trek down the Snowy River undertaken by Mullett's people for millennia from their High Country home all the way to the Victorian coastline. The detail in the story is fantastic as Mullett actually undertook the walk as a little girl. The people followed the river for hundreds of kilometres – the women with grass baskets filled with food slung from their hips and shoulders while they carried sleeping rugs and their babies, the men up ahead with spears and boomerangs. Eventually they reached the sea and the children saw for the first time huge yellow sand dunes and the rolling waves of the ocean. They feasted on fish, mussels and oysters in estuarine lakes then continued along the coast to Mallacoota, where the men had a corroboree. Then they journeyed home, enjoying the fruits of the fire-stick farming they had employed at certain spots along the river on their way south, with plenty of kangaroos to hunt among the fresh growth. The people then returned to the high mountains to participate in the summer bogong moth feast.

Those are three stories of the Snowy River – one mythological, one ecological and one anthropological – and none of them involve horses or heroic rides. Indeed, there's a story that suggests there was no heroic ride. Travelling down the Snowy with Richard Swain in 2019, he pointed out a craggy hill with the unusual name Where Dick Got Frightened. Seems there was a half Aboriginal, half Irish stockman called Dick who chose not to pursue his cattle after they took off down the precipitous slope. The hill is in the Byadbo Wilderness, the dry landscape of pine-clad ridges where Banjo Paterson likely set 'The Man from Snowy River'. So was the daring ride itself a fictional creation, just like the white rider? Did Banjo Paterson transform cows into horses and invent the heroic pursuit? Is the most popular white story in the mountains a glorified version of an Aboriginal story? Was Banjo the ultimate unreliable narrator?

Only in recent decades have High Country Aboriginal stories been widely shared in the public realm so that Australians might hear them and undertake their own metaphorical learning walk. Uncle Rod Mason's story about the creation of the Snowy River appeared in the 2002 book *Snowy River Story: The Grassroots Campaign to Save a National Icon* by Claire Miller. The tale of Dyillagamberra the Rainmaker also comes from Mason, and appeared in a New South Wales National Parks and Wildlife Service leaflet around 2007. The full version of 'The Learning Walk' appeared in a collection called *Nyernila – Listen Continuously: Aboriginal Creation Stories of Victoria* published by Creative Victoria in 2014. And in 2000, National Parks and Wildlife Service publications officer Mike Young compiled *The Aboriginal People of the Monaro* with Ngarigo women Ellen and Debbie Mundy. This was a landmark work. For the first time, the history of the traditional owners of country had been comprehensively captured in print form.

In places, *The Aboriginal People of the Monaro* is a harrowing read. The first European arrivals on the Monaro in the 1820s brought with them smallpox, guns, influenza and alcohol – each lethal in their own way.

The Europeans desecrated sacred sites, causing loss of face among Elders and exacerbating tensions between clans. Land was cleared, destroying the scrub in which game could be hunted. The Europeans over-burned the land in a childishly simplistic and ineffectual imitation of fire-stick farming. And all of this happened in the shadow of a mountain that would soon be named for Kosciuszko, who gave his two favourite pistols to a chief of America's Miami nation and urged him to shoot dead the first man who came to subjugate him or despoil his country.

If one section of *The Aboriginal People of the Monaro* sums up the catastrophic clash of cultures, it's the six pages devoted to blankets. Long farcical story short, the disruption to traditional ways was so abrupt and complete that the Monaro people were unable to make the possum skin rugs that had kept them warm in winter for millennia. That's because making a possum skin rug took more than know-how and possums. A complex social structure was required. Men hunted the possums. Women dressed the skins. Men then sewed the skins into rugs, decorated them and distributed them along kinship lines or through gift exchange. When the traditional way of living on country broke down, social structure went with it and making possum skin rugs became like trying to manufacture automobiles without an assembly line. The European solution? Blankets! What could possibly go wrong? Blankets weren't waterproof like possum skins, that's what. Indeed, possum skin rugs were so waterproof, the Monaro people could sleep snug and dry in almost any weather. Under sodden blankets, many inevitably died of respiratory diseases. Young illustrates this with a memorably deadpan quote from the 1893 book *The Book of the Bush* by Australian author George Dunderdale:

> It had been the commissioner's duty to give one blanket annually to each native, and thus that garment became to

him the Queen's livery, and an emblem of civilisation; it raised the savage in the scale of humanity, and encouraged him to take the first step of the march of progress. His second step was into the grave.

As the surviving Ngarigo people of the Monaro became unable to live on their land in the traditional manner by around the mid-nineteenth century, some men became stockmen and some women joined them as rural labourers managing stock, while other women became housekeepers for white settlers. Others moved to the south coast, where most of the Ngarigo live to this day, unable to return to Country because of massively inflated property prices in ski towns like Jindabyne.

One of the many casualties was language. The grammatical structure of the Ngarigo language is now known by only a handful of people, with most Ngarigo knowing just phrases and words.

A tiny but invaluable fragment was preserved in 1834, when the Austrian naturalist John Lhotsky travelled in early autumn to the Snowy Mountains region via the Monaro plains. Lhotsky climbed several peaks – though almost certainly not the mountain that Strzelecki would name Kosciuszko six years later – but the high point of his journey from a cultural perspective was his presence at the performance of a song by Ngarigo women, the melody and lyrics of which he committed to paper as best he could. Back in Sydney, Lhotsky arranged the song as a piece of parlour music, and it's said to have been the first piece of Australian music ever printed.

The song lives on today, and while the Djinama Yilaga choir didn't perform it in their 2023 performances in Poland, it has become part of their repertoire. In 2021, musicologist Linda Barwick and Ngarigo woman Professor Jakelin Troy re-evaluated Lhotsky's sheet music in the journal *Musicology Australia* in an article entitled 'Claiming the "Song of the Women of the Menero Tribe"'. They argued that the music revealed not just the key role of women in Ngarigo music, but was an insight into the way that the Ngarigo saw themselves as custodians of Country.

> The Song text as analysed appears to be an attempt by Ngarigu to influence the return of the snow and all that is associated with snow and its subsequent melt that sustains the alpine ecosystem. Given the time of year it was performed, it is also possible that the Song marked the end of the bogong season and was part of a ceremony to ensure the right environmental conditions for the moths to again increase in the spring.

Professor Troy is Director of Aboriginal and Torres Strait Islander Research at the University of Sydney with an office in the university's signature sandstone Quadrangle. But it would be a mistake to cast her as an ivory-tower academic. Anyone lucky enough to walk on Country with Troy will soon see she knows and understands it intimately. At the top of Thredbo's Kosciuszko chairlift are two large groups of rocks. Troy says the group on the left as you ride the chair is called the Ancestor Rocks and that you must always greet the ancestors. The cluster to the right of the chairlift top station is called the Sentinel Rocks and the grassy hollows below the rocks were a birthing place and a site of women's business.

I must have ridden that old chairlift a thousand times in winter when you factor in two seasons working on the mountain and however many years as a recreational skier and bushwalker. Often I have admired both groups of rocks. It's impossible to miss them. In the increasingly rare heavy snow seasons, the Ancestor Rocks become partially buried by drifting snow, and are a favourite spot for daring skiers and snowboarders to launch themselves off. The Sentinel Rocks are never buried, and are often coated in other-worldly encrustations of ice called rime, formed by tiny airborne water droplets which freeze on contact when blown by strong winds onto cold surfaces. To most visitors, the groups of rocks are a sign that you've reached the top of Australia's longest chairlift. But who knew they had symbolic value to the traditional owners of Country? Who can imagine how many summer newborns filled their lungs with menthol wafts of alpine mint in their very first breath underneath the giant tors of the Sentinel Rocks? And who knew you had to greet the ancestors as you approach their rocks? Is there some terrible punishment for failing to do so?

'Well, you haven't died yet,' Troy deadpans.

'If I remember to greet them every time I ride the chair for the rest of my life, will that make up for it?'

'You have an obligation to do so, and make sure you tell people you're with to greet them too.'

People, you heard Professor Troy. Ancestor Rocks on the left, Sentinel Rocks on the right as you head up the Kosciuszko chairlift at Thredbo. Pay through the nose for the privilege of riding this thing, and pay your respects to the ancestors because lord knows, the descendants of the ancestors haven't been shown much respect in the last 200 years.

From 1892, many Ngarigo who remained on the Monaro were shunted onto the Aboriginal Reserve at Delegate, south of Jindabyne, a place where people of neighbouring Nations had traditionally camped on their seasonal travels.

In the late nineteenth and early twentieth centuries, governments set aside three types of spaces for Aboriginal people to live on: missions, reserves and managed reserves, each with slightly different forms of administration and regulation. The establishment of these places was framed as 'protection', although as one senior Parks staffer puts it, 'the traditional owners were treated like wildlife, not people'. The advent of the reserves and missions coincided with Federation, in 1901, when the disparate self-governing colonies united to form the modern nation of Australia. One of the first pieces of Federal legislation was the *Immigration Restriction Act*, which formed the basis of what became known as the White Australia Policy. The policy was designed to keep non-Europeans (mostly Asians) out of Australia but it indirectly affected Aboriginal people, fuelling a fresh wave of resentment and suspicion against anyone without white skin. It also laid the foundation for the policy of removing Aboriginal children from their families and assimilating them into white society in what came to be known as the Stolen Generations. The Ngarigo were not immune. Children were taken from across the Monaro district, even from families who had built a life for themselves in towns.

Severed from Country, family ties, language and cultural practices, it's little wonder that the Ngarigo were for so long virtually invisible as the traditional custodians of the land. Aboriginal people have always viewed themselves as inseparable from the land. The word 'Country' as used by Aboriginal people means more than the land and waterways and wildlife. It entails the idea of people living upon it, and the laws and lore of those people dating back to the Dreamtime. Without a living connection to Country, how can stories be told? And without stories, how can people understand anything about Country?

Aboriginal stories of the High Country haven't yet percolated into popular culture in the manner of 'The Man from Snowy River'. But their gradual emergence in National Parks material and elsewhere reflects the broader awakening of all Australians to the rights and traditions of Aboriginal people. In 1962, all Aboriginal Australians were finally granted the right to vote in Federal elections. In 1973, the White Australia Policy was abolished. In 1992, the Mabo decision granting Native Title was handed down. In 2008, the Apology to the Stolen Generations was delivered by then Prime Minister Kevin Rudd. At primary school in the 1980s, history lessons were all about Captain Cook. Kids now know the name of their local Aboriginal Nation. The result of The Voice referendum in 2023 – when sixty per cent of Australians rejected a proposal for the establishment of a parliamentary advisory body comprised of Indigenous representatives – denied Aboriginal people a permanent national voice in the Federal parliament. But you'd better believe they're raising their voice at a local level. And if you want to know what the Ngarigo voice sounds like, there's one standout example.

Every five years, Kosciuszko National Park staff prepare management plans for the park. In the process of drafting the 2006 Plan of Management, regional manager Dave Darlington wanted Aboriginal input. The previous plan only had a perfunctory paragraph about Aboriginal people and their traditional connections to Country. Darlington and his team were keen to include more.

'He wanted to have a statement up front explaining what the park meant to traditional groups,' explains Ngarigo Elder Iris White. 'He wanted to capture what our aspirations were, and that was a really new thing for us. My mum never thought she would have the opportunity.'

Iris grew up on Wallaga Lake Aboriginal Station, a managed reserve on the New South Wales south coast. Her family later moved to a housing commission home in Bomaderry, about two hours south of Sydney. Life wasn't easy. The family was among the first Aboriginal people in a tough part of town and Iris had to leave school at fourteen to care for her brothers and sisters when her parents found work in Nowra. But she had good people around her. She worked at the fish and chip shop in the school holidays, completed a secretarial course at Nowra TAFE, and eventually won a scholarship to go to university in Sydney, graduating with a Bachelor in Adult Education and forging a career in the education and public policy sectors.

While the statement in the Kosciuszko Plan of Management was a collaboration among the Ngarigo themselves and also with other groups whose lands lie nearby, when you meet Iris in her neat home in Moruya on the south coast, you can feel her hands all over it – not in a domineering way but like the hand symbols in Aboriginal rock paintings, which represent belonging and the importance of community.

The statement was called Yerribie/Dhirrayn. Yerribie means 'going' or 'moving' in the Ngarigo language, while Dhirrayn means 'mountains' in the Wiradjuri tongue. Together, that makes 'moving mountains' and in a metaphorical context, that's what the people were trying to do with their statement, as in shifting the way we see the mountains.

It started with the basics:

Our Mother binds us to our laws/lores. This country is our Mother. We – the Aboriginal People of the Mountains – belong to this country. She is our beginning, giving us our identity and culture. She brings us together and takes us away.

The Mountains are very old and an ongoing life force that strengthens the ancestral link of our people. We have a living, spiritual connection with the mountains. We retain family stories and memories of the mountains, which makes them spiritually and culturally significant to us. Our traditional knowledge and cultural practices still exist and need to be maintained.

In the spirit of inclusivity, it mentioned Nations whose territory was close by, or who travelled seasonally to the mountains, even if they didn't live on Country:

> We recognise the diversity of Aboriginal clans and People of the Mountains – Wiradjuri, Wolgalu, Ngunnawal, Monaro Ngarigo … We recognise that Wiradjuri, Wolgalu and Ngunnawal are known by their totem, and acknowledge the matrilineal (mother's) bloodline of the Monaro Ngarigo people. We also acknowledge that many other clans have associations with the mountains.

Mt Kosciuszko isn't mentioned but it's there if you read between the lines:

> The mountains recognise the language names given by our people and naming of places strengthens our living culture.

There was a strong environmental message:

> Living by natural cycles, the land provides our people with life, ceremony, family lore/law and resources, such as tools, plant medicine, plant food, waters, fish, animals and insects e.g. the Bogong moth, while the melting of the snow gives life to the many creeks and rivers that flow out of the mountains. There are places of spiritual and physical significance to our people, and we are committed

to working in partnership with others to protect, maintain and manage these places.

There was a feisty appraisal of the impact of the first white settlers, of the reserves and missions, the Stolen Generations and other cruel policies and practices:

> Forced separation from our land had a profound impact on our family life. European governance disrupted and destroyed our traditional ways. We were moved away from our country and many people were herded onto missions. Aboriginal family lives were torn apart with the removal of children, and people were threatened with death in some instances if they tried to practice their traditional ways, especially lore, language and culture.

And there was a vision expressed for the future, one which entailed spiritual, cultural and economic wellbeing for all:

> It is our vision for the future to cooperatively and collaboratively work with the National Parks and Wildlife Service to manage the park and maintain its spiritual, natural and cultural values. This will build a strong cultural and economic base for future generations of our people. The development and provision of employment, training and economic opportunities will deliver benefits to our people and communities. Our culture will be strengthened by access to our traditional lands and the development and participation of our people in cultural camps and cultural maintenance programs. By passing on knowledge to future generations of Aboriginal children, our culture will stay alive and strong.

Again, you have to realise the significance of that statement. It didn't matter that it would mostly be read by bureaucrats and interest groups. It was out there. For the first time since colonisation, the Ngarigo were publicly expressing what Kosciuszko meant to them. They were telling their story. The Ngarigo had a voice. Unfortunately, maintaining a united voice would not prove straightforward.

Around the same time as the Yerribie/Dhirrayn statement, Dave Darlington and his staff set up two Indigenous groups, one for the Ngarigo, another representing a mix of people in the north of the park where it borders other nations and even includes a portion of Wolgalu country. Darlington commissioned a Memorandum of Understanding for each group – a non-legally-binding document that would formalise a working relationship between Parks and traditional owners, incorporating Aboriginal knowledge into park management. The northern group drafted theirs quickly. Plagued by infighting, the Ngarigo took over a decade. That's why a dual naming proposal for Kosciuszko National Park stalled, even though it was marked as 'high priority' in the draft of the 2006 Plan of Management.

Why the hold-up with what ended up being a simple eleven-page document? Partly, it was because Indigenous societies, like any society, will never be united on any or all issues. It's also worth noting that Australian Aboriginal Nations historically had no chiefs, kings, queens or even Elders who alone have the ultimate right to speak on behalf of Country. But the Ngarigo have a unique source of disharmony. Because most of them have lived off Country for generations, clans often don't know other clans. Complicating matters, many Ngarigo have only recently felt comfortable embracing their heritage. 'Aboriginal ancestry was something to be ashamed of and not something to be curious about,' Wimbledon champ Ash Barty wrote about her Ngarigo paternal grandparents in her memoir *My Dream Time*. Others didn't even know they were Ngarigo until recently. When you've got Elders who grew up in the 1950s and 1960s with the lived experience of poverty and discrimination, and others whose experiences were completely different, and when there's a lack of trust between the two groups, how do you move forward?

Anyway, they got it done. In 2016, the Memorandum of Understanding between the National Parks and Wildlife Service and the Southern Snowy Mountains Aboriginal Community finally saw daylight, with the parties agreeing 'to act cooperatively as partners for management and protection of the Country and culture'. And while a memo never changed the world, ancient knowledge did, and Indigenous knowledge is increasingly being incorporated into land management practices as joint management of national parks between Parks and traditional owners is adopted.

The joint management model has worked well at Uluru–Kata Tjuta National Park since 1985, and the Ngarigo and others will play a hands-on role in Kosciuszko's future if the model is introduced there. There are already hurdles. Kosciuszko National Park's mostly white staff find it difficult to attract young Ngarigo people to junior ranger positions because most of them live off Country and can't bear to leave the close bonds of family. But at least the knowledge carried by the traditional owners is valued in the mountains now, and you'd better believe it's needed.

In 2021, John Barilaro lashed the mountains with his stockwhip one more time before he quit politics later that year. In declaring the Snowy Mountains a Special Activation Precinct, the extremely colourful politician behind the legislation protecting brumbies left the door ajar for the government to employ special planning powers that could potentially override parts of the Kosciuszko National Park Plan of Management. The Special Activation Precinct designation is designed to turbo-charge the local tourist economy, and while there are worthy projects on the SAP agenda, like the Jindabyne bypass, critics worry that the environmental and Aboriginal heritage of the mountains will be shunted aside as lesser concerns, just as they were for the better part of 200 years.

Cut to 2022, when Iris White was asked to conduct a Welcome to Country ceremony for Special Activation Precinct planners in Jindabyne. Some Australians loathe Welcome to Country ceremonies, idiotically arguing that they don't need to be welcomed to their own country, thanks very much. That is missing the point by the length of the Snowy River.

'What we actually do in a Welcome to Country is we are welcoming people into a relationship with us,' Iris explains. 'It's not, "Here's our Country, welcome to it." Our culture is based on relationships and reciprocity and that is what we're actually doing.'

Iris reckons she might have confused a few people at that event. 'I took a rock from the Snowy River and put it on the table. I said, "That rock carries story for this Country and I'm going to leave it with you."' So she left the rock.

Once or twice since, she's asked people what happened to it and they've told her, 'Oh, it's here somewhere.' Maybe that rock now sits on some mid-level bureaucrat's desk as a paperweight. Maybe it's in the bottom drawer of a dusty filing cabinet in a locked room in a poorly lit corridor in the basement of an outbuilding of Snowy Monaro Regional Council, like the Ark of the Covenant in the giant government warehouse at the end of *Raiders of the Lost Ark*. But maybe, just maybe, the rock is in an enthusiastic young town planner's hands and they're trying to learn from it, asking it all the right questions. 'Rock from the Snowy River, what can you tell us about how to care for this country? What stories do you hold that are richer, more meaningful and more relevant to tens of thousands of years of human history than the stories told in the last 200 years?'

CHAPTER 29

A POLISH PICKLE

Just as the Ngarigo were re-establishing their rightful place as a key voice up in Kosciuszko, another player emerged: the Australian Polish community.

Polish Australians have long brimmed with pride at the exploits of Strzelecki and at Kosciuszko's name sitting atop Australia, although for years there was no formal expression of that passion in the mountains. That changed with the delivery of a giant Strzelecki statue to Jindabyne in 1988, Poland's gift to Australia for the bicentenary. Look at the mighty Pole, immortalised in bronze in Banjo Paterson Park on the grassy shores of Lake Jindabyne, all four metres, 3.2 tonnes and $1.5 million dollars of him, pointing toward Mt Kosciuszko with supreme assuredness, like he knew exactly where he was heading, which he absolutely did not. You have to wonder if the delivery truck got lost too. Jindabyne is the base for Kosciuszko National Park tourism, so the statue's location makes sense for visitor traffic, but the town sits on the eastern side of the mountains, while Strzelecki approached from the lower country to the west. It's a bit like if the memorial to Captain Cook's landing in Botany Bay had been situated in

Sydney Harbour, which Cook never sailed into. Anyway, the Strzelecki statue is a fixture in the mountains now and so too is the Australian Polish community.

Blame it all on vodka. After a Polish community event in Sydney in 2006, a small crowd kicked on at the home of Andrzej and Ernestyna Kozek, a warm, energetic pair of academics who were both born in Poland but made their lives in Australia. The merrymakers knocking back late-night vodka shots included members of amateur woodwind ensemble the Sydney Windjammers, who had played at the event earlier that evening. Ernestyna asked a band member if he might consider including Kosciuszko's music in a performance.

'Kosciuszko's miniatures can be described as typical salon pieces of the late 18th century. They are short, charming pieces, suitable for entertaining the audiences in small settings,' wrote Polish American pianist and educator Magdalena Adamek in a piece entitled 'Tadeusz Kosciuszko – a Cosmopolitan and an Artist' in the University of Warmia and Mazury in Olsztyn's 2018 *Artistic Forum*, Volume I.

Kosciuszko's music might have been ideal for small settings but the band member immediately had an idea to play it in a much bigger setting. 'Let's play Kosciuszko music on top of Mt Kosciuszko!' he said. And that's exactly what happened.

The performance took place on 17 February 2007 and it was quite the scene. A Polish flag was draped over the summit plinth. The Windjammers were joined by Polish dancers in traditional costume from Sydney's Lajkonik Polish song and dance ensemble. You couldn't have asked for a milder, more benign, windless day and there were plenty of day-tripping hikers in the impromptu audience. A Polish TV station even covered it. Ursula Lang, artistic director and co-founder of Lajkonik, was thrilled. Australian-born of Polish descent,

Lang had put in long hours working with Kosciuszko National Park regional manager Dave Darlington organising the event. In coming years, she would put in plenty more.

In 2007, Lang and the Kozeks founded Kosciuszko Heritage, an incorporated organisation with the aim of promoting knowledge of Strzelecki and Kosciuszko, especially the latter. They started a cultural festival in the mountains called K'Ozzie Fest which they described as 'an annual, vibrant celebration of the Snowy Mountains, Australia's diverse multicultural society and the ideals of democracy and freedom'. They also invested time and effort building bridges with mountain communities, including the Ngarigo, and developed the website kosciuszkoheritage.com, a goldmine of information on Kosciuszko, Strzelecki and more. Unapologetically, a key objective of Kosciuszko Heritage is to keep Kosciuszko's name on the mountain, but from day one the founders were savvy enough to position that aim as beneficial to all, framing the exemplary deeds and values of both Kosciuszko and Strzelecki as embodying Australian values and aspirations.

Kosciuszko Heritage had a rocky start. The festival enjoyed only moderate success. Meanwhile, some Aboriginal people were outwardly hostile toward both Lang and the Kozeks at cross cultural workshops organised by Parks. 'We gave them a postcard with Strzelecki on it and Aunty Deanna Davison threw it back at us,' Lang recalls.

Lang took a group of Ngarigo people down to the Strzelecki statue to talk about his values and was asked by one member of the group, 'Why are you showing us a statue of a European?'

Attitudes slowly softened as the Poles showed that they were genuinely interested in Aboriginal culture. A cut-through moment came after Lang gave some Aboriginal Elders a copy of the chapter 'The Aborigines' from Strzelecki's 1845 report to Governor Gipps, *Physical Description of New South Wales and Van Diemen's Land*. As mentioned earlier, that chapter contained rare insights for a European of the age, with Strzelecki demonstrating an understanding of the complexity of Aboriginal culture and genuine sympathy toward their plight.

After reading the 23-page chapter, one Elder was sold. 'Strzelecki must have been a good man. The Spirits of the Mountain must have looked after him,' she told Lang.

Within a few years, the Poles had been accepted by most of the Ngarigo. 'Are our Polish friends coming down?' one Elder asked as she organised events in the mountains for NAIDOC Week, the annual national celebration of the history, culture and achievements of Aboriginal and Torres Strait Islander peoples.

Sitting with Ursula Lang and her partner, Tony, in their spacious home on acreage in the hills above the Hawkesbury River on Sydney's far north-western outskirts, it's unbelievably difficult not to make a pig of yourself as they present a generous plate of kielbasa and garlicky homemade Polish pickles. Lang has just retired from her forty-year career as a town planner but remains committed to her Polish song and dance ensemble, Lajkonik. She's also an active member of the Southern Ranges Regional Advisory Committee, which means she retains an input on affairs in Kosciuszko. She's proud that the Australian Polish community is now viewed as a stakeholder in the region and says it's a shame that Australians don't understand more about Tadeusz Kosciuszko, believing it to be a failure of the education system. And she's as determined as ever to keep Kosciuszko's name on the mountain.

'The mountain didn't have one Aboriginal name but it's got the opportunity of keeping one name we can all share and accept and be proud of too because that name represents those values that are dear to us all as Australians,' she says. 'Human rights and equality are important values that we all share in multicultural Australia and I would like to see some sort of formal decision where the name of Mt Kosciuszko is endorsed in perpetuity.'

Still in Sydney's north-west but a little closer to town, Andrzej and Ernestyna Kozek will kill you with kindness and crumbly Polish cherry cake, overlooked by portraits of their heroes, Strzelecki and Kosciuszko. Ernestyna says Strzelecki had a Polish affliction known as pioro w dupie – literally 'a feather in the ass'. It seems to imply that he was an energetic but also somewhat restless soul who just couldn't sit still, always moving from one project to the next.

The Kozeks are a bit like that themselves. Taking a group of Ngarigo to Poland in 2017 on the 200th anniversary of Kosciuszko's death, then again in 2023 on the 150th anniversary of Strzelecki's passing, were just two of their exploits. It seems that they've found their true purpose relatively late in the piece, and that mission is to foster understanding between the Australian Polish community, the Aboriginal people of the mountains and the wider Australian community, all in the name of preserving you-know-what.

'We dream to retain his name on the mountain,' Andrzej says. 'Remember that when Mt Kosciuszko was named in 1840, Poland did not exist. It was a reminder that our country did not vanish, even if it was no longer on the map.'

Poland has indeed done it tougher than most nations over the years, stamped out of existence as an independent nation for well over a century after the failed Kosciuszko Uprising, then sold out to the communists at the end of World War II. But were not Aboriginal societies similarly erased from the

High Country? Were the missions and reserves any less an assault on traditional ways than the Nazi invasion of Poland or Poland's post-war puppet Soviet government? And what about the doctrine of Terra Nullius that said the land was never yours anyway? If Australia's highest mountain is to serve as reminder of a country that did not vanish even though its people were brutalised and robbed of nationhood, should not that country be the land of the Ngarigo and other nearby groups?

To his credit, Andrzej is no denier of Australia's dark past. Like Ursula Lang, he believes that the name Kosciuszko can help Australians reconcile its history and navigate toward a more enlightened future because of the values of Kosciuszko himself and those of Strzelecki, the man who named the mountain.

'It is certain that both Kosciuszko and Strzelecki would have supported the Aboriginal position because the Aborigines barely survived the colonial invasion and so much had been stolen from them,' he says. 'Yet these native people originally requested changing the name of the mountain without knowing anything about who Tadeusz Kosciuszko was, or of his stance on slavery, of the story of his will, or about his strong support for equality.'

Does it change the equation that Strzelecki and Kosciuszko were exemplary characters who championed the rights of the oppressed?

According to Aboriginal man Richard Walley, it does not. 'These places have been there for thousands of years and identify themselves. They are greater than the individuals or groups who claim to have discovered them,' he said in 2005 with specific reference to Mt Kosciuszko.

Walley is a Nyoongar man from Western Australia who is a well-known artist, performer, musician and cultural educator. Along with the actor and TV personality Ernie Dingo, he helped usher the millennia-old Welcome to Country ceremony into everyday use, to the point where it has become a fixture at the opening of proceedings in Federal Parliament. But why was a West Australian Aboriginal man commenting on a mountain almost 4000 kilometres to the east?

It all started with a group called Mt Kosciuszko Inc based in Perth. Like the Sydney-based Kosciuszko Heritage, the passionate Perth Poles incorporated and made a website – in their case mtkosciuszko.org.au. When an early draft version of the 2006 Kosciuszko National Park Plan of Management came to the group's attention, they were incensed at the high priority given to proposed dual naming (even though only the park, not the mountain itself, had been mooted for dual naming status). So they took their outrage to the state's biggest newspaper, *The West Australian*.

The first article appeared on 15 January 2005. That's the one in which Richard Walley gave the quote about the places being greater than the people who claim to have discovered them. A follow-up article appeared on 17 January under the headline, 'Expat Poles rally to defence of Kosciuszko', and the story included a breakout box with two phone numbers that readers could call to express their view, one for yes and one for no, in a very 2005 way of doing reader polls.

The same day, *The West Australian* ran a brief editorial stating that the call a few years earlier by Tumbarumba Mayor George Martin to rename Mt Kosciuszko was 'an unwarranted attempt to interfere with a national icon'. This wasn't the worst op-ed ever to appear in an Australian newspaper on matters relating to mountain names in the High Country. That honour belongs to a piece in *The Border Mail* of Albury Wodonga in 2008, after a range in the Victorian High Country got a long overdue name change to the Jaithmathangs, the name of the local Aboriginal

Nation. A nearby Nation disputed the name change but that's not the point of the story. The point is that for the previous 100-plus years, the range had been known as the Ni--erheads. 'Who gave Gavin Jennings, the Victorian Environmental Minister, the authority to change the name of the mountain range, The Ni--erheads, to some unpronounceable name?' thundered the writer. In case you're wondering, he spelled it out in full.

When people so passionately defend an overtly racist name, you can only imagine how hard they'll fight to keep the name honouring a man of Kosciuszko's character. The poll results published in *The West Australian* on 18 January proved that. Of the 2237 people who responded, ninety-three per cent said no to the idea of a dual name for Mt Kosciuszko. 'If the opposition is so strong against changing the name from Kosciuszko how can they do it now?' asked Mt Kosciuszko Inc founding member Anna Habryn.

Most non-Indigenous Australians have moved forward in their understanding of the relationship of Aboriginal people to the land in recent years, but the huge margin of that 2005 phone poll still suggests you can bank on a great big ugly culture war when a serious, united push to rename Mt Kosciuszko inevitably arises. When that happens, there's one voice we'd all do well to listen to.

CHAPTER 30

THE LAST WISHES OF THE DEPARTED

So let's walk in the footsteps of the Ngarigo people, the Wolgalu, the Wiradjuri, the Ngunnawal, the Jaithmathang, the Dhudhuroa and others. Let's climb Mt Kosciuszko again, this time following the ancient bogong moth pathway taken by so many Nations, which was also the route taken by Strzelecki's party in 1840.

The route today is called Hannels Spur and it remains little-attempted because it's so tough compared to the hikes from Charlotte Pass or from the top of Thredbo. The track starts on the western side of the mountains at Geehi Flats campground, a grassy clearing lined with towering eucalypts. Camp here in summer and you'll fall asleep to the thudding hops of eastern grey kangaroos and the babble of the Swampy Plains River near its confluence with the Geehi River, then awaken to the wail of yellow-tailed black cockatoos. Hoisting a heavy pack on your back and fording the Geehi in swift, thigh-deep, amber-coloured water is the day's first challenge, each step courting catastrophe on slippery river stones. Aunty Rhonda Casey says

Aboriginal people named sections of rivers but not the entire river. It's a bit like the way they had 500 nations but no name for the enormous land now called Australia. She also says the Ngarigo believe that when crossing a river, you must cross and return at the same point or your soul will be left on the other side. With the car parked at Geehi Flats campground, returning the same way was always the plan. Retaining the soul will be a handy bonus.

From the southern bank of the Geehi, you cross a small floodplain dotted with coarse tussocks until a weathered timber sign appears. The sign says very little, and plenty.

Hannels Spur Track
1800m ascent
Moiras Flat 6.5 km
Mt Kosciuszko 15.5 km

In pure linear terms, 15.5 kilometres is hardly daunting. On flat terrain, it'd be half a day's walk for a seasoned bushwalker. But the slopes ahead are anything but level. Forget everything you've read about the modest nature of these mountains by international standards. If there's one place where Australia's highest peaks are intimidating, it's here.

Few Australians see the Main Range from the western side because most approach from Sydney and Canberra via the high Monaro plains to the east. But on this rugged western flank, the mountains plummet to the lowlands, eager to divest themselves of themselves. No North American ski resort has a vertical drop between the valley and the top of the highest ski lift that exceeds the elevation difference from the Geehi River valley to Mt Kosciuszko. That 1800-metre ascent is also more than half the altitude gap between Everest's Base Camp and summit. Climb Hannels Spur and you deserve every moth or muesli bar.

From the weather-beaten sign, the narrow trail disappears into the forest, weaving at first through white gum, red stringybark, broad-leaved peppermint and other lowland eucalypts. There are steep pitches and gentler pitches but always it's upward, upward, relentlessly upward. It feels like a giant hand is pushing you down. Perhaps it's Byamee reminding you who's boss around here. Every so often, fallen trees impede progress. Park rangers clear them periodically with chainsaws but they can never keep up. The vegetation becomes dense and scrubby in places, trapping heat like a rainforest. No-one is around. Macarthur's diary records that it was ninety degrees Fahrenheit (thirty-two Celsius) the day the Strzelecki party started up this route so they decided to wait until evening and ascend by moonlight before camping, probably about a third of the way up the range.

'A fine lyre-bird furnished an ample supper and consoled us for the want of water,' Macarthur wrote of that evening. It's a revealing entry. Despite all those swift rivers down below and the innumerable clear streams up high fed by snow drifts and sphagnum bog, this brutal shoulder of the range is devoid of drinking water. The path is damp and even muddy in places but there's nothing to drink. That's why backpacks are so heavy on this ascent – carrying three litres for the first section is the absolute minimum.

Upward. The cicadas are screaming. A leech hitches a ride. What is this madness? Why this obsession with Kozzie and Strezza? That's who they are right now. Too hard to say Kosciuszko and Strzelecki. Every step a slog, every syllable an effort. Speaking to one Ngarigo woman, she said the abbreviation Kozzie was disrespectful. Did she mean it was inconsiderate to Kosciuszko himself, or that it was a sign of over-familiarity for a man whose name doesn't belong here? Unclear at this time. Anyway, Strezza's two Aboriginal guides were called Charley Tarra and Jacky and there's no way that Charley and Jacky were the birth names of two Aboriginal men in 1840, so really, it's just levelling the playing field. If Europeans couldn't be bothered calling Aboriginal people by their real names, they ain't gettin' theirs on this climb. Charley and Jacky. Kozzie and Strezza. All men are created equal. These are the unfiltered neural firings on this brutal, waterless ascent. It's like a sweaty fever dream.

Three hours, four hours, five hours, nearly six hours. At last the forest opens up at Moiras Flat, a small clearing among burnt snow gums with a nearby trickling creek, the first water since the Geehi. Strezza and his party made it here around 10 am on 12 March 1840 and Macarthur recorded that the place showed unmistakable signs of human activity:

> The spot we had now reached was the favourite camping-ground of the natives during their annual visit to feast on the Boogan Moth. Traces of their camps were visible in all directions. Our sable friends arrive thin and half-starved; and in a few weeks' revelling on this extraordinary food, clothe their skinny frames in aldermanic contrast.

Upward still through the snow gum woodland. As the trees thin out, the world explodes in 'aldermanic contrast' – that is, it appears to become much bigger, as a quick Google search of Macarthur's archaic term reveals that 'aldermanic' apparently means large or plump. Gibbo, Pinnibar, then eventually Bogong appear, mountains of the Victorian High Country which have kept their Aboriginal names, the latter far in the distance, the first two rising blue and hulking above the Murray River valley with grey spines of burnt snow gums. The grass in the river valleys is yellow, a stark contrast to the palette of mountain colours. The air is now welcomingly cool and the first small snow patches come into view, still much further up. Strzelecki's description of a 'region of perpetual snows' was more poetic than accurate. Year-round snows have not covered this country since the Ice Age and as Strzelecki was climbing in mid-March – the start of autumn – it's unlikely there were more than a few remnant patches from the previous winter. Let's pick up his journey from this point.

Two hours after leaving Moiras Flat, Macarthur recorded that he had reached the 'open summit', by which he meant the tree line – the level at which trees will no longer grow due to a combination of temperature, wind and other localised factors. The going can't have been easy as they carried all sorts of gear, including a heavy mercury barometer – an instrument that measures air pressure, from which a mountain's height could be determined with reasonable accuracy. Later that day, Strzelecki would tell Macarthur that Mt Kosciuszko was 7800 feet. Five years later, in his report to Governor Gipps, he would write that it was 6510 feet. The mountain is in fact 7316 feet, or 2228 metres, so if you average out the two figures and cut Strzelecki a bit of scientific slack, you'd have to say he got close enough.

The final section from the tree line was tougher than expected for Strzelecki's party. Macarthur recorded that upper reaches of the range were covered with a thick, tall, nearly impassable grass which he called 'monnong grass', which probably meant ribbon grass, a species conspicuously absent today, another legacy of the bovine bulldozers that blitzed the Main Range.

In the early afternoon, in air that Macarthur described as 'bitterly cold', he sent Jacky and Charley to make camp lower down, possibly at the site of what today is called Byatts Camp, where they had left blankets and other provisions. He and Strzelecki continued upward, with Macarthur describing the final slog as a 'toilsome ascent' and 'laborious climb'. And then they were on the summit of Australia.

Except that they weren't.

From Geehi Flats, the highest visible peak is Mt Townsend, Australia's second-highest peak at 2209 metres, just nineteen metres lower than Kosciuszko. That's what Strzelecki had been aiming for all along, believing it to be the highest point in the land. But after clambering up Townsend's summit boulders, they soon realised they were mistaken, as Macarthur wrote:

> We found the actual summit divided into six or more points. The Count by the aid of his instruments quickly detected one of them as being in fact considerably higher than where we stood. A deep ravine, separating us from this, did not deter my adventurous friend; he determined to reach it. As the day was far advanced, I thought it more prudent to return toward the point where I had ordered the natives to await our return. Before leaving the Count he told me of his intention of recording his visit to the highest point in Australia by associating the name of Kosciusko with our successful ascent.

Two points worth quickly fleshing out: by 'the actual summit divided into six or more points', Macarthur clearly meant the crest of the range rather than the summit of one particular mountain. It's also worth revisiting the line about Strzelecki declaring his intention to name the highest mountain Kosciuszko. Again, the wording of that passage surely leaves open the strong possibility that Strzelecki had the name in mind from the start of the trip, long before he noticed that the mountain strongly resembled the Kosciuszko Mound in Krakow.

Reams have been written about what happened next. The most authoritative dissection of events was written by Lieutenant Colonel Hugh Powell Gough Clews, a Yorkshireman who became a leading Australian surveyor and an indispensable figure in the mountains during the construction of the Snowy Mountains Scheme in the 1950s. And if you're not sold on his qualifications, let the man himself sell them to you:

> Many descriptions have been written of the ascent of Mount Kosciusko by Paul Edmund Strzelecki. Most of these have been written by people not intimately acquainted with the topographical features of the approaches to Mount Kosciusko, and perhaps most of the writers have been persons normally working in an office, not being field men, and also having no personal experience of pushing into absolutely unknown, or unmapped country.

That's from the introduction to Clews' 1973 book *Strzelecki's Ascent of Mount Kosciusko*, a work both concise and precise. In it, Clews concludes that Strzelecki summited Mt Kosciuszko in late afternoon before remaining on the summit until around 7.30 pm, performing a range of scientific observations with his sextant and geological tools. Based on Clews' meticulously researched timeline, it seems certain that Strzelecki had enough time to summit Kosciuszko after Townsend, even though his progress was again slowed by that long, thick, no-longer-existent grass in the bowl-shaped valley between the two peaks, which lie about four kilometres apart. We know also that Strzelecki returned to camp in darkness, arriving with Jacky, whom Macarthur had dispatched to look for him. This again suggests he summited Kosciuszko. What else was he doing up on the range for so many hours?

But there's still that tiny sliver of doubt. In Strzelecki's account in his report to Governor Gipps, he describes Kosciuszko as 'a pinnacle, rocky and naked' which absolutely fits Townsend but not Kosciuszko. Of the view from Kosciuszko, Strzelecki wrote that 'the eye plunges into a fearful gorge 3000 feet deep …' That is absolutely, all day long, a description of the view from Townsend, not Kosciuszko, because Townsend sits at the edge of the massif whereas Kosciuszko has views to all horizons but none that are immediately precipitous.

So here's a theory: maybe mist rolled in, as it often does on the Main Range, and Strzelecki got lost. Maybe Byamee had the final say on who travelled on Country. Maybe Strzelecki, as a matter of honour, pretended he climbed Kosciuszko. Whatever elevation and other measurements he took, rock specimens he examined and souvenirs he gathered – like the flower he sent to Adyna Turno – would have been close enough to identical on Townsend. Then again, maybe Strzelecki did as history records and climbed both mountains, then muddled the details when he wrote his report five years later. In the end, it matters little either way. What matters is not the truth about Strzelecki but the true story of the mountains.

To this day, people are still actively trying to downplay the area's Aboriginal history, not least on Mt Kosciuszko itself. One falsehood put forward by those opposed to removing the name Kosciuszko is that the mountain wasn't a significant Aboriginal site as it had no obvious boulder outcrops for bogong moths. This is wrong. While the grassy summit has only small rocks, there are larger outcrops a short way down the mountain's northern flank where moths congregated. More broadly, stories like the Byamee creation story told by Aunty Rhonda Casey prove that the mountain was significant. How could the country's highest point not be?

Others have written that Aboriginal people wouldn't have known that Mt Kosciuszko was the highest point as it's so close in elevation to nearby peaks, so how could it be a place of significance? This argument is best swatted away by again borrowing Lieutenant Colonel Clews' deliciously disdainful line: 'Perhaps most of the writers have been persons normally working in an office.' Of course the Aboriginal people knew which mountain was highest. Can you imagine living on Country your whole life, travelling it, harvesting food on it, conducting ceremony on it and not being able to discern subtle differences in elevation? It's like arguing that a city dweller wouldn't recognise the street they live on without a street sign.

This first, inarguable truth is that the place has been desecrated. From the immeasurable damage done by grazing animals to the scars of ski resorts and megaprojects like the Snowy Scheme to the increasing ravages of human-caused climate change to the theft of the traditional owners' traditions and Country, the Kosciuszko area has changed more in the last 200 years than during any similar time frame in its history. Not for nothing is Kosciuszko National Park denied World Heritage status, even though there is nowhere quite like it on Earth.

But we can salvage it. To do that, we must listen to the old stories. The Ice Age is still telling its 10,000-year-old story with its cirques, lakes and granite boulders. The very shape of the mountains tells a 500-million-year-old tale, rounded and beaten down by the elements unlike those jagged Johnny-come-lately Himalayas, which can count a mere fifty million birthdays. Now it's time to understand the Aboriginal history.

Ongoing storytelling and education are crucial in these mountains. YouTube is full of inane videos showing people's day hikes up Kosciuszko without the faintest inquiry about the area's ecology or timeless history. There should be interpretive signage from the Ancestor Rocks and Sentinel Rocks at the top of the Thredbo chairlift all the way along the path to the summit, pointing out the significance of key places and explaining everything from traditional Aboriginal cultural practices like the annual bogong moth feast to the forced displacement of the Ngarigo and nearby Nations. The summit walk should be a learning walk for everyone who undertakes it, just as this book has been for me.

My personal learning walk through these mountains started with a literal walk – an attempted 700-kilometre trek across the length of the High Country which was interrupted toward the end by the Black Summer bushfires, as detailed in my book *From Snow to Ash*. Then came *The Brumby Wars*, phase two of the learning walk as human passions burned no less fiercely than the fires. Then came this book, which started as a hero quest: 'The setting of my previous two books is named after a guy who did what?! Australians should know about him! The world should know about him!' And it's true. It's hard these days to find a hero to believe in, and every minute, hour and day of research has shown Kosciuszko to be the most admirable, fascinating and unappreciated figure imaginable. But in researching and writing the Australian section of the book, it became clear that the most important learning was not about Kosciuszko the man. It was about Kosciuszko the mountain, the Country that surrounds it, the people who are the traditional custodians of that Country and the stories that Country tells through those people.

The good news is we don't all need to walk the length of the High Country to understand this place. We just need to open our eyes and ears to the stories and knowledge of the area's traditional owners. The great humanist Strzelecki could see that. The Pole who named Mt Kosciuszko understood that Aboriginal voices were being drowned out as their traditional way of life was being attacked. He grasped that we desperately need to listen.

As he wrote in quite beautiful words in his report to Governor Gipps:

> Amidst the wrecks of schemes, efforts and attempts to Christianise, civilise, utilise and preserve the Aboriginal race, there remains yet to be adopted one measure worthy of the liberality of the English Government, – viz., to listen and attend to the last wishes of the departed, and to the voice of the remaining few.

In a sense, that's all anyone from the Ngarigo and nearby Nations is asking. Listen and attend to the last wishes of the departed, and to the voice of the remaining few. It's like a Welcome to Country or Acknowledgement of Country ceremony where the speaker pays their respects to Aboriginal Elders past, present and emerging. No-one is saying the country doesn't belong to everyone. No-one is saying one group of Australians is more important or authentic than any other. It's the opposite. It's inclusive, not exclusive: they're saying listen to those with knowledge of Country and we can all get on with caring for Country together.

'When it comes to the name of the mountain, we all need to know the real story, the ancient story, and respect that,' says Ngarigo woman Cheryl Davison, the sister of Iris White. A talented artist, Davison runs a gallery in the New South Wales south coast town of Narooma. She cites the example of Gulaga, the prominent peak just south of Narooma which Captain Cook named Mt Dromedary on account of its humped shape, and which was widely known as such until recently. 'They no longer call it Dromedary, everyone calls it Gulaga now and I think the same respect has to be given to our sacred mountain,' she says. 'I don't know what the right name for Kosciuszko is right now, but I think between us all, we'll work it out.'

Iris White won't commit to one particular name for the time being either, and that's not only because her people are yet to agree on a name and may not do so for years. In a drop-in visit to her home that turns into a three-hour chin-wag over several coffees, you sense she's trying to say something that lies deep beneath the conversation. It's about the name of the mountain but it's about more than that. It might be about the obsession of non-Aboriginal Australians with the quick-fix, with the symbolic gesture like changing a name that makes us feel, 'Okay, we've done that, we are good people, this issue is done and dusted now.' While dual naming or a full name change from Mt Kosciuszko would absolutely make a difference to Aboriginal people, there's more at stake than just the mountain's name.

And then Iris finds the words. 'I don't think Country needs a certain name to carry the story,' she says. 'I would rather see the stories of the people connected to the mountains get told because Country carries the story.'

That's the all-important voice we have to listen to: the voice of Country. And listening to Country means listening to Aboriginal people because, as mentioned earlier, they see themselves as inseparable from Country. People are Country and Country is people. That hasn't changed, despite many Ngarigo being forced to live off Country.

While Iris White and her sister Cheryl Davison are content to wait for consensus to change the mountain's name either through dual naming or with what you might call a 'new old name', other folk with Ngarigo heritage feel a greater sense of urgency. Professor Jakelin Troy is an advocate of the name Kunama Namadgi and while she acknowledges that Kosciuszko was a great humanist, she says his name doesn't bring anything to the mountains.

'Kosciuszko never was of this place. His name does not have any connection at all. It doesn't call out to the mountains, it doesn't speak to the mountains, it erases what the mountains are.'

As for old Koz himself, you can only imagine he'd willingly give up his name, just as many felt he would want the Black Lives Matter graffiti to remain on his statue in Washington, DC to show his support for the cause. We know from countless episodes of Kosciuszko's life that he never sought personal glory, and this was the case even when his pay packet and career advancement were part of the package. When Kosciuszko was up for promotion during the Revolutionary War, his first thought was to avoid creating resentment among lesser skilled but fiercely ambitious French and American engineers, so he wrote to his senior officer, Colonel Robert Troup: 'My dear Colonel, if you see that my promotion will make a great many jealous, tell the General that I will not accept of one because I prefer peace more than the greatest rank in the world.' Kosciuszko was duly not promoted and was only made brigadier general after the war.

Kosciuszko was a kind man, a humble man, a noble man, a truly great man, but it doesn't much matter in the Australian context if he was greater than the person who invented pierogi. If Kosciuszko was willing to lay down his life for human rights and dignity, he'd surely be the first to advocate removing his name from the mountain, if that's what its traditional owners want. At the very least, he'd be desperate to foster a civil debate on the issue. Perhaps we can all play our part now that we know his story, and through him, the story of the mountain's traditional custodians.

It'd be just like old Koz to keep working his magic, to keep inspiring humanity to be better, even in death.

SOURCES

Books

Anderson, John. *James Macarthur – The Untold Story of Naming Kosciuszko*. Self-published, 2021.

Andrews, Alan EJ. *Kosciusko: The Mountain in History*. Tabletop Press, 1991.

Clews, Lt Colonel Hugh Powell G. *Strzelecki's Ascent of Mount Kosciusko 1840*. Australia Felix Literary Club, 1973.

Conwill, Kinshasha Holman & Gardullo, Paul (editors). *Make Good the Promises: Reclaiming Reconstruction and its Legacies*. Amistad, 2021.

Egleston, Thomas. *The Life of John Paterson, Major-General in the Revolutionary Army*. G.P. Putnam's Sons, 1898.

Evans, Anthony Walton White. *Memoir of Thaddeus Kosciuszko, Poland's Hero and Patriot, an Officer in the American Army of the Revolution*. Self-published through the Society of the Cincinnati, 1883.

Finkelman, Paul. *Slavery and the Founders: Race and Liberty in the Age of Jefferson*. M.E. Sharpe, 2014.

Gardner, Monica M. *Kosciuszko: A Biography*. George Allen & Unwin Ltd, 1920.

Heney, Helen. *In a Dark Glass: The Story of Paul Edmond Strzelecki*. Angus & Robertson, 1961.

Jefferson, Thomas. *Notes on the State of Virginia*. Lilly and Wait, Boston, 1832.

Meacham, Jon. *Thomas Jefferson: The Art of Power*. Random House, 2013.

Mullett, Aunty Rachel. 'The Learning Walk' in *Nyernila – Listen Continuously: Aboriginal Creation Stories of Victoria*. Creative Victoria in association with the Victorian Aboriginal Corporation for Languages, 2014.

Nash, Gary B and Hodges, Graham Russell Gao. *Friends of Liberty: Thomas Jefferson, Tadeusz Kosciuszko, and Agrippa Hull*. Basic Books, 2008.

Pula, James S. *Kosciuszko: The Purest Son of Liberty*. Hippocrene Books. 1998.

Slattery, Deirdre and Worboys, Graeme. *Kosciuszko: A Great National Park*. Envirobook, 2020.

Smith, Clint. *How the Word is Passed: A Reckoning with the History of Slavery Across America*. Little, Brown, 2021.

Storozynski, Alex. *The Peasant Prince: Thaddeus Kosciuszko and the Age of Revolution*. St Martin's Press, 2009.

Strzelecki, PE. *Physical Description of New South Wales and Van Diemen's Land*. Longman, Brown, Green and Longmans, 1845.

Young, Michael with Mundy, Ellen & Mundy, Debbie. *The Aboriginal People of the Monaro*. NSW National Parks and Wildlife Service, 2000.

Zamoyski, Adam. *Poland: A History*. HarperCollins, 2015.

Aboriginal stories in NSW National Parks Service leaflets, bulletins and other publications

'The Southern Snowy Mountains Aboriginal Community Memorandum of Understanding.' NSW National Parks and Wildlife Service, Office of Environment and Heritage and the Southern Snowy Mountains Aboriginal Community, 2016.

'Dyillagamberra – the local Rainmaker'. *Kosciuszko Today* winter 2007 issue. NSW National Parks and Wildlife Service.

'Garugalla – the spirit in the clouds'. *Kosciuszko Today* summer 2007/08 issue. NSW National Parks and Wildlife Service.

'Gurrangatti – the river spirit'. *Kosciuszko Today* winter 2008 issue. NSW National Parks and Wildlife Service.

'Yerribie/Dhirrayn'. *Kosciuszko National Park Plan of Management 2006*. NSW National Parks and Wildlife Service, Australian Alps Cooperative Management Program, Department of Environment and Conservation (NSW).

Articles, stories and poems

Adamek, Magdalena. 'Tadeusz Kosciuszko – a Cosmopolitan and an Artist: Case of Two Polonaises and the Waltz'. *Forum Artystyczne*, University of Warmia and Mazury in Olsztyn, 2018.

Andrews, Alan EJ. 'Mt Kosciuszko'. *Polish Council of Australia and New Zealand Bulletin*, Issue 1, Autumn 2005.

Angry Staff Officer. 'Thaddeus Kosciusko: The Polish Engineer You Never Heard of who Saved America'. angrystaffofficer.com. 9 July, 2019.

Ashford, Evan. 'The Privilege of Blackness: Black Empowerment and the Fight for Liberation in Attala County, Mississippi 1865–1915' (doctoral thesis). University of Massachusetts, Amherst, November 2018.

Banner, Stuart. 'Why Terra Nullius? Anthropology and Property Law in Early Australia'. *Law and History Review*, Vol. 23, No. 1 (Spring, 2005), pp. 95–131. American Society for Legal History.

Bajdek, Anthony J. 'The Patron Saint of West Point: Tadeusz Kościuszko and His Academy Disciples'. *Polish American Studies*, Vol. 76, No. 2 (Autumn 2019), pp. 47–63.

Brumfield, Bentley. 'Tylertown'. *My Town Mississippi Poetry Project*, Mississippi Department of Education, 2022.

Burczak, Michał. 'The Creation of an Enduring Legend of the National Hero: A Comparison of Tadeusz Kościuszko and George Washington. *The Polish Review*, Vol. 59, No. 3 (2014), pp. 25–39. University of Illinois Press.

Coates, Ta-Nehisi. 'Thomas Jefferson and the Divinity of the Founding Fathers'. *The Atlantic*, 10 December 2012.

Coates, Ta-Nehisi. 'Some Clarification on Thomas Jefferson'. *The Atlantic*, 11 December 2012.

Coates, Ta-Nehisi. 'Thomas Jefferson, Tadeusz Kosciusko, and Slavery: Annette Gordon-Reed Responds'. *The Atlantic*, 18 December 2012.

Cohen, Amy. 'Revolutionary War Hero Thaddeus Kościuszko Ages Well in New Era of Social Justice'. hiddencityphila.org. 24 August, 2020.

Czubaty, Jarosław. 'A Republican in a Changing World: The Political Position and Attitudes of Tadeusz Kościuszko, 1798–1817'. *The Polish Review*, Vol. 59, No. 3 (2014), p. 80. University of Illinois Press.

'Empty Pedestals: What Should be Done with Civic Monuments to the Confederacy and its Leaders?' *Civil War Times Magazine*, 18 July, 2017.

Flera, Wojciech. 'Does the Life of Tadeusz Kościuszko Provide Lessons for Today?' *Polish American Studies*, Vol. 64, No. 1 (Spring, 2007), pp. 75–78. University of Illinois Press.

Gliński, Mikołaj. 'Tadeusz Kościuszko's Last Will & Testament: An Unwritten Chapter in American History'. Culture.pl, 12 October, 2017.

Gonzalez, Jill Walker. 'Broken and Broke: Financial Loss and Fragmentation in A. Walton White Evans's Memoir of Thaddeus Kosciuszko'. *Polish American Studies*, Vol. 75, No. 2 (Autumn 2018), pp. 9–30. University of Illinois Press.

Grudnicki, Lindsey. 'True to a Single Object: The Character of Tadeusz Kościuszko'. Ashbrook Statesmanship Thesis Recipient of the 2013 Charles E. Parton Award.

Haiman, Miecislaus. 'American Influences on Kosciuszko's Act of Insurrection'. *Polish American Studies*, Vol. III, No. 1–2, January–June 1946.

Halecki, Oscar. 'The Third of May, Kosciuszko, and Polish Democracy'. *Bulletin of the Polish Institute of Arts and Sciences in America*, Vol. 2, No. 4 (July 1944), pp. 914–931.

Hapanowicz, Piotr. 'Tadeusz Kościuszko and Liberty'. *The Polish Review*, Vol. 67, No. 4, 2022. University of Illinois Press.

Hillar, Marian. 'The Polish Constitution of May 3, 1791: Myth and Reality'. *The Polish Review*, Vol. 37, No. 2 (1992), pp. 185–207. University of Illinois Press.

'Historical Perspectives on Kosciuszko'. Kosciuszkoatwestpoint.org.

Hodges, Graham Russell Gao. 'Kościuszko and African-American History'. *The Polish Review*, Vol. 59, No. 3 (2014), pp. 41–56. University of Illinois Press.

Kadziela, Łukasz and Strybel, Robert. 'The 1794 Kościuszko Insurrection'. *The Polish Review*, Vol. 39, No. 4 (1994), pp. 387–392. University of Illinois Press.

Kajencki, Francis C. 'Kościuszko's Role in the Siege of Ninety-Six'. *Polish American Studies*, Vol. 54, No. 2 (Autumn, 1997), pp. 9–22. University of Illinois Press.

'Kościuszko Uprising – the last attempt to save the Republic of Poland'. dzieje.pl (Portal Historyczny), 23 March 2018.

Kozek, A. 'The known and less familiar history of the naming of "Mt Kosciuszko"'. Polish Museum and Archives in Australia.

Kusielewicz, Eugene and Krzyżanowski, Ludwik. 'Julian Ursyn Niemcewicz's American Diary'. *The Polish Review*, Vol. 3, No. 3 (Summer, 1958), pp. 83–115. University of Illinois Press.

Lockwood, Alan. 'In the Footsteps of Kraków's European Identity: The Rynek Underground Archaeological Exhibit'. *The Polish Review*, Vol. 57, No. 4 (2012), pp. 87–99. University of Illinois Press.

Magnis, Nicholas E. 'Thomas Jefferson and Slavery: An Analysis of His Racist Thinking as Revealed by His Writings and Political Behavior'. *Journal of Black Studies*, Vol. 29, No. 4 (March 1999), pp. 491–509.

Majmurek, Jakub. 'Kościuszko Knew That Black Lives Matter'. dissentmagazine.org. 25 June 2020.

Morgan, Ron. 'Arthur St. Clair's Decision to Abandon Fort Ticonderoga and Mount Independence'. *Journal of the American Revolution*, 16 May 2016.

Nash, Gary B and Hodges, Graham Russell Gao. 'Why We Should All Regret Jefferson's Broken Promise to Kościuszko.' Historynetwork.org.

Ottenberg, Louis. 'A Testamentary Tragedy: Jefferson and the Wills of General Kosciuszko'. *American Bar Association Journal*, Vol. 44, No. 1 (January 1958), pp. 22–26.

Palmer, Dave R. 'Fortress West Point: 19th Century Concept in an 18th Century War'. *The Military Engineer*, May–June 1976, Vol. 68, No. 443, Bicentennial Issue (May–June 1976), pp. 171–174. Society of American Military Engineers.

Petigru, Charles (with an introduction by James Pula). 'Fellow Cadets'—Charles Petigru's Dedication of the Kościuszko Column at West Point. *The Polish Review*, Vol. 59, No. 3 (2014), pp. 95–106. University of Illinois Press.

Pula, James S. 'The American Will of Thaddeus Kosciuszko'. *Polish American Studies*, Spring, 1977, Vol. 34, No. 1 (Spring, 1977), pp. 16–25.

Pula, James S. 'Kościuszko's Influence as an American Military Leader'. *The Polish Review*, Vol. 59, No. 3 (2014), pp. 5–23. University of Illinois Press.

Pula, James S. 'Tadeusz Kościuszko: A Case Study in Constructed Historical Symbolism'. *The Polish Review*, Vol. 53, No. 2 (2008), pp. 159–182. University of Illinois Press.

Rose, William. 'Stanisław Konarski, Preceptor of Poland'. *The Slavonic Review*, Vol. 4, No. 10 (June 1925), pp. 23–41.

Rosner, Anna M. 'Jewish Participation in the Kościuszko Uprising'. *The Polish Review*, Vol. 59, No. 3 (2014), pp. 57–71. University of Illinois Press.

Sedgwick, Catharine. 'West Point'. Juvenile Miscellany, 1833, *Sedgwick Stories: The Periodical Writings of Catharine Maria Sedgwick*.

Solak, Anita. 'Tadeusz Kościuszko: For Our Freedom and Yours'. Blog of the Textual Records Division at the National Archives, 15 September 2020.

Storozynski, Alex. 'Thaddeus Kosciuszko, a man who bridged so many divides'. *New York Daily News*, 8 April 2018.

'The 500 Greatest Albums of All Time'. *Rolling Stone*, December 2023.

Troy, Jakelin and Barwick, Linda. 'Claiming the "Song of the Women of the Menero Tribe"'. *Musicology Australia*, Volume 42 (2020), pp 85–107.

Tzur, Nissan. 'Reclaiming Jewish Property in Krakow'. *The Krakow Post*, 18 November 2012.

Uminski, Sigmund H. 'Julian Ursyn Niemcewicz in America'. *Polish American Studies*, Vol. 2, No. 3/4 (July–Dec 1945), pp. 89–94. University of Illinois Press.

Wiencek, Henry. 'The Dark Side of Thomas Jefferson'. *The Smithsonian Magazine*, (October 2012).

Winter, Nevin O. 'Kosciuszko, Hero of Poland and the USA.' Excerpt article on the website tota.world from the book *Poland of To-Day and Yesterday*. L.C. Page & Company, Boston, 1913.

Wojdon, Joanna and Tyszkiewicz, Jakub. 'The Image of Tadeusz Kościuszko in Postwar Polish Education'. *The Polish Review*, Vol. 59, No. 3 (2014), pp. 81–94. University of Illinois Press.

Wood, Gordon. 'Jefferson in His Time'. *The Wilson Quarterly*, Vol. 17, No. 2 (Spring, 1993), pp. 38–51.

ACKNOWLEDGEMENTS

Researching and writing this book was both thrilling and exhausting. As I write these words huddled in my draughty garden shed in the depths of the Sydney winter with only a small bar heater defending a chill as belligerent as Catherine the Great herself, I can't believe the mountain has finally been climbed.

The first thank-you obviously goes to Kate the Great and my children Stella and Leo. Fam, life is busy and complicated. We've all got stuff going on and I tried hard never to make my stuff more important than your stuff while I was neck-deep in Koz. I acknowledge that I didn't always succeed, so thank you for believing in Kosciuszko, for still being here emotionally and physically, and for the occasional cheese and pickle sandwich thrown over the back porch in the direction of the shed.

This thing doesn't happen without Sophie Hamley, publisher of non-fiction at Hachette Australia. I am so lucky to know Sophie, and not just because she is smart, chirpy and sends the most upbeat text messages, but because Sophie is also a believer. When I told her that I wanted to recount key moments of Kosciuszko's life episodically (not chronologically) as I took readers on a road trip, she didn't go 'You're mixing spaghetti Bolognese and chocolate ice cream in the same bowl here, Anthony.' She was just like 'Tell this engrossing story your way. Readers will go with you.' I love her for that. We even coined a new literary fusion genre: 'travelography'.

The whole team at Hachette Australia has been a pleasure to work with over the three books of my Australian alpine trilogy. Copy editor Libby Turner misses nothing and always knows when I have wisecracked once too often. Senior editor Karen Ward has this unbelievably reassuring way of making you feel like she is across every single thought bubble in the manuscript five minutes after you've delivered it. Designer Luke Causby gave the *Kosciuszko* cover the perfect amount of nostalgic dreaminess. Everyone at Hachette from editorial to marketing to sales to finance to the CEO Louise Stark has shown incredible enthusiasm for this project. As the publication date drew near, it felt like a great big shiny engine was revving in the Hachette garage. You should all be proud of your contribution to Australian literary life. Kosciuszko the man and Kosciuszko the alpine region have been ignored for too long by major Australian publishers. Hachette has helped fill a huge gap in our national imagination.

Thank you to DTN, the parent company of my Australian employer Weatherzone, and to my managers and colleagues on the Weatherzone consumer content team including Rick Thornton, Ron Wong, Krisha Patel, Ben Domensino, Ashleigh Madden, Joel Pippard and Karen P'ng. Thanks also to all the meteorologists with whom I speak daily. Working half the week helping shape Australia's finest weather news feed continues to be an excellent way to stay productive and sane while undertaking these book projects. I learn so much from all of you, and I love our daily weather discussions and life banter.

Thanks to Mum, Dad, Lynn, Helen, Soy, Ali, and my in-laws Bill and Jenni Pearcy for your unwavering support, and for always asking the right questions about these projects.

Thanks to my Australian friends who checked in regularly during this project. I'd get a cramp if I listed you all, but you

ACKNOWLEDGEMENTS

include Peter Lewis, Ann King, Andrew 'Naiba' Heys, Glenn Cullen, Steve Rosanove, Jason Harty, Bradley and Linda Roche, Toby Stenberg, Catriona Carver, Denis Carnahan and Ben Doherty.

Thanks to the Americans I met on this project who accommodated me in ways large or small. Special thanks for reading large chunks of the manuscript must go to Paul Finkelman, and to John Benjamin and his wife Agnieszka Makles. Thanks to my New Jersey cousins Karen and Debbie, and your families, for always making me feel at home on America's east coast. Thanks to David Green and especially Donna Holdiness in Kosciusko, Mississippi for being the epitome of Southern hospitality. Cheers to Barry Johnson for being the king of Nashville. Thanks to James Pula, Steve Olejasz and Graham Hodges for your time, patience, and invaluable insights into Kosciuszko's character and military prowess. Thanks to my awesome trio of mates in Kingston for being the best hosts and tour guides in upstate New York. Thanks to India Spartz and Joshua Hall at the Stockbridge Library, Museum & Archives for sharing a chilly Massachusetts afternoon and your passion for history. Huge thanks to Rick Wilcox for dropping by that day.

In Europe, I am deeply grateful to Dr Leszek Marek Krzesniak, President of Poland's Kosciuszko Foundation, and to the eminent and very friendly historian Piotr Hapanowicz, who has the gift of making complicated ideas simple. Big thanks also to Mieczyslaw 'Mietek' Bielawski and Mat Schulz for being outstanding geographical and intellectual guides in Krakow. And a huge thanks to Teresa Ackermann for specially opening the Kosciuszko Museum for me on a rainy Monday in Solothurn, Switzerland.

In Australia I must thank Ernestyna and Andrzej Kozek for their friendship, generosity and ongoing hard work in making information on Strzelecki and Kosciuszko freely available to all. Felix Molski and Ursula Lang were two other kind and helpful Australians of Polish heritage. Thanks to Richard Chirgwin for the great deal up at Bunjaree Cottages in the Blue Mountains during the final push to finish this thing. Massive thanks to the usual suspects in Kosciuszko National Park, including Rob Gibbs, Di Thompson and Dave Darlington. Thanks as always to the entire crew on the forum of the website ski.com.au, who remain the most supportive, knowledgeable and entertaining bunch of idiots on the internet. All three of these books don't happen without you lot. Rob Mann and Stefaan Steyn deserve special praise. Those pastries seriously saved my life that day, Rob. And as ever, thanks to Sun's Noodle, Kosta the barista with charisma at Ibrahim Espresso, and Rockdale Library – for food, coffee and shelter on days when the fridge was empty and the shed was too hot/cold/dank/lonely.

Most importantly, I thank the traditional owners of the area that most Australians today call Kosciuszko. As mentioned in the final chapter of this book, it's ironic that my obsession with an old European guy led me to sit down with Monero-Ngarigo people and listen at length to your stories for the first time. In no particular order, I would like to thank Iris White, Rhonda Casey, Cheryl Davison, John Dixon, Michelle Davison, Rod Mason (whom I never met but whose published work was invaluable) and Paul Paton. I only spoke to Paul once on the phone, but he is the grandson of Aunty Rachel Mullett, whose story 'The Learning Walk' provides both the title and the philosophical backbone of the Australian section of this book. A matriarch of the mountains, Aunty Rachel sadly died a few weeks before this book was printed. I thank her for her contribution to Australian life and I thank her people for allowing parts of her ancestral story to be shared here.

ACKNOWLEDGEMENTS

Lastly, I want to thank you, the reader, for getting off TikTok or YouTube and reading these words. Without you, these literary adventures do not happen. I hope you think of them as your adventures too.

Anthony Sharwood is a Walkley Award-winning journalist who has worked in TV, newspapers, magazines and online news. Formerly a sportswriter who covered several Olympic Games, he now specialises in the environment, climate and weather. In 2020 he released the acclaimed *From Snow to Ash*, a love letter to the Australian High Country written after walking the Australian Alps Walking Track, and in 2021 he explored the passionate environmental and cultural battle over Australia's wild horses in *The Brumby Wars*. His books *Kosciuszko* and *Bring Your A Game* are both 2024 releases.